Practice Commentaries—FRCrP

The Practice Commentaries Series

Practice Commentaries—FRCrP

2002/2003 Edition

Louis M. Natali
Temple University Beasley School of Law

Inga L. Parsons
New York University School of Law

Steven M. Statsinger
The Legal Aid Society, Federal Defender Division
Southern District of New York

Susan C. Wolfe
Hoffman Pollok & Pickholz

National Institute for Trial Advocacy

NITA Editorial Board

Kenneth S. Broun, Chair
University of North Carolina
Chapel Hill, North Carolina

Joseph R. Bankoff
King & Spalding
Atlanta, Georgia

James J. Brosnahan
Morrison & Foerster
San Francisco, California

Jo Ann Harris
Pace University School of Law
White Plains, New York

Deanne C. Siemer
Wilsie Co. LLC.
Washington, D.C.

© 2001 National Institute for Trial Advocacy
PRINTED IN THE UNITED STATES OF AMERICA
ALL RIGHTS RESERVED

No part of this work may be reproduced or transmitted in any form or by any means, electronic or mechanical, including photocopying and recording, or by any information storage or retrieval system without the prior written approval of the National Institute for Trial Advocacy unless such copying is expressly permitted by federal copyright law. Address inquiries to:

Reproduction Permission
National Institute for Trial Advocacy
Notre Dame Law School
Notre Dame, Indiana 46556
(800) 225-6482   Fax (219) 271-8375
E-mail: nita.1@nd.edu   www.nita.org

Natali, Louis M., Inga L. Parsons, Steven M. Statsinger, Susan C. Wolfe, *Practice Commentaries—FRCrP* (NITA, 2001).

ISBN 1-55681-762-2

Library of Congress Cataloging-in-Publication Data
Practice commentaries-FRCrP / Louis M. Natali ... [et al.].--2002/2003 ed.
   p. cm. -- (The practice commentaries series)
   ISBN 1-55681-762-2 (pbk. : alk. paper)
   1. United States. Supreme Court. Rules of criminal procedure for the United States district courts. 2. Criminal procedure--United States.
I. Natali, Louis M., 1942- II. Series.
KF9606.515 .P73 2001
345.73'05--dc21

2001054672

Table of Contents

Preface xi

Acknowledgments xiii

Introduction xv

About the Authors xvii

I. Scope, Purpose, and Construction 1
    Rule 1. Scope 1
    Commentary 1
    Rule 2. Purpose and Construction 2
    Commentary 3

II. Preliminary Proceedings 4
    Rule 3. The Complaint 4
    Commentary 4
    Rule 4. Arrest Warrant or Summons Upon
    Complaint 5
    Commentary 6
    Rule 5. Initial Appearance Before the Magistrate
    Judge 7
    Commentary 8
    Rule 5.1. Preliminary Examination 9
    Commentary 11

III. Indictment and Information 13
    Rule 6. The Grand Jury 13
    Commentary 17
    Rule 7. The Indictment and the Information . . . 20
    Commentary 21
    Rule 8. Joinder of Offenses and of Defendants . . . 23
    Commentary 23

Rule 9. Warrant or Summons Upon Indictment or
Information 25
Commentary 27

IV. Arraignment and Preparation for Trial 32
Rule 10. Arraignment 32
Commentary 32
Rule 11. Pleas. 36
Commentary 40
Rule 12. Pleadings and Motions Before Trial;
Defenses and Objections. 43
Commentary 45
Rule 12.1. Notice of Alibi 46
Commentary 48
Rule 12.2. Notice of Insanity Defense or Expert
Testimony of Defendant's Mental Condition. . . . 51
Commentary 52
Rule 12.3. Notice of Defense Based Upon Public
Authority 58
Commentary 59
Rule 13. Trial Together of Indictments or
Informations 61
Commentary 61
Rule 14. Relief From Prejudicial Joinder 65
Commentary 65
Rule 15. Depositions 67
Commentary 69
Rule 16. Discovery and Inspection. 70
Commentary 75
Rule 17. Subpoena 79
Commentary 80
Rule 17.1. Pretrial Conference. 81
Commentary 81

V. Venue 82
   Rule 18. Place of Prosecution and Trial 82
   Commentary 82
   Rule 19. Transfer Within the District (Rescinded) . 83
   Rule 20. Transfer From the District for Plea and Sentence 83
   Commentary 83
   Rule 21. Transfer From the District for Trial 85
   Commentary 85
   Rule 22. Time of Motion To Transfer 86
   Commentary 86

VI. Trial 87
   Rule 23. Trial by Jury or by the Court 87
   Commentary 87
   Rule 24. Trial Jurors 88
   Commentary 90
   Rule 25. Judge; Disability 93
   Commentary 93
   Rule 26. Taking of Testimony 97
   Commentary 97
   Rule 26.1. Determination of Foreign Law 98
   Commentary 98
   Rule 26.2. Production of Witnesses Statements . . 101
   Commentary 103
   Rule 26.3. Mistrial 103
   Commentary 103
   Rule 27. Proof of Official Record 107
   Commentary 107
   Rule 28. Interpreters 109
   Commentary 109
   Rule 29. Motion for Judgment or Acquittal 118

Commentary. 119
Rule 29.1. Closing Argument 126
Commentary. 126
Rule 30. Instructions. 131
Commentary. 131
Rule 31. Verdict 132
Commentary. 132

VII. Judgment 134
Rule 32. Sentence and Judgment. 134
Commentary. 139
Rule 32.1. Revocation or Modification of
Probation or Supervised Release 159
Commentary. 160
Rules 32.2 Criminal Forfeiture 167
Commentary. 170
Rule 33. New Trial. 174
Commentary. 174
Rule 34. Arrest of Judgment 179
Commentary. 179
Rule 35. Correction or Reduction of Sentence . . 183
Commentary. 184
Rule 36. Clerical Mistakes 189
Commentary. 189

VIII. Appeal 193
Rule 37. Taking Appeal; and Petition for Writ
of Certiorari (Abrogated) 193
Rule 38. Stay of Execution 193
Commentary. 194
Rule 39. Supervision of Appeal (Abrogated) . . . 197

IX. Supplementary and Special Proceedings. . . 198
Rule 40. Commitment to Another District 198

Commentary. 199
Rule 41. Search and Seizure 203
Commentary. 207
Rule 42. Criminal Contempt 216
Commentary. 217

X. General Provisions 221
Rule 43. Presence of the Defendant 221
Commentary. 222
Rule 44. Right to and Assignment of Counsel. . . 226
Commentary. 226
Rule 45. Time 233
Commentary. 234
Rule 46. Release From Custody 238
Commentary. 240
Rule 47. Motions 251
Commentary. 251
Rule 48. Dismissal 257
Commentary. 257
Rule 49. Service and Filing of Papers 261
Commentary. 261
Rule 50. Calendars; Plans for Prompt Disposition . 263
Commentary. 263
Rule 51. Exceptions Unnecessary 266
Commentary. 267
Rule 52. Harmless Error and Plain Error 269
Commentary. 269
Rule 53. Regulation of Conduct in the Court Room 273
Commentary. 273
Rule 54. Application and Exception 274
Commentary. 277

Rule 55. Records. 278
Commentary. 279
Rule 56. Courts and Clerks. 282
Commentary. 282
Rule 57. Rules by District Courts. 282
Commentary. 283
Rule 58. Procedure for Misdemeanors and
Other Petty Offenses 284
Commentary. 289
Rule 59. Effective Date. 298
Rule 60. Title 298

Preface

The *Practice Commentaries—FRCrP* is the second in a new series of Practice Commentaries published by the National Institute for Trial Advocacy. These publications are designed to bring practical understanding of the Federal Rules of Criminal Procedure to the experienced litigator, the newly arrived associate and the law student alike. Experienced litigators have written the commentaries and the commentaries reflect real life problems and practice.

The *Practice Commentaries—FRCrP* was first written for on-line distribution and is intended to be a collection of succinct and practical overviews of each rule.

Acknowledgments

The *Practice Commentaries—FRCrP*, the second in the Practice Commentaries series, owes its existence to the many professional who are a part of the National Institute for Trial Advocacy. This series is unique in NITA's history in that the commentaries were first written for electronic distribution and now, with this publication, the FRCrP commentaries are being distributed in printed form. In addition to the first book in this series, *Practice Commentaries—FRCP*, we anticipate another book of commentaries on the Federal Rules of Evidence in the immediate future and an ongoing series of books thereafter as our authors continue to share their experience and advice about federal litigation.

I want to thank the Board of Directors of NITA whose foresight and vision got the Commentaries Project started. Professor Anthony Bocchino, our editor-in-chief, provides the editorial guidance and continues to set the highest standards for the Commentaries Project.

Special thanks to Sue Toth, manager of electronic business; Frank Alan, editor, Electronic Legal Publishing; Peg Hartman, general manager of programs and publications; Ashley Smith, editor; Barbara VanHolsbeke, editorial manager; Lisa Michalak, senior staff assistant and all the other staff members at NITA Central and at Lexis who have done so much to this publication.

Most of all, however, I want to thank all the authors who worked so hard to share their experiences and their insights about the litigation nuances and complexities of the Federal Rules of Criminal Procedure.

Raymond White
Chief Operating Officer,
National Institute for Trial Advocacy

Introduction

The Practice Commentaries is a new series of publications by the National Institute for Trial Advocacy and those publications are derived from the commentaries first written for electronic distribution on Lexis and as part of the printed and CD version of Lexis' United States Code Service. This book, *Practice Commentaries FRCrP*, is the second of three books in the Practice Commentaries series.

The rules are printed in their entirety and each rule is followed by a commentary. This book is designed to be used by both practicing attorneys and law students. With respect to attorneys, this book provides a ready reference and for the law student it provides insight as to how the rules are applied in practice, recognizing that practical application often departs from the theory one finds in law school.

The Federal Rules of Criminal Procedure deal with an ever-changing range of issues subtly changing to meet new circumstances and revisiting old ones. These commentaries examine the basic litigation issue raised by the rules and we have tried to anticipate the upcoming changes to the rules by discussing the anticipated changes. NITA will continue to update the commentaries online and that permits the reader to use the electronic medium to access current observations and unanticipated changes. Combining electronic availability with the convenience of hard copy distribution gives readers the best of the two worlds.

The authors bring their own perceptions and styles to the commentaries and we hope the different styles will present useful and thoughtful views of the rules. The authors generally have come from the defense side of the bar but the issues they raise and the observations they make are of value to prosecutors and defense attorneys alike.

We have stressed the practical through out the commentaries and offer suggested strategies for dealing with issues raised by the rules but as with all legal material we do not represent that the commentaries are exhaustive in their analysis.

We have included several sample Lexis queries through out this book which will help the reader find the NITA commentaries on Lexis.

As is always the case, NITA reserves all intellectual property rights for the original material in this publication but not for public domain material.

Anthony Bocchino, Editor-in-chief

Frank Alan, Electronic Publishing Editor

About the Authors

Professor Louis Natali, Professor Inga Parsons, Steven Statsinger, and Susan Wolfe are experienced litigators as well as students of the law. These authors bring years of courtroom experience in dealing with the practical aspects of the Federal Rules of Criminal Procedures.

Professor Louis Natali is a professor of law at Temple University Law School in Philadelphia, teaching courses in death penalty litigation, criminal law, evidence, professional responsibility, interviewing, negotiating and counseling.

In 1971, Professor Natali formed the law firm of Segal, Appel, and Natali, specializing in criminal defense. Professor Natali was associate professor at Rutgers-Camden Law School in 1974, leaving that position in 1976 to become First Assistant Defender at the Philadelphia Defender's Association. Professor Natali has published numerous articles on evidence and trial advocacy.

Professor Natali graduated from Georgetown Law Center in 1966 where he was an associate editor of the *Georgetown Law Journal*. He clerked on the United States Court of Appeals for the Fourth Circuit. He was a graduate fellow in criminal law and litigation at the University of Pennsylvania Law School.

He has published numerous articles on evidence and trial advocacy including *In Re Grooten*, a trial file in professional responsibility. Professor Natali co-published, with Professor Ohlbaum, an article on the Supreme Court's decision to uphold the constitutionality of the federal preventive detention statue, which appears in 62 Temp. L. Rev. 1225 (1989). He has been a teacher with NITA since 1973.

Professor Inga L. Parsons has been an acting assistant professor of Clinical Law at NYU School of Law since 1995 and is the co-supervisor of the New York University Federal Defender Clinic.

Professor Parsons teaches criminal procedure and practice and specializes in teaching criminal procedure through federal criminal case simulation. In addition to her instructional activities about Federal Sentencing Guidelines and trial advocacy, Professor Parsons' scholarship involves indigent defense, federal criminal practice and the Federal Sentencing Guidelines.

Her article, "Making it a Federal Case: A Model for Indigent Representation," was published in the 1997 Annual Survey of American Law 101 (1999) and she recently published an op-ed article in the *National Law Journal* on discovery rules in the federal system generally and the Timothy McVeigh case specifically. She has been responsible for supervising the placement of the clinic case files on an interactive secured Web site and has written a student manual, *Guide to Assisting Federal Defenders*, and is the originator and editor-in-chief of the Clinical Law Center's Newsletter: *NYU Clinic News*.

Professor Parsons was one of three NYU faculty members to receive the Student Bar Association's Community Recognition Award for devoted service, outstanding leadership and commitment to the community of NYU School of Law in 1996–97.

She was an Assistant Federal Defender in the Southern District of New York from 1990 to 1995.

Professor Parsons received her A.B. from Harvard in 1985, her J.D. from Columbia in 1989 and clerked for the Honorable William P. Gray, C.D.CA in 1989–90.

Steve Statsinger is a staff attorney at the Legal Aid Society, Federal Defender Division SDNY. Mr. Statsinger was a staff attorney with the Appeals Bureau, Federal Defender Division and the Criminal Appeals Bureau of The Legal Aid Society. He is also an adjunct associate professor of paralegal studies at New York University, School of Continuing and Professional Studies in the Department of Finance, Law and Taxation.

His publications include *Practice Under the Federal Sentencing Guidelines* and a contribution entitled "Appeals in Guideline Sentencing" to a comprehensive guide to the appeals process incases involving the United States Sentencing Guidelines. He has also written several articles on federal criminal practice for *Defense News*, an in-house quarterly publication distributed to defense attorneys nationwide.

He received his B.S. from Brown University in 1984, where he received a Department of Psychology Teaching Fellowship, and his J.D. in 1987 from Columbia University School of Law.

Susan C. Wolfe is a partner with Hoffman, Pollok & Pickholz. She has been practicing criminal defense in the state federal courts in New York City for over fifteen years. Ms. Wolfe and her law firm handle high profile white-collar criminal cases, particularly in the securities field.

She is a member of the National Association of Criminal Defense Lawyers and is a visiting instructor in the Intensive Trial Advocacy program at Cardoza Law School.

She received her B.A. from Cornell University in 1981 and her J.D. from Boston University School of Law in 1984.

I. Scope, Purpose, and Construction

Rule 1. Scope

These rules govern the procedure in all criminal proceedings in the courts of the United States, as provided in Rule 54(a); and, whenever specifically provided in one of the rules, to preliminary, supplementary, and special proceedings before United States magistrate judges and at proceedings before state and local judicial officers.

Commentary

By Prof. Inga L. Parsons
New York University School of Law

The Federal Rules of Criminal Procedure (the Rules) govern procedure in criminal proceedings in the courts of the United States enumerated in FRCrP 54, which includes the District of Guam, the Virgin Islands, and the District for the Northern Mariana Islands. *See* FRCrP 1; FRCrP 54(a).

There are certain exceptions to the application of the Rules. In the Virgin Islands, for example, trial may proceed by information; an indictment is not required. FRCrP 54(a). If an attorney will be practicing in a court outside the United States, but under federal jurisdiction, a careful reading of FRCrP 54 is necessary. Helpful to this endeavor will be the stylistic amendments to FRCrP 54 that are set to be codified by the end of 2001, which will combine FRCrP 54 with FRCrP 1 and make the application provisions of FRCrP 54 more accessible and easier to understand. Significant terms for the Rules are defined in FRCrP 54(c) such as what is meant by "Attorney for the government," "Law," and "State"; attorneys should be familiar with those terms, for example, the term "State" encompasses the District of Columbia and Puerto Rico.

The Rules do not apply to extradition proceedings, civil forfeiture, or the collection of fines. *See* FRCrP 54(b)(5). Habeas corpus proceedings are regarded as civil proceedings and thus not governed by the Rules. Military proceedings are not ordinarily subject to the Rules either.

Juvenile delinquency proceedings are governed by the procedures set out in the juvenile delinquency provisions of the criminal code (18 USCS §§ 5031–5042) and may be governed by the Rules to the extent the Rules are not inconsistent with those provisions. The one specific federal criminal procedure rule applying to a juvenile is FRCrP 20(d) regarding the transfer of a juvenile's case from the charging jurisdiction to the jurisdiction of arrest. See FRCrP 20(d).

Misdemeanors are subject to the Rules to the extent provided by FRCrP 58, which has special provisions applying specifically to misdemeanors and other petty offenses in federal court. See FRCrP 58 and the Commentary for FRCrP 58.

State offenses removed to federal court are governed by the Rules, except state law governs dismissal by the prosecutor. FRCrP 54(b)(1). In general, state law controls the substantive law of transferred state cases, including states cases assimilated into the federal system pursuant to 18 USCS § 13. Procedure is governed by federal law. See, e.g., *United States v. Wilmer*, 799 F.2d 495, 499–500 (9th Cir. 1986). If a person is arrested in a federal park for unlicensed operation of a vehicle, that is strictly a state crime because there is no federal unlicensed operation offense. In order to prosecute the case in federal court, the state offense is assimilated into the federal system because the offense occurred on federal property. Federal procedural and constitutional law applies to the offense, including the law on Fourth and Fifth Amendment rights, *e.g.*, whether a defendant's statement is admissible. In some states a defendant's statement would be suppressed or not admitted under that state's constitution, but would be admissible under the federal constitution. Such cases may be transferred to the federal system so the evidence will be allowed. State substantive law applies to the elements of the assimilated state offense, *e.g.*, what is meant by the term operation of a vehicle. The Federal Rules of Evidence would apply to the hearings and trial of transferred and assimilated cases.

Rule 2. Purpose and Construction

These rules are intended to provide for the just determination of every criminal proceeding. They shall be construed to secure simplicity in procedure, fairness in administration and the elimination of unjustifiable expense and delay.

Commentary

By Prof. Inga L. Parsons
New York University School of Law

The Federal Rules of Criminal Procedure (the Rules) were adopted to bring uniformity and simplicity to the common law that had developed to adjudicate federal criminal cases. Before the Rules, federal criminal procedure was haphazard and hyper-technical. Failure to follow certain pleading requirements could bar a prosecution or defense, and certain motions could not be brought if the term of court had expired. Indictments were dismissed because of minor errors and defendants were perceived as "getting off on a technicality" that was unrelated to guilt or innocence. The Rules were intended to avoid such technical niceties. *See United States v. Claus*, 5 F.R.D. 278, 279 (EDNY 1946).

FRCrP 2 explains that the Rules are intended to provide for a "just determination . . . [and] be construed to secure simplicity in procedure, fairness in administration, and the elimination of unjustifiable expense and delay." FRCrP 2 has something for everyone in its broad and vague terms, and as a result it is both meaningful and meaningless.

If litigants run up against a technical requirement, FRCrP 2 can be employed in an attempt to convince the judges to use their equitable powers and the generosity of FRCrP 2 to do what is just. On the other hand, opposing counsel could invoke FRCrP 2 to counter the claim by arguing for simplicity and avoidance of expense and delay. Nevertheless, it is useful to have FRCrP 2 in the advocate's arsenal when a certain requirement or deadline should be overlooked based on the compelling circumstances in the case or when a judge is looking for a way to "do the right thing" despite the requirements of the Rules. FRCrP 2 is of no assistance, however, when a fixed deadline for filing post-trial motions under FRCrP 29, 33, 34, and 35 is missed because the court will lack jurisdiction to hear the claim. *See* the Commentaries for FRCrP 29, 33, 34, and 35.

II. Preliminary Proceedings

Rule 3. The Complaint

The complaint is a written statement of the essential facts constituting the offense charged. It shall be made upon oath before a magistrate judge.

Commentary

By Prof. Louis M. Natali
Temple University Beasley School of Law

Rules 3 and 4 should be read together. Rule 3 defines the complaint, which is a first step in the process of commencing criminal proceedings. The other method is by indictment.

The complaint must be made under oath before a magistrate. If the magistrate is satisfied that probable cause exists, an arrest warrant will issue. Rule 4 provides the probable cause must be stated in order for a valid arrest warrant to issue. Only that information which lies within the four corners of the complaint and affidavits may be used in the probable cause determination upon which a court will ultimately rule.

Neither rule defines probable cause. The definition is left to development by the courts and is beyond the ambit of this commentary. It is enough to say that the decision in *Illinois v. Gates*, 462 U.S. 213, 76 L. Ed. 2d 527, 103 S. Ct. 2317 (1983), has employed a totality of the circumstances test rather than a rigid categorical analysis of reliable informant and corroboration.

These rules are significant for arrests which have evidentiary consequences. If physical evidence, a confession, and identification or a witness is the fruit of an illegal arrest, a motion to suppress should be filed. In this connection a discovery motion should be made pursuant to Rule 16 in order to learn what evidence the prosecution possesses.

While Rule 4(b) permits hearsay "in whole or in part" to be used in the probable cause determination, case law fully delineates the role that hearsay plays in the probable cause determination.

An illegal arrest without the seizure of any evidence will not result in the defendant's discharge or the dismissal of the indictment. It has often been said that a defendant cannot suppress its person.

Statements in a complaint or affidavit should be seriously studied for two other reasons. First, the statements may lead to discoverable information or form the bases for a discovery motion to obtain witness statements or other information. *See* Rule 16.

Second, such statements may be useful to impeach the testimony of the author of the complaint, who will usually be the case agent or one of the other agents who may testify.

Rule 4. Arrest Warrant or Summons Upon Complaint

(a) Issuance. If it appears from the complaint, or from an affidavit or affidavits filed with the complaint, that there is probable cause to believe that an offense has been committed and that the defendant has committed it, a warrant for the arrest of the defendant shall issue to any officer authorized by law to execute it. Upon the request of the attorney for the government a summons instead of a warrant shall issue. More than one warrant or summons may issue on the same complaint. If a defendant fails to appear in response to the summons, a warrant shall issue.

(b) Probable cause. The finding of probable cause may be based upon hearsay evidence in whole or in part.

(c) Form.

(1) Warrant. The warrant shall be signed by the magistrate judge and shall contain the name of the defendant or, if the defendant's name is unknown, any name or description by which the defendant can be identified with reasonable certainty. It shall describe the offense charged in the complaint. It shall command that the defendant be arrested and brought before the nearest available magistrate judge.

(2) Summons. The summons shall be in the same form as the warrant except that it shall summon the defendant to appear before a magistrate at a stated time and place.

(d) Execution or service; and return.

(1) By whom. The warrant shall be executed by a marshal or by some other officer authorized by law. The summons may be served by any person authorized to serve a summons in a civil action.

(2) Territorial limits. The warrant may be executed or the summons may be served at any place within the jurisdiction of the United States.

(3) Manner. The warrant shall be executed by the arrest of the defendant. The officer need not have the warrant at the time of the arrest but upon request shall show the warrant to the defendant as soon as possible. If the officer does not have the warrant at the time of the arrest, the officer shall then inform the defendant of the offense charged and of the fact that a warrant has been issued. The summons shall be served upon a defendant by delivering a copy to the defendant personally, or by leaving it at the defendant's dwelling house or usual place of abode with some person of suitable age and discretion then residing therein and by mailing a copy of the summons to the defendant's last known address.

(4) Return. The officer executing a warrant shall make return thereof to the magistrate judge or other officer before whom the defendant is brought pursuant to Rule 5. At the request of the attorney for the government any unexecuted warrant shall be returned to and canceled by the magistrate judge by whom it was issued. On or before the return day the person to whom a summons was delivered for service shall make return thereof to the magistrate judge before whom the summons is returnable. At the request of the attorney for the government made at any time while the complaint is pending, a warrant returned unexecuted and not canceled or summons returned unserved or a duplicate thereof may be delivered by the magistrate judge to the marshal or other authorized person for execution or service.

Commentary

See the Commentary for FRCrP 3.

Rule 5. Initial Appearance Before the Magistrate Judge

(a) **In general.** Except as otherwise provided in this rule, an officer making an arrest under a warrant issued upon a complaint or any person making an arrest without a warrant shall take the arrested person without unnecessary delay before the nearest available federal magistrate judge or, if a federal magistrate judge is not reasonably available, before a state or local judicial officer authorized by 18 U.S.C. § 3041. If a person arrested without a warrant is brought before a magistrate judge, a complaint, satisfying the probable cause requirements of Rule 4(a), shall be promptly filed. When a person, arrested with or without a warrant or given a summons, appears initially before the magistrate judge, the magistrate judge shall proceed in accordance with the applicable subdivisions of this rule. An officer making an arrest under a warrant issued upon a complaint charging solely a violation of 18 U.S.C. § 1073 need not comply with this rule if the person arrested is transferred without unnecessary delay to the custody of appropriate state or local authorities in the district of arrest and an attorney for the government moves promptly, in the district in which the warrant was issued, to dismiss the complaint.

(b) **Misdemeanors and other petty offenses.** If the charge against the defendant is a misdemeanor or other petty offense triable by a United States magistrate judge under 18 U.S.C. § 3401, the magistrate judge shall proceed in accordance with Rule 58.

(c) **Offenses not triable by the United States Magistrate Judge.** If the charge against the defendant is not triable by the United States magistrate judge, the defendant shall not be called upon to plead. The magistrate judge shall inform the defendant of the complaint against the defendant and of any affidavit filed therewith, of the defendant's right to retain counsel or to request the assignment of counsel if the defendant is unable to obtain counsel, and of the general circumstances under which the defendant may secure pretrial release. The magistrate judge shall inform the defendant that the defendant is not required to make a statement and that any statement made by the defendant may be used against the defendant. The magistrate judge shall also inform the defendant of the right to a preliminary examination. The magistrate judge shall allow the defendant reasonable time and opportunity to consult counsel and shall detain or conditionally release the defendant as provided by statute or in these rules.

A defendant is entitled to a preliminary examination, unless waived, when charged with any offense, other than a petty offense, which is to be tried by a judge of the district court. If the defendant waives preliminary examination, the magistrate judge shall forthwith hold the defendant to answer in the district court. If the defendant does not waive the preliminary examination, the magistrate judge shall schedule a preliminary examination. Such examination shall be held within a reasonable time but in any event not later than 10 days following the initial appearance if the defendant is in custody and no later than 20 days if the defendant is not in custody, provided, however, that the preliminary examination shall not be held if the defendant is indicted or if an information against the defendant is filed in district court before the date set for the preliminary examination. With the consent of the defendant and upon a showing of good cause, taking into account the public interest in the prompt disposition of criminal cases, time limits specified in this subdivision may be extended one or more times by a federal magistrate judge. In the absence of such consent by the defendant, time limits may be extended by a judge of the United States only upon a showing that extraordinary circumstances exist and that delay is indispensable to the interests of justice.

Commentary

By Prof. Louis M. Natali
Temple University Beasley School of Law

Rule 5 has several significant features.

Rule 5 requires prompt presentation before the magistrate upon arrest within or without a warrant. It does not apply to indicted cases. The preliminary appearance and examination are extremely important proceedings and should not be waived or taken lightly.

The initial appearance guarantees that a judicial official will read the complaint. It also triggers the accused's right to counsel, to bail and to a determination of probable cause unless there is an indictment. If in custody, the accused is entitled to a hearing within ten days and, if on bail, within twenty days. The hearing can result in the defendant's discharge if there is insufficient evidence to hold him. It may also result in the discovery of evidence, the ability to impeach witnesses and the limiting of the case against the defendant. Finally it may result in a bail reduction or the reconsideration of a decision to detain the defendant. *See* comments to Rule 5.1.

The major thrust of this rule was to protect the accused from police overreaching through prolonged detention. The McNabb, 318 U.S. 332, 87 L. Ed. 819, 63 S. Ct. 608 (1943), and Mallory, 354 U.S. 449, 1 L. Ed. 2d 1479, 77 S. Ct. 1356 (1957), line of cases hold that any evidence obtained as a result of such delay must be suppressed. While this attack on illegally obtained evidence has been foreshadowed by Miranda, 384 U.S. 436, 16 L. Ed. 2d 694, 86 S. Ct. 1602 (1966), and the right to counsel cases, it still has vitality for lawyers practicing in the federal system. Most of the decided cases are from the District of Columbia, with a metropolitan police department.

Counsel should proceed pursuant to Rule 16 to discover if there are any statements made by his client. If there are, then the time frame between arrest and the initial appearance is critical. The only permissible delay is the delay incident to booking, fingerprinting and otherwise processing the defendant. This should rarely exceed a few hours. A motion to suppress on the grounds that this rule was violated should be made whenever it is felt that a statement was made by police exploiting the delay in a prompt presentment to the magistrate. The hearing on the motion may also result in discoverable information to use at trial and for impeachment. This is also meaningful where counsel may be required or desire to relitigate the voluntariness issue before a jury.

Rule 5.1. Preliminary Examination

(a) **Probable cause finding.** If from the evidence it appears that there is probable cause to believe that an offense has been committed and that the defendant committed it, the federal magistrate judge shall forthwith hold the defendant to answer in district court. The finding of probable cause may be based upon hearsay evidence in whole or in part. The defendant may cross-examine adverse witnesses and may introduce evidence. Objections to evidence on the ground that it was acquired by unlawful means are not properly made at the preliminary examination. Motions to suppress must be made to the trial court as provided in Rule 12.

(b) Discharge of defendant. If from the evidence it appears that there is no probable cause to believe that an offense has been committed or that the defendant committed it, the federal magistrate judge shall dismiss the complaint and discharge the defendant. The discharge of the defendant shall not preclude the government from instituting a subsequent prosecution for the same offense.

(c) Records. After concluding the proceeding the federal magistrate judge shall transmit forthwith to the clerk of the district court all papers in the proceeding. The magistrate judge shall promptly make or cause to be made a record or summary of such proceeding.

(1) On timely application to a federal magistrate judge, the attorney for a defendant in a criminal case may be given the opportunity to have the recording of the hearing on preliminary examination made available to that attorney in connection with any further hearing or preparation for trial. The court may, by local rule, appoint the place for and define the conditions under which such opportunity may be afforded counsel.

(2) On application of a defendant addressed to the court or any judge thereof, an order may issue that the federal magistrate judge make available a copy of the transcript, or of a portion thereof, to defense counsel. Such order shall provide for prepayment of costs of such transcript by the defendant unless the defendant makes a sufficient affidavit that the defendant is unable to pay or to give security therefor, in which case the expense shall be paid by the Director of the Administrative Office of the United States Courts from available appropriated funds. Counsel for the government may move also that a copy of the transcript, in whole or in part, be made available to it, for good cause shown, and an order may be entered granting such motion in whole or in part, on appropriate terms, except that the government need not prepay costs nor furnish security therefor.

(d) Production of statements.

(1) In general. Rule 26.2(a)–(d) and (f) applies at any hearing under this rule, unless the court, for good cause shown, rules otherwise in a particular case.

(2) Sanctions for failure to produce statement. If a party elects not to comply with an order under Rule 26.2(a) to deliver a statement to the moving party, the court may not consider the testimony of a witness whose statement is withheld.

Commentary

By Prof. Louis M. Natali
Temple University Beasley School of Law

Rule 5.1 deals with the conduct of the preliminary examination as required by Rule 5. The hearing is required for a defendant in custody for ten days who remains unindicted. There are several important limits on the hearing. Hearsay is admissible to establish probable cause, objections as to how the evidence was obtained are not heard and no motion to suppress will be entertained. The logic of these limitations lies in the fact that the only issue for decision is whether probable cause exists. A long line of cases and the rule itself allow the probable cause decision to be made on hearsay. Moreover the magistrate may not make credibility assessments of the witnesses. This will be done at trial by the fact finder.

The key decision for counsel is whether to ask any questions at all. If the government has not made out its case, counsel should move for a discharge on the grounds that the evidence, even if believed, does not establish probable cause. In this way counsel should try to limit the information and not open doors to buttress a weak case. In reality, however, most cases will be held to answer in the district court via indictment. In that event counsel must pursue a different course. Instead of making useless objections, counsel should use this hearing to learn as much about the evidence that exists and to learn the full extent of what absent witnesses have said about the defendant. Once it is clear that the case will not be discharged, it will not matter if the magistrate hears all the damaging evidence in the prosecutor's possession. Better that it comes out at the earliest moment than subsequently. The prosecutor will likely object after it becomes clear that the object is discovery and not an attack on probable cause.

In appropriate cases counsel should consider calling other agents or lay witnesses to discover and record their testimony. However, this right is rarely accorded and, when it is, it is usually limited by the magistrate. The thrust of the response must be that the witness will aid the court in making the probable cause determination.

III. Indictment and Information

Rule 6. The Grand Jury

(a) **Summoning grand juries.**

(1) **Generally.** The court shall order one or more grand juries to be summoned at such time as the public interest requires. The grand jury shall consist of not less than 16 nor more than 23 members. The court shall direct that a sufficient number of legally qualified persons be summoned to meet this requirement.

(2) **Alternate jurors.** The court may direct that alternate jurors may be designated at the time a grand jury is selected. Alternate jurors in the order in which they were designated may thereafter be impanelled as provided in subdivision (g) of this rule. Alternate jurors shall be drawn in the same manner and shall have the same qualifications as the regular jurors, and if impanelled shall be subject to the same challenges, shall take the same oath and shall have the same functions, powers, facilities and privileges as the regular jurors.

(b) **Objections to grand jury and to grand jurors.**

(1) **Challenges.** The attorney for the government or a defendant who has been held to answer in the district court may challenge the array of jurors on the ground that the grand jury was not selected, drawn or summoned in accordance with law, and may challenge an individual juror on the ground that the juror is not legally qualified. Challenges shall be made before the administration of the oath to the jurors and shall be tried by the court.

(2) **Motion to dismiss.** A motion to dismiss the indictment may be based on objections to the array or on the lack of legal qualification of an individual juror, if not previously determined upon challenge. It shall be made in the manner prescribed in 28 U.S.C. § 1867(e) and shall be granted under the conditions prescribed in that statute. An indictment shall not be dismissed on the ground that one or more members of the grand jury were not legally qualified if it appears from the

record kept pursuant to subdivision (c) of this rule that 12 or more jurors, after deducting the number not legally qualified, concurred in finding the indictment.

(c) Foreperson and deputy foreperson. The court shall appoint one of the jurors to be foreperson and another to be deputy foreperson. The foreperson shall have power to administer oaths and affirmations and shall sign all indictments. The foreperson or another juror designated by the foreperson shall keep a record of the number of jurors concurring in the finding of every indictment and shall file the record with the clerk of the court, but the record shall not be made public except on order of the court. During the absence of the foreperson, the deputy foreperson shall act as foreperson.

(d) Who may be present.

(1) While grand jury is in session. Attorneys for the government, the witness under examination, interpreters when needed and, for the purpose of taking the evidence, a stenographer or operator of a recording device may be present while the grand jury is in session.

(2) During deliberations and voting. No person other than the jurors, and any interpreter necessary to assist a juror who is hearing or speech impaired, may be present while the grand jury is deliberating or voting.

(e) Recording and disclosure of proceedings.

(1) Recording of proceedings. All proceedings, except when the grand jury is deliberating or voting, shall be recorded stenographically or by an electronic recording device. An unintentional failure of any recording to reproduce all or any portion of a proceeding shall not affect the validity of the prosecution. The recording or reporter's notes or any transcript prepared therefrom shall remain in the custody or control of the attorney for the government unless otherwise ordered by the court in a particular case.

(2) General rule of secrecy. A grand juror, an interpreter, a stenographer, an operator of a recording device, a typist who transcribes recorded testimony, an attorney for the government, or any person to whom disclosure is made under paragraph (3)(A)(ii) of this subdivision shall not disclose matters occurring before the grand jury, except as otherwise provided for in these rules. No obligation of secrecy may be imposed on any person except in accordance with this rule. A knowing violation of Rule 6 may be punished as a contempt of court.

(3) Exceptions.

(A) Disclosure otherwise prohibited by this rule of matters occurring before the grand jury, other than its deliberations and the vote of any grand juror, may be made to—

(i) an attorney for the government for use in the performance of such attorney's duty; and

(ii) such government personnel (including personnel of a state or subdivision of a state) as are deemed necessary by an attorney for the government to assist an attorney for the government in the performance of such attorney's duty to enforce federal criminal law.

(B) Any person to whom matters are disclosed under subparagraph (A)(ii) of this paragraph shall not utilize that grand jury material for any purpose other than assisting the attorney for the government in the performance of such attorney's duty to enforce federal criminal law. An attorney for the government shall promptly provide the district court, before which was impaneled the grand jury whose material has been so disclosed, with the names of the persons to whom such disclosure has been made, and shall certify that the attorney has advised such persons of their obligation of secrecy under this rule.

(C) Disclosure otherwise prohibited by this rule of matters occurring before the grand jury may also be made–

(i) when so directed by a court preliminarily to or in connection with a judicial proceeding;

(ii) when permitted by a court at the request of the defendant, upon a showing that grounds may exist for a motion to dismiss the indictment because of matters occurring before the grand jury; or

(iii) when the disclosure is made by an attorney for the government to another federal grand jury; or

(iv) when permitted by a court at the request of an attorney for the government, upon a showing that such matters may disclose a violation of state criminal law, to an appropriate official of a state or subdivision of a state for the purpose of enforcing such law. If the court orders disclosure of matters occurring before the grand jury, the disclosure shall be made in such manner, at such time, and under such conditions as the court may direct.

(D) A petition for disclosure pursuant to subdivision (e)(3)(C)(i) shall be filed in the district where the grand jury convened. Unless the hearing is ex parte, which it may be when the petitioner is the government, the petitioner shall serve written notice of the petition upon (i) the attorney for the government, (ii) the parties to the judicial proceeding if disclosure is sought in connection with such a proceeding, and (iii) such other persons as the court may direct. The court shall afford those persons a reasonable opportunity to appear and be heard.

(E) If the judicial proceeding giving rise to the petition is in a federal district court in another district, the court shall transfer the matter to that court unless it can reasonably obtain sufficient knowledge of the proceeding to determine whether disclosure is proper. The court shall order transmitted to the court to which the matter is transferred the material sought to be disclosed, if feasible, and a written evaluation of the need for continued grand jury secrecy. The court to which the matter is transferred shall afford the aforementioned persons a reasonable opportunity to appear and be heard.

(4) Sealed indictments. The federal magistrate judge to whom an indictment is returned may direct that the indictment be kept secret until the defendant is in custody or has been released pending trial. Thereupon the clerk shall seal the indictment and no person shall disclose the return of the indictment except when necessary for the issuance and execution of a warrant or summons.

(5) Closed hearing. Subject to any right to an open hearing in contempt proceedings, the court shall order a hearing on matters affecting a grand jury proceeding to be closed to the extent necessary to prevent disclosure of matters occurring before a grand jury.

(6) **Sealed records.** Records, orders and subpoenas relating to grand jury proceedings shall be kept under seal to the extent and for such time as is necessary to prevent disclosure of matters occurring before a grand jury.

(f) Finding and return of indictment. A grand jury may indict only upon the concurrence of 12 or more jurors. The indictment shall be returned by the grand jury, or through the foreperson or deputy foreperson on its behalf, to a federal magistrate judge in open court. If a complaint or information is pending against the defendant and 12 jurors do not vote to indict, the foreperson shall so report to a federal magistrate judge in writing as soon as possible.

(g) Discharge and excuse. A grand jury shall serve until discharged by the court, but no grand jury may serve more than 18 months unless the court extends the service of the grand jury for a period of six months or less upon a determination that such extension is in the public interest. At any time for cause shown the court may excuse a juror either temporarily or permanently, and in the latter event the court may impanel another person in place of the juror excused.

Commentary

By Prof. Louis M. Natali
Temple University Beasley School of Law

Generally

The rule on grand juries is complex and not well written. It also must be read together with Rule 12(b).

Challenges to the Panel or Individual Grand Jurors

Subdivisions (a) and (b) deal with how the grand jury is created and with challenges to it because it was not "selected, drawn or summoned" in accordance with law. This language refers to both constitutional and statutory rights to have a fair and representative array. In practice issues arise with respect to (1) biased or prejudiced grand jurors and (2) problems of under-representation by race, gender, or ethnic group.

In order to make such a challenge via a motion to quash the indictment under Rule 12, it is necessary to obtain the names of the panel and to conduct some study or investigation because this objection must be made pretrial. While the grand jurors are sworn in open court, counsel will rarely know of this event or whether or not his client will be indicted. Thus it may be impossible to make this motion until after indictment and investigation. The names of grand jurors may be obtained from the clerk of court or upon motion to the court.

Challenges to panels because of underrepresentational issues are also complex and often require expert testimony and statistical analysis to prove the elements of a claim for under-representation. However, the doctrinal law based on the equal protection clause provides that it is not necessary that one be a member of the affected group to make such a challenge. Grand jury witnesses may not make such a challenge.

Secrecy of the Proceedings

Grand jury secrecy is the general rule. The proceedings are, however, required to be recorded. Rule 6(e)(3)(C) provides the possible grounds for exceptions to the secrecy requirement. Subdivisions (C)(i) and (ii) provide the most practical basis for defense counsel to obtain the entire proceeding.

Misconduct

Informal discovery or Jencks Act (18 USCS § 3500) discovery will result in counsel's receiving the grand jury testimony of all witnesses the government will use in its case-in-chief. These transcripts should be read as early as possible. They will often be the source of valuable impeachment material. But they may also reveal grand juror and prosecutor comments. Such comments may provide the factual basis for a motion for disclosure under Rule 6(e)(3)(C)(ii) and to serve as a ground to dismiss for grand juror or prosecutorial misconduct.

Impeachment

Although most indictments are secured on the summary testimony of a single federal law enforcement agent, trial witnesses can be called to testify before the grand jury in order to lock in their testimony. There are two ways to obtain their testimony. One is through informal discovery pursuant to Rule 16, the other is under the Jencks Act (18 USCS § 3500) and Rule 26.2 which requires that the government provide the testimony after the witness has testified on direct examination.

The first method is obviously the preferred method but careful counsel will always ask, as part of cross-examination, as to whether she is in possession of all witness statements and testimony. If there are additional statements either by way of grand jury follow-up appearances or subsequent statements, the court will order their production before cross-examination is to be completed. Counsel should insure that there is sufficient time to read these statements. A recess may be necessary.

Many courts will suggest to the prosecution that such Jencks material be provided the evening before the witness' appearance. Any inconsistencies between the witness' trial testimony and his grand jury testimony may be exploited on cross-examination, closing, and via a request for an instruction about witness credibility and the jury's right to reject entirely the testimony of a witness who has been impeached on an important point.

Lexis Search Tip

To find a commentary on a particular rule using a table-of-content lookup of the USCS Federal Rules, do the following:

1. Click Federal Legal – U.S.

2. Click USCS Federal Rules.

3. Click Federal Rules of Criminal Procedure.

4. Click Article III The Indictment and the Information.

5. Click Rule 6 Grand Jury.

Click on "Review expert commentary from The National Institute for Trial Advocacy" which appears just before Rule 6 and view the commentary written by Professor Louis M. Natali.

Rule 7. The Indictment and the Information

(a) **Use of indictment or information.** An offense which may be punished by death shall be prosecuted by indictment. An offense which may be punished by imprisonment for a term exceeding one year or at hard labor shall be prosecuted by indictment or, if indictment is waived, it may be prosecuted by information. Any other offense may be prosecuted by indictment or by information. An information may be filed without leave of court.

(b) **Waiver of indictment.** An offense which may be punished by imprisonment for a term exceeding one year or at hard labor may be prosecuted by information if the defendant, after having been advised of the nature of the charge and of the rights of the defendant, waives in open court prosecution by indictment.

(c) **Nature and contents.**

(1) **In general.** The indictment or the information shall be a plain, concise and definite written statement of the essential facts constituting the offense charged. It shall be signed by the attorney for the government. It need not contain a formal commencement, a formal conclusion or any other matter not necessary to such statement. Allegations made in one count may be incorporated by reference in another count. It may be alleged in a single count that the means by which the defendant committed the offense are unknown or that the defendant committed it by one or more specified means. The indictment or information shall state for each count the official or customary citation of the statute, rule, regulation or other provision of law which the defendant is alleged therein to have violated.

(2) **Criminal forfeiture.** No judgment of forfeiture may be entered in a criminal proceeding unless the indictment or the information provides notice that the defendant has an interest in property that is subject to forfeiture in accordance with the applicable statute.

(3) **Harmless error.** Error in the citation or its omission shall not be ground for dismissal of the indictment or information or for reversal of a conviction if the error or omission did not mislead the defendant to the defendant's prejudice.

(d) Surplusage. The court on motion of the defendant may strike surplusage from the indictment or information.

(e) Amendment of information. The court may permit an information to be amended at any time before verdict or finding if no additional or different offense is charged and if substantial rights of the defendant are not prejudiced.

(f) Bill of particulars. The court may direct the filing of a bill of particulars. A motion for a bill of particulars may be made before arraignment or within ten days after arraignment or at such other later time as the court may permit. A bill of particulars may be amended at any time subject to such conditions as justice requires.

Commentary

By Prof. Louis M. Natali
Temple University Beasley School of Law

This Rule concerns itself with the wording of the indictment (used for felonies) and the information (used for misdemeanor and where indictment is waived). It also contains authority to obtain a bill of particulars when the indictment provides inadequate information to prepare a defense.

Generally the indictment will be the method of charging a serious case. However, under subdivision (b) informations may be used for those pleading guilty to felonies where there may be a plea bargain and it will not be necessary to put the prosecution to the trouble of presenting evidence to a grand jury. The defendant must waive the constitutional right to indictment in open court after a colloquy.

Subdivision (c) deals with the content of the indictment which must always be read with care. The indictment will be divided into counts each charging a separate crime and stating the statute violated. An effective way to prepare for trial is to compare the counts to the code and to the jury instructions for each offense. Counsel should then ask which facts prove which elements of each offense as stated in the Code and in the jury instructions. Both pattern instructions and case law should be consulted in carrying out this task.

Often it will appear that the indictment charges in broad statutory language which may contain different factual theories. It may be necessary to use subdivision (f) to request a bill of particulars to force the prosecutor to opt for one theory or another. Courts have ceded much discretion to prosecutors and do not smile upon such motions. However, they are granted when a compelling showing is made that the defense is impaired.

Each count should only contain one offense, and a motion to dismiss on grounds of duplicity should be considered if this is not the case. On the other hand, multiplicity is the charging of a single offense in more than one count. However, each victim will usually constitute a separate offense.

Conspiracy indictments pose special problems in pleading. A conspiracy count will describe the purposes and goals of the conspiracy and also set out sufficient overt acts committed by the coconspirators to put them on notice as to how to defend. It may aver more than one goal, *e.g.*, the delivery of cocaine and heroin. It will also provide the names of unindicted coconspirators who will probably be witnesses against those indicted. Unindicted coconspirators will often have made deals with the prosecutor (pleading guilty via the information) or have been granted immunity. The other method for presenting their testimony will be via tapes made through electronic or telephonic surveillance.

One may need to seek a bill of particulars to learn and limit the proof at trial. An indictment which is grudging in providing overt acts should be the subject of a bill. The date of the indictment is also significant in all cases but especially in conspiracy cases. The government may use coconspirator statements only made during the pendency of the conspiracy and in furtherance thereof. Thus the date is critical. The conspiracy usually ends with arrest or indictment and post-arrest/post-indictment statements are inadmissible. *See* Federal Rule of Evidence 801(d).

Where the prosecutor uses both a conspiracy and a complicity theory, counsel should attempt to force an election of theories. Notice, the right to prepare a defense, and jury confusion should be the basis of this motion.

Subdivision (d) provides for a motion to strike surplusage. Surplusage may include outrageous reference to a defendant which suggest he has committed other crimes such as "the enforcer" or the "killer." *See* Federal Rule of Evidence 404(b). Or the indictment may plead information and material that is inadmissible and irrelevant.

Insufficiency

A motion to quash on grounds of insufficiency may be made if a particular count does not state an offense. But this will only result in a pyrrhic victory because, so long as the statute of limitations has not run, the prosecutor will simply amend the indictment. It is far better not to alert the prosecutor and move for a judgment of acquittal at the close of the government's case. See Rule 29. If it turns out that there is an element that has not been proved, the court should grant the motion. But courts, in their discretion, may allow the government to reopen if they are easily able to prove a missing element. It may be best to wait until the close of all the evidence to make such a motion or as part of a motion for new trial.

Rule 8. Joinder of Offenses and of Defendants

(a) Joinder of offenses. Two or more offenses may be charged in the same indictment or information in a separate count for each offense if the offenses charged, whether felonies or misdemeanors or both, are of the same or similar character or are based on the same act or transaction or on two or more acts or transactions connected together or constituting parts of a common scheme or plan.

(b) Joinder of defendants. Two or more defendants may be charged in the same indictment or information if they are alleged to have participated in the same act or transaction or in the same series of acts or transactions constituting an offense or offenses. Such defendants may be charged in one or more counts together or separately and all of the defendants need not be charged in each count.

Commentary

By Prof. Louis M. Natali
Temple University Beasley School of Law

Generally

This Rule defines when offenses and defendants may be joined in the same indictment. It must be read together with Rule 14 which sets out when one may seek relief from a prejudicial joinder of either offenses or codefendants. Each crime must be charged in a separate count.

Offenses

A single defendant may be charged with more than one offense in separate counts under this rule if the crimes are of the same or similar "character," if based on the same transaction, or if two or more transactions are part of a common scheme or plan.

Same Character Offenses

This is an unfortunate phrase since such evidence may be barred under Federal Rule of Evidence 404(b). But in this connection, if a defendant is charged with a spree of similar offenses, *e.g.*, bank robberies or drug sales, they may be joined in a single indictment. While Federal Rules of Evidence 403 and 404(b) should be the basis for a severance, the prosecutor may argue that Federal Rule of Criminal Procedure 9 is an exception. However, the extreme prejudice that joinder brings about should be stressed and unless the offenses meet a 404(b) exception, a severance should be granted.

Same Transaction

This refers to cases where several crimes may have been committed together as a part of one transaction such as auto theft, bank robbery, and illegal weapon possession, where it is averred that the accused stole a car, and used a sawed-off shotgun to rob a bank. These types of crimes will rarely be severed. *See* the Commentary for FRCrP 14.

Part of a Scheme

This refers to charges of conspiracy, mail fraud, and wire fraud where the goal results in the commission of a series of offenses each time the conspirators accomplish their goal, *e.g.*, a conspiracy to commit a number of bank robberies using stolen cars and prohibited weapons. Again, it will be difficult to sever these offenses unless you meet one of the conditions discussed in the treatment of Rule 14.

Joinder of Defendants

Defendants may be joined in a single indictment if they are alleged to have participated in the commission of the same crime or crimes or in the same series of "acts or transactions" which constitute an offense. Co-participants will normally be charged as coconspirators under 18 USCS § 371 and as aiders and abettors under 18 USCS § 2. There is a preference for trying all participants together. Unless the court is persuaded by the reasons of a constitutional violation under *Bruton*, 391 U.S. 123, 20 L. Ed. 2d 476, 88 S. Ct. 1620 (1968), or because of prejudice (*see* the Commentary for FRCrP 14), all participants will be tried together.

The fact that one codefendant has made a confession is the single best ground for a severance. Thus, before rejecting this ground (Rule 14) for relief, counsel should engage in both formal and Rule 16 discovery. Co-counsel must also be consulted to determine which defendants made statements.

Rule 9. Warrant or Summons Upon Indictment or Information

(a) Issuance. Upon the request of the attorney for the government the court shall issue a warrant for each defendant named in an information supported by a showing of probable cause under oath as is required by Rule 4(a), or in an indictment. Upon the request of the attorney for the government a summons instead of a warrant shall issue. If no request is made, the court may issue either a warrant or a summons in its discretion. More than one warrant or summons may issue for the same defendant. The clerk shall deliver the warrant or summons to the marshal or other person authorized by law to execute or serve it. If a defendant fails to appear in response to the summons, a warrant shall issue. When a defendant arrested with a warrant or given a summons appears initially before a magistrate judge, the magistrate judge shall proceed in accordance with the applicable subdivisions of Rule 5.

(b) Form.

(1) Warrant. The form of the warrant shall be as provided in Rule 4(c)(1) except that it shall be signed by the clerk, it shall describe the offense charged in the indictment or information and it shall command that the defendant be arrested and brought before the nearest available magistrate judge. The amount of bail may be fixed by the court and endorsed on the warrant.

(2) Summons. The summons shall be in the same form as the warrant except that it shall summon the defendant to appear before a magistrate judge at a stated time and place.

(c) Execution or service; and return.

(1) Execution or service. The warrant shall be executed or the summons served as provided in Rule 4(d)(1), (2) and (3). A summons to a corporation shall be served by delivering a copy to an officer or to a managing or general agent or to any other agent authorized by appointment or by law to receive service of process and, if the agent is one authorized by statute to receive service and the statute so requires, by also mailing a copy to the corporation's last known address within the district or at its principal place of business elsewhere in the United States. The officer executing the warrant shall bring the arrested person without unnecessary delay before the nearest available federal magistrate judge or, in the event that a federal magistrate judge is not reasonably available, before a state or local judicial officer authorized by 18 U.S.C. § 3041.

(2) Return. The officer executing a warrant shall make return thereof to the magistrate judge or other officer before whom the defendant is brought. At the request of the attorney for the government any unexecuted warrant shall be returned and cancelled. On or before the return day the person to whom a summons was delivered for service shall make return thereof. At the request of the attorney for the government made at any time while the indictment or information is pending, a warrant returned unexecuted and not cancelled or a summons returned unserved or a duplicate thereof may be delivered by the clerk to the marshal or other authorized person for execution or service.

Rule 9. Warrant or Summons Upon Indictment or Information

Commentary

By Prof. Inga L. Parsons
New York University School of Law

FRCrP 9 sets forth the requirements for issuance of a summons or warrant for a defendant upon grand jury indictment or prosecutor's information. These requirements are similar to FRCrP 4 providing for issuance of an arrest warrant or summons upon a complaint.

Sufficiency of Probable Cause

If the prosecutor has obtained an indictment, no further evidence of probable cause is required to obtain a warrant or summons under FRCrP 9. Strategically, the prosecutor may wish to proceed by indictment rather than complaint or information for issuance of the arrest warrant, since grand jury proceedings are secret and the grand jury is essentially a rubber stamp for whatever the prosecutor places before it, be it probable cause or a ham sandwich. The prosecutor can proceed by information if the charge is a misdemeanor. For felonies, the prosecution must proceed by indictment unless the defendant waives indictment. *See* the Commentary for FRCrP 7.

If the prosecution proceeds by information, FRCrP 9 requires that the request be supported by probable cause. Probable cause must be set out in a sworn affidavit detailing the necessary facts, typically sworn to by the case agent. A prosecutor's information alone, without an affidavit setting forth the facts to establish probable cause, is insufficient. *Gerstein v. Pugh*, 420 U.S. 103, 43 L. Ed. 2d 54, 95 S. Ct. 854 (1975). Neither FRCrP 4 nor FRCrP 9 define probable cause; thus, the totality of the circumstances standard is used.

The defendant has a right to challenge the sufficiency of the facts in the affidavit offered to support probable cause. The defendant does not have a right to challenge the issuance of a summons or warrant based on indictment since the grand jury's determination of probable cause is a sufficient finding, provided the grand jury is properly constituted under FRCrP 6. When the prosecution has proceeded by information with a sworn affidavit, defense counsel should obtain the affidavit and review it to see whether it indeed sufficiently sets forth probable cause to believe an offense was committed and that it was the defendant who committed it.

In addition to assessing the sufficiency of the probable cause, the affidavit can provide additional discovery to the defense which is particularly useful if the case was not initiated with a complaint but through a prosecutor's information that merely tracked the language of the statute. The affidavit may also provide grounds for impeaching the officer at a future hearing or trial. With that in mind, prosecutors should be careful about what is included and not included in the affidavit. It is a good idea to include a clause stating that not all information known in the case is detailed in the affidavit, but only what is necessary to support the application. If a complaint was already filed, prosecutors should rely, when possible, on the original complaint to obtain the warrant under FRCrP 4, rather than create a whole separate affidavit under FRCrP 9. If additional information is required, the better practice for prosecutors would be to supplement the complaint, rather than file a full new affidavit that defense counsel will try to use for impeachment if there are any inconsistencies with the original complaint or other documents in the case. Of course, if the prosecutor obtains an indictment, no affidavit is required.

Strategies to Avoid Issuance of a Warrant

The prosecutor will sometimes notify defense counsel (if present in the case at that time) in advance of seeking a warrant. This advance notice is more likely to happen in white collar crimes or with low-level, nonviolent offenders. It is also more likely to happen when defense counsel and the prosecutor have a good working relationship. To paraphrase a common adage: a good lawyer knows the law, a great lawyer knows the judge, and a really great lawyer knows the federal prosecutor. If defense counsel learns of a pending warrant or expects a warrant to be issued, counsel should try to persuade the prosecutor to proceed by a summons. It is in the prosecutor's discretion to request the issuance of a summons rather than a warrant under FRCrP 9(a). The summons provides for a voluntary appearance at a set time and place. When the prosecutor cannot be convinced to proceed by a summons, defense counsel should make arrangements to have the defendant surrender voluntarily on the warrant by asking that the prosecutor "hold off the dogs" (meaning the U.S. Marshals) with the understanding that the defendant will surrender posthaste. If the defendant does not show up by a set deadline, the U.S. Marshals can then act on the warrant.

A voluntary appearance on a warrant, like a voluntary appearance on a summons, avoids an often degrading and embarrassing arrest and is extremely helpful in obtaining release on the defendant's own recognizance, since it bolsters the defense's argument that there is very little risk that the defendant will flee in the future. If defense counsel is unable to contact the defendant to surrender voluntarily or to convince the prosecutor to request a summons, counsel should ask that bail be set on the warrant to allow for immediate release when the defendant is arrested. *See* FRCrP 9(b)(1). If the client voluntarily surrenders and the warrant is still outstanding, defense counsel should ensure that the prosecutor vacates the unexecuted warrant under FRCrP 9(c)(1). Otherwise, the U.S. Marshals, an agency independent from the U.S. Attorney's Office, will act on the warrant and arrest a client unnecessarily.

"Unnecessary Delay" Considerations

If a warrant is issued, the defendant may be arrested any time thereafter (unlike a search warrant issued under FRCrP 41 requiring execution within 10 days). Once a defendant is arrested pursuant to FRCrP 9, the officer executing the warrant must bring the defendant "without unnecessary delay" before the nearest available magistrate judge for an initial appearance pursuant to FRCrP 5. Neither FRCrP 9 nor FRCrP 4 (also requiring the defendant be brought without unnecessary delay) defines the term "unnecessary delay," although the 1944 Advisory Committee Notes to FRCrP 5 provide that unnecessary delay must be "determined in light of all the facts and circumstances of the case."

When a defendant is arrested on a warrant issued by complaint, the Supreme Court provides for a safe harbor from challenges of undue delay if there is a judicial determination of probable cause within forty-eight hours from the time of arrest. *County of Riverside v. McLaughlin*, 500 U.S. 44, 114 L.Ed.2d 49, 111 S.Ct. 1661 (1991). A warrant issued on an indictment or information does not require a judicial determination of probable cause, so the forty-eight-hour rule is not binding, but can be a context for the defense to argue that the delay was unnecessary. Since there is no set time when a delay is unreasonable, defense counsel must argue why this delay is unreasonable under the circumstances.

Unfortunately for the defense motion, post-indictment delays of as long as five days have been upheld under FRCrP 9, *see United States v. Purvis*, 768 F.2d 1237 (11th Cir. 1985). Nevertheless, many of the cases finding no unnecessary delay may be distinguished, and the role of defense counsel is to show that the reasons proffered by this prosecutor justifying the delay are insufficient, as well as to individualize the prejudice to this particular client.

At the appearance on the warrant, defense counsel should ensure that the court inquire on the record as to the date and time the defendant was arrested. The present date and time should also be noted so that any delay can be calculated. If the delay seems at all unreasonable—even a delay of an hour may be undue if the defendant was arrested outside the agency office—defense counsel should ask the judge to have the prosecution set down the reasons for the delay. Defense counsel should insist that there be a hearing to determine why the delay occurred and what transpired during the delay (often it is to interrogate the defendant). Defense counsel should also insist that the arresting agents take the stand under oath on the matter, rather than allow the prosecution to proceed by proffer. Since probable cause itself cannot be established solely by prosecutor information, the defense can argue that something as important as unnecessary delay should likewise be based on facts to which the declarant has personal knowledge given under oath. A hearing on the issue of unnecessary delay could lead to discovery of additional information, as well as provide the basis for the court to determine that the delay was necessary.

The remedy for unnecessary delay is not necessarily dismissal of the indictment or information. *See* the Commentary for FRCrP 48. There are technically no Speedy Trial Act violations which the defense can invoke because the speedy trial clock begins to run when the defendant is brought before a magistrate judge or the filing of an indictment or information—whichever is later. 18 USCS § 3161(c)(1). Thus, although the speedy trial clock began to run from the time the indictment or information was filed, once the defendant appeared before the magistrate judge the clock is, in a sense, restarted.

If evidence is obtained during an unnecessary post-indictment delay, the remedy will be suppression. *See United States v. Perez-Torribio*, 987 F.Supp 245, 247 (S.D.N.Y. 1998) (government conceded thirty-two-day post-indictment presentment delay

Rule 9. Warrant or Summons Upon Indictment or Information

was unnecessary, but court found dismissal was not an available remedy since Speedy Trial Act did not apply but that remedy was suppression of statements taken during period of delay). Although extremely unlikely to prevail, defense counsel should still consider whether the delay was so prejudicial that it may have violated the defendant's due process or Sixth Amendment trial rights (only available if the defendant is detained), particularly if the delay resulted in the loss of defense witnesses or was done deliberately by the government to obtain a strategic advantage.

IV. Arraignment and Preparation for Trial

Rule 10. Arraignment

Arraignment shall be conducted in open court and shall consist of reading the indictment or information to the defendant or stating to the defendant the substance of the charge and calling on the defendant to plead thereto. The defendant shall be given a copy of the indictment or information before being called upon to plead.

Commentary

By Prof. Inga L. Parsons
New York University School of Law

The purpose of a formal arraignment under FRCrP 10 is to advise the defendant of the indictment or information, and to have the defendant plead guilty or not guilty to the charges. Many federal practitioners, and even judges, refer to the initial appearance under FRCrP 5 as an "arraignment," though it is not properly an arraignment of the defendant as prescribed by FRCrP 10.

Notification of the Charges

Although FRCrP 10 provides for a reading of the indictment, defendants routinely waive their right to have the indictment or information read in its entirety in open court. There is little to be gained by a formal reading (particularly a lengthy indictment), unless a defendant insists on such a reading. Defense counsel should ensure that the defendant has a copy of the indictment and that it has been read out loud to the defendant by counsel or an interpreter prior to the arraignment.

Omissions or technical failures at an arraignment are not ordinarily grounds for vacating convictions where the defendant is otherwise aware of the charges and no prejudice is shown. *See, e.g., United States v. Reynolds*, 781 F.2d 135, 136, n.2 (8th Cir. 1986) (absence of arraignment on superceding indictment was "of little consequence" where defendant had sufficient notice of the accusation and an adequate opportunity to defend himself).

Plea Strategies

The arraignment is when the case is typically assigned to a judge unless the case has been assigned to a judge in advance by the court clerk. In districts where the defendant may plead guilty before the intake district judge, defense counsel should be cognizant of who the sitting judge will be and the possibility of having the defendant enter a guilty plea at that stage to secure a favorable judge. As the saying goes, a good lawyer knows the law, a great lawyer knows the judge. In many cases, however, the arraignment stage is too early to make a determination of whether the defendant should plead guilty. Moreover, in most districts this so-called "judge shopping" is unavailable for felony indictments either because the district court judge is assigned randomly by the court clerk in advance or because a magistrate judge presides over the arraignment. Counsel should become familiar with the local practice on arraignment procedure, which differs from district to district.

FRCrP 5 provides that a defendant shall not be called upon to plead at an initial appearance if the offense is not triable by the magistrate judge. (Under 18 USCS § 3401 a magistrate judge only has jurisdiction to try and sentence defendants accused of misdemeanors.) Thus, the defendant accused of a felony who is arraigned by a magistrate judge necessarily enters a not guilty plea and the case is "wheeled out" to a district court judge typically by pulling a judge's card randomly out of a wheel. Defendants accused of misdemeanors only may be arraigned at the initial appearance in front of the magistrate judge, and defense counsel representing defendants accused of misdemeanors should be prepared at the initial appearance for the defendant to also enter a guilty or not guilty plea. See the Commentary for FRCrP 58.

In many districts, felony guilty pleas are referred to magistrate judges with the consent of the defendant. Although a magistrate judge cannot accept a guilty plea to a felony, the magistrate judge will conduct the FRCrP 11 allocution, and refer the plea and the record back to the district court judge with a recommendation to accept the plea of guilty. District court judges appear to rubber stamp these recommendations.

Not all district judges refer guilty pleas to magistrate judges. In many cases it may be useful to have the district judge conduct the allocution to humanize the defendant in front of the sentencing judge. On the other hand, it may be preferable to have the allocution before the sentencing judge in black-and-white print instead, particularly if the defendant's demeanor is such that it could detract from remorse or acceptance of responsibility.

It would be the rare case where a judge referred a plea to a magistrate judge and a defendant did not consent. Defense counsel may rightly fear that failure to consent could irritate the sentencing judge who will then have to conduct the plea. However, if it is crucial to have the judge conduct the allocution, the defendant may avoid such referral by refusing, artfully of course, to give consent, albeit with some risk.

There may be other strategic advantages in having the defendant plead guilty before the magistrate judge rather than the district court judge. If the defendant decides to withdraw his plea (*see* FRCrP 32(e)) before the district court judge has acted on the magistrate judge's recommendation, defense counsel might argue that a formal guilty plea had not been entered. A felony guilty plea before a magistrate judge by referral may provide an additional ground for granting a motion to withdraw a plea since it was not taken before a district court judge who technically has sole jurisdiction over the felony plea. Any challenge based on the insufficiency of the arraignment proceedings such as the entry of a guilty plea before a magistrate judge not empowered to take a felony plea should be made before trial, or it may be considered waived.

Assignment of Counsel and Bail Considerations

If the government has proceeded against the defendant by way of indictment rather than complaint, the arraignment may also be the initial appearance for the defendant in federal court. Both the prosecution and defense counsel should ensure that the judge inform the defendant of his or her applicable rights under FRCrP 5 including the right to counsel, bail, and the right to remain silent. Arraignment has been deemed a critical stage of the proceedings and the defendant is entitled to the assistance of counsel. *See, e.g., McConnell v. United States,* 375 F.2d 905 (5th Cir. 1967) (the arraignment in a federal criminal prosecution is a vital part of the criminal process and the accused is entitled to the assistance of counsel).

Defense counsel should be prepared to argue for bail. If it is the initial appearance in federal court, as well as arraignment, this will be the first opportunity to request that the defendant be released. If bail has been denied at the initial appearance, defense counsel may want to make another bail application or supplement the previous application either to the sitting magistrate judge (who may be more receptive to granting bail than the one who denied bail previously) or to the newly assigned district court judge, depending on the practice of the court and the individual practices of the assigned judge. Some district judges will refer a bail hearing to a magistrate judge. Since the defendant will have been charged in an information or indictment, he or she will not be entitled to a preliminary examination under Rule 5.1 because the issue of probable cause will have been satisfied by the grand jury indictment or prosecutor's information.

Speedy Trial Issues

When a district court judge is assigned by an intake judge or a magistrate judge, the judge frequently provides instructions either to go directly to the court for a status conference or for the parties to set an immediate date for a status conference. If the judge is assigned in advance, the arraignment is typically combined with the first status conference. Such urgency to hold a status conference arises because the speedy trial clock is triggered from the date the indictment or information is filed, or the initial presentment before the magistrate judge under FRCrP 5, whichever is later. *See* 18 USCS § 3161(c)(1). In most cases the later date is the date the indictment is filed, since most defendants are initially presented on a complaint under FRCrP 4.

Judges ordinarily require an immediate conference at which future delays for negotiations, motions, etc., can be excluded from speedy trial calculations. However, the time between the date the indictment was filed until the date of the status conference is ordinarily counted against the seventy days within which a defendant is supposed to be brought to trial. Future delays, not specifically excluded under the Speedy Trial Act, can be excluded if the ends of justice outweigh the public and the defendant's interest in a speedy trial. *See* 18 USCS § 3161(h)(8)(A). This "interests of justice" catchall exclusion under the Speedy Trial Act cannot be excluded by the court retroactively increasing the need for an immediate conference.

At the initial conference, the assigned judge will usually set a discovery schedule, a motions schedule, if necessary, and even a trial date in order to meet Speedy Trial Act considerations.

Counsel should know how much time has elapsed on the speedy trial clock, the status of discovery, possible motions to be filed and whether the case is likely to go to trial.

Defense counsel should resist any attempt by the court to pin down the defense as to the length of the defense case, whether an alibi or insanity or public authority defense will be invoked at any trial, or whether the defendant will take the stand. Usually the court will accept a tactful explanation that such issues require additional investigation and consideration, but that the defense is mindful of its notice obligations under FRCrP 12.1–12.3.

Defense counsel should also consider what its position will be with respect to consenting to exclusions of time under the Speedy Trial Act. The decision whether to consent to exclusions becomes particularly important where the defendant is incarcerated. If an unnecessary delay has already occurred, it may be advantageous not to consent to exclusions. Although the judge can independently exclude the time if a proper basis exists, objecting to exclusions may bolster a future motion for dismissal on speedy trial grounds.

Rule 11. Pleas

(a) Alternatives.

(1) In general. A defendant may plead guilty, not guilty, or nolo contendere. If a defendant refuses to plead, or if a defendant organization, as defined in 18 U.S.C. § 18, fails to appear, the court shall enter a plea of not guilty.

(2) Conditional pleas. With the approval of the court and the consent of the government, a defendant may enter a conditional plea of guilty or nolo contendere, reserving in writing the right, on appeal from the judgment, to review of the adverse determination of any specified pretrial motion. A defendant who prevails on appeal he shall be allowed to withdraw the plea.

(b) Nolo contendere.
A defendant may plead nolo contendere only with the consent of the court. Such a plea shall be accepted by the court only after due consideration of the views of the parties and the interest of the public in the effective administration of justice.

(c) Advice to defendant. Before accepting a plea of guilty or nolo contendere, the court must address the defendant personally in open court and inform the defendant of, and determine that the defendant understands, the following:

(1) the nature of the charge to which the plea is offered, the mandatory minimum penalty provided by law, if any, and the maximum possible penalty provided by law, including the effect of any special parole or supervised release term, the fact that the court is required to consider any applicable sentencing guidelines but may depart from those guidelines under some circumstances, and, when applicable, that the court may also order the defendant to make restitution to any victim of the offense; and

(2) if the defendant is not represented by an attorney, that the defendant has the right to be represented by an attorney at every stage of the proceeding and, if necessary, one will be appointed to represent the defendant; and

(3) that the defendant has the right to plead not guilty or to persist in that plea if it has already been made, the right to be tried by a jury and at that trial the right to the assistance of counsel, the right to confront and cross-examine adverse witnesses, and the right against compelled self-incrimination; and

(4) that if a plea of guilty or nolo contendere is accepted by the court there will not be a further trial of any kind, so that by pleading guilty or nolo contendere the defendant waives the right to a trial; and

(5) if the court intends to question the defendant under oath, on the record, and in the presence of counsel about the offense to which the defendant has pleaded, that the defendant's answers may later be used against the defendant in a prosecution for perjury or false statement; and

(6) the terms of any provision in a plea agreement waiving the right to appeal or to collaterally attack the sentence.

(d) Insuring that the plea is voluntary. The court shall not accept a plea of guilty or nolo contendere without first, by addressing the defendant personally in open court, determining that the plea is voluntary and not the result of force or threats or of promises apart from a plea agreement. The court shall also inquire as to whether the defendant's willingness to plead guilty or nolo contendere results from prior discussions between the attorney for the government and the defendant or the defendant's attorney.

(e) Plea agreement procedure.

(1) In general. The attorney for the government and the attorney for the defendant—the defendant when acting pro se—may agree that, upon the defendant's entering a plea of guilty or nolo contendere to a charged offense, or to a lesser or related offense, the attorney for the government will:

(A) move to dismiss other charges; or

(B) recommend, or agree not to oppose the defendant's request for a particular sentence or sentencing range, or that a particular provision of the Sentencing Guidelines, or policy statement, or sentencing factor is or is not applicable to the case. Any such recommendation or request is not binding on the court; or

(C) agree that a specific sentence or sentencing range is the appropriate disposition of the case, or that a particular provision of the Sentencing Guidelines, or policy statement, or sentencing factor is or is not applicable to the case. Such a plea agreement is binding on the court once it is accepted by the court. The court shall not participate in any discussions between the parties concerning any such plea agreement.

(2) Notice of such agreement. If a plea agreement has been reached by the parties, the court shall, on the record, require the disclosure of the agreement in open court or, on a showing of good cause, in camera, at the time the plea is offered. If the agreement is of the type specified in subdivision (e)(1)(A) or (C), the court may accept or reject the agreement, or may defer its decision as to the acceptance or rejection until there has been an opportunity to consider the presentence report. If the agreement is of the type specified in subdivision (e)(1)(B), the court shall advise the defendant that if the court does not accept the recommendation or request the defendant nevertheless has no right to withdraw the plea.

(3) Acceptance of a plea agreement. If the court accepts the plea agreement, the court shall inform the defendant that it will embody in the judgment and sentence the disposition provided for in the plea agreement.

(4) Rejection of a plea agreement. If the court rejects the plea agreement, the court shall, on the record, inform the parties of this fact, advise the defendant personally in open court or, on a showing of good cause, in camera, that the court is not bound by the plea agreement, afford the defendant the opportunity to then withdraw the plea, and advise the defendant that if the defendant persists in a guilty plea or plea of nolo contendere the disposition of the case may be less favorable to the defendant than that contemplated by the plea agreement.

(5) Time of plea agreement procedure. Except for good cause shown, notification to the court of the existence of a plea agreement shall be given at the arraignment or at such other time, prior to trial, as may be fixed by the court.

(6) Inadmissibility of pleas, plea discussions, and related statements. Except as otherwise provided in this paragraph, evidence of the following is not, in any civil or criminal proceeding, admissible against the defendant who made the plea or was a participant in the plea discussions:

(A) a plea of guilty which was later withdrawn;

(B) a plea of nolo contendere;

(C) any statement made in the course of any proceedings under this rule regarding either of the foregoing pleas; or

(D) any statement made in the course of plea discussions with an attorney for the government which do not result in a plea of guilty or which result in a plea of guilty later withdrawn. However, such a statement is admissible (i) in any proceeding wherein another statement made in the course of the same plea or plea discussions has been introduced and the statement ought in fairness be considered contemporaneously with it, or (ii) in a criminal proceeding for perjury or false statement if the statement was made by the defendant under oath, on the record, and in the presence of counsel.

(f) Determining accuracy of plea. Notwithstanding the acceptance of a plea of guilty, the court should not enter a judgment upon such plea without making such inquiry as shall satisfy it that there is a factual basis for the plea.

(g) Record of proceedings. A verbatim record of the proceedings at which the defendant enters a plea shall be made and, if there is a plea of guilty or nolo contendere, the record shall include, without limitation, the court's advice to the defendant, the inquiry into the voluntariness of the plea including any plea agreement, and the inquiry into the accuracy of a guilty plea.

(h) Harmless error. Any variance from the procedures required by this rule which does not affect substantial rights shall be disregarded.

Commentary

By Prof. Louis M. Natali
Temple University Beasley School of Law

Generally

Rule 11 provides the types of pleas a defendant may enter and the procedure for taking these, especially the guilty plea. The sentencing guidelines have much to say about the way plea bargains are now structured and this rule must be read together with both the general and special guidelines governing each count to which a client will enter a plea.

Subdivision (a) provides for the alternatives and stipulates that a defendant may enter a plea of not guilty, guilty, or nolo contendere. However, subdivision (a)(1) provides for a conditional plea. Conditional pleas are used to preserve appellate issues but also to spare the time and expense of trial. They require the approval of the court and the consent of the government. The defendant has no right to enter such a plea.

A conditional plea is often employed after the denial of a motion to suppress or some other pretrial issue where counsel believes he or she may be successful on appeal. Since defendant has very limited rights to interlocutory appeal, this plea is the only effective way to preserve appellate issues and yet get some benefit for entering a guilty plea. There is nothing to prevent the defendant from attempting to negotiate a favorable bargain with the prosecutor. In the event the defendant is successful on appeal, the plea and sentence will be set aside and the parties will proceed according to whatever appellate ruling has been entered. These plea arrangements were approved by the Supreme Court in *Lefkowitz v. Newsome*, 420 U.S. 283, 43 L.Ed. 2d 196, 95 S. Ct. 886 (1975).

Subdivision (b) deals with pleas of nolo contendere. Such a plea literally means that the accused does not contest the charges and is tantamount to a plea of guilty in the criminal case but may not be used in any civil proceeding such as a civil antitrust action or a civil tax matter. It is disfavored by prosecutors, but may be accepted by the court after it considers the views of the parties and the interests of the public. The court will attempt to determine the benefits to the public by requiring a guilty plea which may be admitted in a civil suit as opposed to allowing or forcing the parties to prove difficult factual issues.

While there is no right to enter a nolo plea, the court may be impressed with such considerations as cost, convenience, impact on prosecution witnesses, and efficiency. Such pleas are not uncommon.

Advice to the Defendant Who Enters a Guilty or Nolo Plea

Subdivision (c) deals with the content of the colloquy the court must engage in with a defendant before accepting a guilty or nolo plea. These provisions are in part constitutionally required by the *Boykin*, 395 U.S. 238, 23 L. Ed. 2d 274, 89 S. Ct. 1709 (1969), and *McCarthy*, 394 U.S. 459, 22 L. Ed. 2d 418, 89 S. Ct. 1166 (1969), decisions. The provisions of Rule 11(c)(1)–(5) are set out in a rather straightforward manner and will not be reiterated here, but counsel should review them before a client enters a guilty or nolo plea. Counsel should also review them with the client and role play the questions that the court will ask. Subdivision (5) makes it clear that the client's responses may be used against him in a subsequent perjury trial and must be read together with Rule 410 of the Federal Rules of Evidence. But such a use of colloquy answers is rare. More importantly, the client should be told that the court will ask whether or not he or she committed the offense(s), and why, under subdivisions (d) and (f), the court is given the responsibility to inquire in order to be satisfied that the plea is voluntary and that there is a factual basis for the plea. Often the court will ask a defendant to tell the court in their own words exactly what the defendant did. If the plea bargain fails these statements may not be used at the trial for any purpose, but they may be used in a subsequent perjury prosecution. *See* subdivision (e)(6).

The court will reject a plea where the defendant does not admit all the elements, especially the mens rea elements. Claims of mistake, ignorance, accident, or a lack of complete understanding are taken seriously by judges. No one wants to see a person who maintains their innocence enter a guilty plea. The client should be prepared on all these points. If there is a genuine issue, the court and the prosecutor should be advised in advance of the colloquy that a defendant may deny a particular mental or factual element. The government is officially opposed to a *North Carolina v. Alford*, 400 U.S. 25, 27 L. Ed. 2d 162, 91 S. Ct. 160 (1970) plea arrangement (a plea in which defendant refuses to admit his guilt but concedes that the facts will establish it and that it is in his best interest to plead guilty), but may agree that matters that are delicate for a particular defendant are not to be touched in detail during the colloquy.

Moreover, the court will be concerned that the plea is involuntary if the defendant complains that he or she is not satisfied with defense counsel or that facts and motions or other legal issues have not been adequately investigated. Thus these issues should be resolved with the client well in advance of the colloquy.

Guilty Plea Procedure—Rule 11(e)

Subdivision (e) deals with the procedure for entering a plea agreement. Essentially, the courts will allow a plea bargain but the judge must not participate in it. However, the bargain must be disclosed in open court during the colloquy. If the court does not agree with the bargain that has been struck, the court will so advise the defendant. At this point the defendant may withdraw the plea and go to trial or take the risk that the court may sentence the defendant to a harsher sentence than the one agreed to in the plea bargain. *See* subdivision (e)(4). However, a defendant may not attempt to enter the plea before a different judge.

Subdivision (e)(1)(A)–(C) deals with the more common types of agreements which contemplate the dismissal of charges, sentence recommendations or agreements not to oppose defense requests, and agreement as to a specific sentence.

It must be stressed that since the advent of the Sentencing Guidelines (18 USCS Appx) this rule must be read with the guidelines because sentencing recommendations may include recommendations as to any number of specific downward departures, which may significantly lower a sentence or result in a probationary sentence. In addition, many plea bargains may be arrived at before the indictment is entered, in anticipation of problems concerning all of the defendant's criminal participation, which a probation officer might taken into account when the officer works out the sentencing range in a PSI.

Finally, each judicial district and each judge behave a little differently, and many judges dislike the guidelines. Counsel should consult with experienced counsel, most notably the federal defenders who practice before a particular judge. The judge's law clerks and deputy clerk are also valuable sources of information on sentencing practices.

Rule 12. Pleadings and Motions Before Trial; Defenses and Objections

(a) Pleadings and motions. Pleadings in criminal proceedings shall be the indictment and the information, and the pleas of not guilty, guilty and nolo contendere. All other pleas, and demurrers and motions to quash are abolished, and defenses and objections raised before trial which heretofore could have been raised by one or more of them shall be raised only by motion to dismiss or to grant appropriate relief, as provided in these rules.

(b) Pretrial motions. Any defense, objection, or request which is capable of determination without the trial of the general issue may be raised before trial by motion. Motions may be written or oral at the discretion of the judge. The following must be raised prior to trial:

(1) Defenses and objections based on defects in the institution of the prosecution; or

(2) Defenses and objections based on defects in the indictment or information (other than that it fails to show jurisdiction in the court or to charge an offense which objections shall be noticed by the court at any time during the pendency of the proceedings); or

(3) Motions to suppress evidence; or

(4) Requests for discovery under Rule 16; or

(5) Requests for a severance of charges or defendants under Rule 14.

(c) Motion date. Unless otherwise provided by local rule, the court may, at the time of the arraignment or as soon thereafter as practicable, set a time for the making of pretrial motions or requests and, if required, a later date of hearing.

(d) Notice by the government of the intention to use evidence.

(1) At the discretion of the government. At the arraignment or as soon thereafter as is practicable, the government may give notice to the defendant of its intention to use specified evidence at trial in order to afford the defendant an opportunity to raise objections to such evidence prior to trial under subdivision (b)(3) of this rule.

(2) At the request of the defendant. At the arraignment or as soon thereafter as is practicable the defendant may, in order to afford an opportunity to move to suppress evidence under subdivision (b)(3) of this rule, request notice of the government's intention to use (in its evidence in chief at trial) any evidence which the defendant may be entitled to discover under Rule 16 subject to any relevant limitations prescribed in Rule 16.

(e) Ruling on motion. A motion made before trial shall be determined before trial unless the court, for good cause, orders that it be deferred for determination at the trial of the general issue or until after verdict, but no such determination shall be deferred if a party's right to appeal is adversely affected. Where factual issues are involved in determining a motion, the court shall state its essential findings on the record.

(f) Effect of failure to raise defenses or objections. Failure by a party to raise defenses or objections or to make requests which must be made prior to trial, at the time set by the court pursuant to subdivision (c), or prior to any extension thereof made by the court, shall constitute waiver thereof, but the court for cause shown may grant relief from the waiver.

(g) Records. A verbatim record shall be made of all proceedings at the hearing, including such findings of fact and conclusions of law as are made orally.

(h) Effect of determination. If the court grants a motion based on a defect in the institution of the prosecution or in the indictment or information, it may also order that the defendant be continued in custody or that bail be continued for a specified time pending the filing of a new indictment or information. Nothing in this rule shall be deemed to affect the provisions of any Act of Congress relating to periods of limitations.

(i) Production of statements at suppression hearing. Rule 26.2 applies at a hearing on a motion to suppress evidence under subdivision (b)(3) of this rule. For purposes of this subdivision, a law enforcement officer is deemed a government witness.

Commentary

By Prof. Louis M. Natali
Temple University Beasley School of Law

This rule sets out the timing and procedure for filing pretrial motions. The time for filing motions is usually determined at arraignment by either the judge or the magistrate as is provided in subdivision (c).

Subdivision (a) provides that all common law types of motions have been abolished and the procedure set out in this rule is the one that governs the filing of motions.

Subdivision (b) applies to any defense, objection, or request which is capable of determination without the trial of the case. Such motions are made in writing but may, at the court's discretion, be made orally. There are five categories of pretrial motions:

1. Defenses and objections based on defects in the institution of the proceedings. These typically include grand jury challenges, the denial of a speedy trial, and the right to challenge the composition of the petit jury panel.

2. Defenses and objections based on defects in the indictment or information. These include defenses such as sufficiency, duplicity/multiplicity, the statute of limitations, double jeopardy,

selective prosecution, and venue or other irregularities, *e.g.* improper removal.

3. Motions to suppress physical evidence, confessions or statements, and identifications must be made before trial. The grounds for this motion will depend on the facts and legal issues at hand and are beyond the scope of this commentary. Any constitutional violation or violation of a statute or Rule of Criminal Procedure should be raised under this rule. If properly pled this motion will result in a hearing before the court and will proceed according to the issues raised. Generally if there has been an arrest warrant or search warrant, the burden shifts to the defendant to prove the evidence was illegally obtained. However, the government will bear the burden to prove the legality of evidence seized via a warrantless search or seizure, or the legality of a confession. If the court does hold a hearing this may be a valuable source of discovery of the prosecution's case. The agents who seized the physical evidence or who obtained the confession will have to testify in order to meet the government's burden. This may lead to discovery of other defenses such as insanity, lack of possession, or lack of knowledge. However, statements of government witnesses will not be discoverable because of Rule 26.2.

4. Requests for discovery. If informal discovery has not been successful, or is incomplete, it may be necessary to have the court order discovery. This may include witnesses, statements, or even bills of particulars and motions for the entire grand jury proceedings in order to properly prove prosecutorial misconduct. *See* the Commentary for FRCrP 6.

5. Requests for severance under Rule 14 must also be made pretrial. While this will not result in a factual hearing, the court will want to discuss redaction of codefendant confessions or other alternatives to a severance as discussed in the Commentary to Rule 14.

Rule 12.1. Notice of Alibi

(a) Notice by defendant. Upon written demand of the attorney for the government stating the time, date, and place at which the alleged offense was committed, the defendant shall serve within ten days, or at such different time as the court may direct, upon the attorney for the government a written notice of the

Rule 12.1. Notice of Alibi

defendant's intention to offer a defense of alibi. Such notice by the defendant shall state the specific place or places at which the defendant claims to have been at the time of the alleged offense and the names and addresses of the witnesses upon whom the defendant intends to rely to establish such alibi.

(b) Disclosure of information and witness. Within ten days thereafter, but in no event less than ten days before trial, unless the court otherwise directs, the attorney for the government shall serve upon the defendant or the defendant's attorney a written notice stating the names and addresses of the witnesses upon whom the government intends to rely to establish the defendant's presence at the scene of the alleged offense and any other witnesses to be relied on to rebut testimony of any of the defendant's alibi witnesses.

(c) Continuing duty to disclose. If prior to or during trial, a party learns of an additional witness whose identity, if known, should have been included in the information furnished under subdivision (a) or (b), the party shall promptly notify the other party or the other party's attorney of the existence and identity of such additional witness.

(d) Failure to comply. Upon the failure of either party to comply with the requirements of this rule, the court may exclude the testimony of any undisclosed witness offered by such party as to the defendant's absence from or presence at, the scene of the alleged offense. This rule shall not limit the right of the defendant to testify.

(e) Exceptions. For good cause shown, the court may grant an exception to any of the requirements of subdivisions (a) through (d) of this rule.

(f) Inadmissibility of withdrawn alibi. Evidence of an intention to rely upon an alibi defense, later withdrawn, or of statements made in connection with such intention, is not, in any civil or criminal proceeding, admissible against the person who gave notice of the intention.

Commentary

By Prof. Inga L. Parsons
New York University School of Law

The alibi defense, as it is called, is not a true affirmative defense. An alibi defense is simply a characterization of a denial of the government's charges on the basis that the defendant was at another place and could not have committed the crime. As it is not an affirmative defense, the defendant has no burden of proof when relying on the defense of alibi. However, to avoid unfair surprise and unnecessary delay, FRCrP 12.1 requires defense counsel to provide written notice of a defense of alibi to the prosecution.

Alibi Notice Strategies

Notice of an alibi defense is triggered only by a written demand from the prosecution that includes the date, time, and place of the offense. If the date, time, and place of the offense are unclear from the government's demand, the defense should seek a bill of particulars under FRCrP 7(f) before providing alibi notice. After being served with the defense notice, which includes where the defendant claims he or she was at the time and the names and addresses of the defense's alibi witnesses, FRCrP 12.2 requires reciprocal notice by the government to provide its list of rebuttal witnesses.

Attorneys for the government should always include a routine request for notice under FRCrP 12.1 in their response to the defense's discovery requests under FRCrP 16. Before providing an alibi notice, defense counsel should ensure that such a request by the prosecution has indeed been made. If the defense gratuitously hands over the names of alibi witnesses, without a specific demand from the attorney for the government, the government's reciprocal duty to disclose rebuttal witnesses is not triggered. When the government fails to make the demand for alibi notice, the defense can proceed on an alibi defense without giving notice under 12.1. Even when a demand is made and defense counsel fails to provide adequate notice, the defendant can still take the stand and raise an alibi defense. In that case, the defense would ordinarily be precluded from offering supporting witnesses, although for good cause shown, a court may grant exceptions to the notice requirements under FRCrP 12 or continue the proceedings. If the government neglects to provide reciprocal discovery, its witnesses may also be precluded, and defense counsel should make a timely objection if such witnesses are called.

Should the defense decide ultimately not to offer an alibi at trial, any notice or statements made in connection with the alibi notice cannot be admitted against the defendant. Nevertheless, defense counsel should be scrupulous in its investigation and preparation of alibi witnesses before giving notice of an alibi defense. Otherwise, witnesses who may not otherwise be known to the government will be interviewed, which could result in additional evidence against the defendant that may be admissible despite a withdrawn alibi notice. Defense counsel should notify "alibi witnesses" that they will be contacted by the government. They may be advised that they are free to talk to the government agents but that they are not required to do so. Defense counsel should be careful not to dissuade or discourage witnesses from speaking to the government in any way that could be interpreted as witness tampering.

Defense counsel may want to hold off raising the issue of "alibi" at trial until the end of the government's case. By waiting until after the government's case, the defense is likely to have a better context in which to determine whether to inject alibi into the case. However, if the defense wishes to include the defense in its opening statement or raise the issue during cross-examination, the government would likely be permitted to bring in witnesses in its case-in-chief, rather than wait until a rebuttal case. If the defense wants to keep the issue out of the case until after the government rests, counsel should notify the court and have the judge instruct the government not to have its witnesses discuss any alibi until the issue is injected into the case by the defense.

Avoiding Use of the Term "Alibi"

The term "alibi" has negative associations of being a "story" or even a "lie" rather than the simple fact that the defendant could not have committed the crime because he was in another place at the time. Thus, before trial, defense counsel should move in limine to preclude the use of the terms "alibi defense" and "alibi" to the jury. The term "alibi defense" is particularly problematic since it suggests, erroneously, that the defendant has some burden of proof. Although a request to preclude the government's use of the term "alibi" in every instance is unlikely to be successful, simply making the motion may lead to self-regulation by the government.

If the court will not preclude the use of the term "alibi," defense counsel should ask that the judge instruct the jury that an alibi is a proper, lawful response to the charges since the government must prove beyond a reasonable doubt that the defendant committed the crime at the time and place alleged.

Because alibi is such a loaded word in today's crime show culture, the defense should use the issue to particularize the need for attorney-conducted voir dire under FRCrP 24(a). At a minimum, defense counsel should submit proposed voir dire questions to the judge that probe those issues and hope that the judge will ask them. Counsel for both sides should be prepared to ask follow-up questions depending on the jurors' response. In those rare instances when a federal judge will allow attorney-conducted voir dire, the few minutes allotted can be used by the defense to flush out the preconceptions of alibi (if the term will be used), and to dispel any negative perceptions by emphasizing that it is the government's burden to show beyond a reasonable doubt that the defendant committed the crime at the time and place alleged.

Alibi Jury Instruction Considerations

The defense is entitled to have the jury instructed on alibi upon request where there is any evidence to establish the alibi. In such an instruction, it is crucial that the judge not refer to the instruction as an "alibi instruction" or an "alibi defense." Instead, the judge should be asked to use explanatory phrases such as "not present at the time and place of the alleged offense." The instructions should emphasize that it is the government's burden of proof to prove beyond a reasonable doubt that the defendant was at a particular place on the date and time alleged. Defense counsel should craft a balanced instruction for the judge to use without the use of the term "alibi" in any manner and object to any instruction by the government with that term.

If defense counsel believes that the judge's instruction to the jury in any way shifts the burden to the defense, counsel should object to the charge. Defense counsel should also object to any instruction or oral addition by the judge that characterizes an alibi defense as easily manufactured or indicates that the jury should receive such a defense with caution or heightened scrutiny. Such statements are erroneous. *See, e.g., United States v. Robinson*, 602 F.2d 760 (6th Cir. 1979). Defense counsel should be certain to object to the language itself as not required in an alibi case and also to the possible shifting of the burden to the defendant. Defense counsel should request to see the judge's exact charge in advance (a standard request with respect to all jury instructions in every case) in order to make objections before the instructions are given to the jury. Should the judge overrule the defense's objections and give the offensive or burden-shifting language to the jury, defense counsel should renew all objections following the giving of the instructions to the jury to preserve the issues for any appeal.

Rule 12.2. Notice of Insanity Defense or Expert Testimony of Defendant's Mental Condition

(a) Defense of insanity. If a defendant intends to rely upon the defense of insanity at the time of the alleged offense, the defendant shall, within the time provided for the filing of pretrial motions or at such later time as the court may direct, notify the attorney for the government in writing of such intention and file a copy of such notice with the clerk. If there is a failure to comply with the requirements of this subdivision, insanity may not be raised as a defense. The court may for cause shown allow late filing of the notice or grant additional time to the parties to prepare for trial or make such other order as may be appropriate.

(b) Expert testimony of defendant's mental condition. If a defendant intends to introduce expert testimony relating to a mental disease or defect or any other mental condition of the defendant bearing upon the issue of guilt, the defendant shall, within the time provided for the filing of pretrial motions or at such later time as the court may direct, notify the attorney for the government in writing of such intention and file a copy of such notice with the clerk. The court may for cause shown allow late filing of the notice or grant additional time to the parties to prepare for trial or make such other order as may be appropriate.

(c) Mental examination of defendant. In an appropriate case the court may, upon motion of the attorney for the government, order the defendant to submit to an examination pursuant to 18 U.S.C. 4241 or 4242. No statement made by the defendant in the course of any examination provided for by this rule, whether the examination be with or without the consent of the defendant, no testimony by the expert based upon such statement, and no other fruits of the statement shall be admitted in evidence against the defendant in any criminal proceeding except on an issue respecting mental condition on which the defendant has introduced testimony.

(d) Failure to comply. If there is a failure to give notice when required by subdivision (b) of this rule or to submit to an examination when ordered under subdivision (c) of this rule, the court may exclude the testimony of any expert witness offered by the defendant on the issue of the defendant's guilt.

(e) Inadmissibility of withdrawn intention. Evidence of an intention as to which notice was given under subdivision (a) or (b), later withdrawn, is not, in any civil or criminal proceeding, admissible against the person who gave notice of the intention.

Commentary

By Prof. Inga L. Parsons
New York University School of Law

FRCrP 12.2 requires the defendant to give notice of an insanity defense or the intended use of expert testimony regarding the defendant's mental condition. Unlike the alibi defense notice under FRCrP 12.1, the duty to give insanity and mental condition notice does not require a prosecutor's demand. Defense counsel should be mindful that the burden of proof is on the defendant to show by clear and convincing evidence a defense of insanity. *See* 18 USCS § 17(b).

Notice Obligations

The defense has an affirmative obligation to give such notice ordinarily within the time for filing pretrial motions. If there is no pretrial motion schedule, the notice must be filed within a reasonable time and defense counsel should be prepared to argue why any delay is necessarily reasonable. Judges do not like delaying a proceeding, but would no doubt grant a continuance to give the government sufficient time to prepare should the judge find the prosecution has been prejudiced by late notice. Worse, the court could preclude defense witnesses should the judge view the delay as intentional or unreasonable.

Once the defense has decided to give notice of insanity, it should be explicit and in writing. If the judge views the notice inadequate under 12.2, the defense will have lost any strategic

Rule 12.2. Notice of Insanity Defense or Expert Testimony of Defendant's Mental Condition

advantage of nondisclosure and still be prevented from presenting expert testimony.

Defense counsel should be aware that some defenses that do not ordinarily appear to be mental conditions might be interpreted as such and require notice under FRCrP 12.2. For example, there is a split in the circuits as to whether the defense of entrapment requires 12.2 notice if the defense argues a susceptibility to entrapment. See *United States v. Sullivan*, 919 F.2d 1403, 1421 (10th Cir. 1990) (12.2 applies to testimony going to susceptibility to entrapment), c.f. *United States v. Hill*, 655 F.2d 512, 517 (3rd Cir. 1981) (Rule 12.2 not applied to exclude proffered expert testimony on entrapment).

Expert Witness Strategies

Before giving notice under FRCrP 12.2, defense counsel should have the defendant examined by its own qualified psychiatrist, preferably one who has been accepted in the past as a government's expert as well. Any prior medical and psychiatric records of the defendant should be obtained either with a consent form signed by the defendant and/or by subpoena if required by the hospital. See FRCrP 17. If the defendant is unable to afford an expert, 18 USCS § 3006A(e) allows for an ex parte application to the court for expert services. Defense counsel should further request that the application and order be sealed to prevent the government from ascertaining that the defense of insanity will be relied on, until the defense gives formal notice.

Since the psychiatric community for these cases is relatively small, most experts know where other experts come out on many issues. As in any case where experts may be called, the experts for both the defense and prosecution can be invaluable not only in testifying in the case, but also preparing the attorneys on the issues and assisting counsel in preparing to cross-examine the other party's expert. Counsel on both sides should be aware of preliminary offers of proof with respect to expert testimony that are required under FRE 702–704 when an expert witness is intended to be called. Specifically, counsel should note that FRE 704 does not allow an expert witness to state an opinion as to whether the defendant had the requisite mental state, since it is an ultimate issue for the trier of fact. Offers of proof should be made outside the presence of the jury.

The defense is not required to give notice of actual witnesses or a list of experts under FRCrP 12.2. However, the parties may be required to provide notice of expert testimony under FRCrP 16(a)(1)(E) if the defense requests disclosure of government expert testimony and the government complies. Disclosure of expert testimony under FRCrP 16(a)(1)(E) requires a summary of the witnesses' opinions, the basis and the reasons for those opinions, and the witnesses' qualifications. Defense counsel should weigh carefully the decision to make a request for experts because the obligation to create witness testimony summaries that must be turned over to opposing counsel is triggered by a defense request. In a case where the government is not likely to offer expert testimony unless compelled by the existence of defense experts, it may be advisable not to ask for prosecution experts. Certainly such a request should not be routinely listed in a standard discovery letter, simply because it is listed under FRCrP 16.

Court-Ordered Psychiatric Examinations

One of the most troublesome provisions of FRCrP 12.2 from the defense perspective is that upon motion of the government, the court may order the defendant to submit to a psychological examination to determine mental competency to stand trial pursuant to 18 USCS § 4241, or to determine the existence of insanity at the time of the offense pursuant to 18 USCS § 4242. Such an examination could provide helpful discovery for the prosecution since psychiatrists typically go into the facts of the alleged offense and detailed background of the defendant in addition to the purely psychological issues. Even though FRCrP 12.2(c) precludes essentially any use of this information by the prosecution against the defendant, it does not preclude its use when the defense introduces testimony on an issue related to a mental condition, *i.e.*, insanity or diminished capacity.

With respect to competency, the court can order the examination upon its own motion. However, an examination for insanity requires a motion from the attorney for the government. *See* 18 USCS § 4242(a). Prosecutors should make such a request as a matter of course. The defense should generally object to the examination. Since the wording of the rule is "in an appropriate case," the court may order such an examination. The rule in no way anticipates that a court-ordered examination is required in every case. The defense should demand specific, individualized reasons why

Rule 12.2. Notice of Insanity Defense or Expert Testimony of Defendant's Mental Condition

the examination is necessary in a particular case. However, if the defendant refuses to submit to a court-ordered examination, the judge can preclude the insanity or mental condition defense. See FRCrP 12.2(d).

If a competency or insanity examination is ordered, the defendant has a right to consult with defense counsel before the examination. (See *Estelle v. Smith*, 451 U.S. 454, 68 L. Ed. 2d. 359, 101 S.Ct. 1866 (1981)). The defense may want to proffer its own expert as qualified to do the examination. If the defense expert has previously been approved by the court or been used by the government, it will be easier to get such an expert appointed.

Although defense counsel does not have a right to be present at the examination, the defense attorney should make a request to the judge to be present, since background, criminal history, and the offense conduct are often discussed. If the examination is ordered over objection and without counsel present, defense counsel should advise the defendant not to discuss immigration status, criminal history or other extraneous incriminating facts. A defendant's Fifth Amendment rights are implicated where the examination is not defense initiated. See *Buchanan v. Kentucky*, 438 U.S. 402, 97 L. Ed. 2d. 33, 107 S.Ct. 2906 (1987). Where the examination is defense initiated or confined solely to the issue of competency, Fifth Amendment rights may not be implicated. *Id.*

The defense should object to the presence of the attorney for the government. Since the government's attorney is not obligated to protect Fifth Amendment rights, defense counsel can make a distinction between the presence of the defendant's attorney and the presence of the government's attorney.

In those cases where the defense's own expert is proffered or will be called to testify, defense counsel should be somewhat cautious in what materials and facts are given to the expert in the initial examination of the defendant. If the defense introduces testimony on an issue "respecting mental condition" at trial, the defendant's statements and the psychiatrist's opinion based on those statements may come out at trial. FRCrP12(c). If an intention to rely on insanity or mental defect is withdrawn, the notice cannot be used against the defendant. FRCrP 12(e).

Jury Questionnaires and Instructions in 12.2 Cases

Once the defense is certain that it will rely on insanity or a mental defect, counsel should prepare a detailed jury questionnaire—ideally jointly with the prosecution. A jury questionnaire can assist counsel in determining preliminarily a juror's relationship to the mental health profession, any previous experience with mental illness or psychiatrists, etc. To tease out these complex and personal issues, individualized jury voir dire and attorney-conducted voir dire are essential. The public has become less receptive to so-called excuse defenses and there is considerable suspicion and even hostility from jurors who assume outright that the defendant is pretending to be insane just to get off. This particularized need could convince the judge to allow attorney-conducted voir dire and individualized voir dire, rather than the standard practice in federal court of having the judge conduct the voir dire. *See*, generally, FRCrP 24.

Counsel for both sides should prepare detailed jury instructions. The critical issue will often be the extent to which there exists a diminished capacity or diminished responsibility defense. The Insanity Reform Act of 1984 requires the defendant to prove by clear and convincing evidence that: (1) the defendant suffers from a severe mental disease or defect; (2) rendering him unable to appreciate the nature and quality or the wrongfulness of his acts. 18 USCS § 17(a). The Act further provides that mental disease or defect does not otherwise constitute an offense. *Id.* However, many courts have allowed the use of a mental condition by psychiatric evidence to negate mens rea, whether termed diminished capacity, diminished responsibility or something else. Counsel should be aware of the law of the circuit and craft instructions accordingly.

In order to compel the judge to give an insanity defense jury charge, defense counsel should be prepared to show evidence of both prongs of 18 USCS § 17(a): severe mental defect and effect on wrongfulness. A judge is unlikely to give an instruction regarding the effect of a not guilty by reason of insanity verdict, unless the government asserts in summations that the defendant would go free or "get off" by such a verdict. Defense counsel should object to any such assertion or implication and request that the court immediately correct counsel's error by advising the jury that the defendant would be hospitalized, and even institutionalized, upon a finding of not guilty by reason of insanity.

Rule 12.2. Notice of Insanity Defense or Expert Testimony of Defendant's Mental Condition

Competency Considerations

Giving notice under 12.2 arguably obligates defense attorneys to consider whether the defendant is competent to stand trial, *i.e.*, does the defendant have the "capacity to understand the nature and object of the proceedings against him . . ." *See Drope v. Missouri*, 420 U.S. 162, 43 L. Ed. 2d. 103, 95 S.Ct. 896 (1975). It is a very low standard. As one prominent New York lawyer quipped, the courts consider a defendant competent if he can tell the difference between the judge and a Bartlett pear.

Where counsel believes the defendant incompetent, defense may have an ethical duty to inform the court that the defendant may not be competent. If the government or the court, sua sponte, believe that the defendant is incompetent, which is more likely in a case where 12.2 notice has been given, they may request or require a competency determination. If defense counsel believes the client to be competent, defense counsel should object to the competency hearing, unless strategically it is better for the defendant to be found incompetent and not stand trial at that time.

Defense counsel should be mindful that a finding of incompetence or insanity does not mean that the defendant is released. If the court finds by a preponderance of the evidence that the defendant is incompetent, the court commits the defendant to the custody of the Attorney General who must hospitalize the defendant for treatment for up to four months until he is competent to stand to trial. *See* 18 USCS § 4244.

If the defendant is still not competent to stand trial, the defendant may be institutionalized if the court finds by clear and convincing evidence that the mental defect "creates a substantial risk of bodily injury to another person or serious damage to property of another." *See* 18 USCS § 4246. There are similar restrictions for defendants deemed not guilty by reason of insanity. Even when a defendant is found competent to stand trial, he may still assert an insanity defense and his competency cannot be admitted against him.

There are other ethical issues that arise in cases where the defendant believes himself to be competent and defense counsel believes the defendant to be incompetent, or where the court orders the defendant to take drugs to make him competent. These issues go beyond the scope of this commentary; however, defense counsel should be aware of the many legal, ethical and professional requirements that govern decision making in cases in which the client suffers from a mental disease or defect.

Rule 12.3. Notice of Defense Based Upon Public Authority

(a) **Notice by defendant; Government response; disclosure of witnesses.**

(1) **Defendant's notice and Government's response.** A defendant intending to claim a defense of actual or believed exercise of public authority on behalf of a law enforcement or Federal intelligence agency at the time of the alleged offense shall, within the time provided for the filing of pretrial motions or at such later time as the court may direct, serve upon the attorney for the Government a written notice of such intention and file a copy of such notice with the clerk. Such notice shall identify the law enforcement or Federal intelligence agency and any member of such agency on behalf of which and the period of time in which the defendant claims the actual or believed exercise of public authority occurred. If the notice identifies a Federal intelligence agency, the copy filed with the clerk shall be under seal. Within ten days after receiving the defendant's notice, but in no event less than twenty days before the trial, the attorney for the Government shall serve upon the defendant or the defendant's attorney a written response which shall admit or deny that the defendant exercised the public authority identified in the defendant's notice.

(2) **Disclosure of witnesses.** At the time that the Government serves its response to the notice or thereafter, but in no event less than twenty days before the trial, the attorney for the Government may serve upon the defendant or the defendant's attorney a written demand for the names and addresses of the witnesses, if any, upon whom the defendant intends to rely in establishing the defense identified in the notice. Within seven days after receiving the Government's demand, the defendant shall serve upon the attorney for the Government a written statement of the names and addresses of any such witnesses. Within seven days after receiving the defendant's written statement, the attorney for the Government shall serve upon the

defendant or the defendant's attorney a written statement of the names and addresses of the witnesses, if any, upon whom the Government intends to rely in opposing the defense identified in the notice.

(3) Additional time. If good cause is shown, the court may allow a party additional time to comply with any obligation imposed by this rule.

(b) Continuing duty to disclose. If, prior to or during trial, a party learns of any additional witness whose identity, if known, should have been included in the written statement furnished under subdivision (a)(2) of this rule, that party shall promptly notify in writing the other party or the other party's attorney of the name and address of any such witness.

(c) Failure to comply. If a party fails to comply with the requirements of this rule, the court may exclude the testimony of any undisclosed witness offered in support of or in opposition to the defense, or enter such other order as it deems just under the circumstances. This rule shall not limit the right of the defendant to testify.

(d) Protective procedures unaffected. This rule shall be in addition to and shall not supersede the authority of the court to issue appropriate protective orders, or the authority of the court to order that any pleading be filed under seal.

(e) Inadmissibility of withdrawn defense based upon public authority. Evidence of an intention as to which notice was given under subdivision (a), later withdrawn, is not, in any civil or criminal proceeding, admissible against the person who gave notice of the intention.

Commentary

By Prof. Inga L. Parsons
New York University School of Law

FRCrP 12.3 requires the defendant to give notice to the prosecution of a defense based on actual or believed exercise of public authority. The defense may arise when the defendant is cooperating with the authorities and claims that he reasonably relied on the instructions of a government agent to engage in criminal activity.

The defense is unusual and FRCrP 12.3 requires notice to the government to avoid unfair surprise.

Notice Considerations

Notice under FRCrP 12.3 is defense initiated and does not require a demand from the prosecution. Defense notice must include the name of the agency, the names of the agents, and the dates for which the defendant claims he or she was acting with authority. FRCrP 12.3(a)(1). If the notice identifies a federal intelligence agency, the court notice must be filed under seal. *Id.* Thereafter, the government is required to provide a written response admitting or denying the allegation of public authority and may ask for the defense to supply a list of names and addresses of defense witnesses. FRCrP 12.3(a)(2). Defense compliance with a witness request triggers a requirement that the government provide a reciprocal witness list. *Id.*

As with the notice of alibi under FRCrP 12.2, defense counsel should be scrupulous in its investigation and preparation of witnesses before giving notice of a defense based on government authority, particularly where the witnesses may be non-government agents. Otherwise, witnesses who may not otherwise be known to the government could be interviewed and result in additional evidence against the defendant which may be admissible. This is true even when notice of public authority is later withdrawn, since only the withdrawn notice itself is inadmissible at trial. FRCrP 12.3(e).

Once the decision to give notice is made, the notice should be adequate and timely. FRCrP 12.3 provides specific time restrictions for compliance and defense counsel should be aware of those requirements. If the judge views the notice as inadequate under FRCrP 12.3, the defense will have lost any strategic advantage of nondisclosure and may still be prevented from presenting witnesses. Where the defense is precluded from presenting witnesses due to noncompliance with the notice requirements of FRCrP 12.3, the defendant still has the right to take the stand and claim the defense.

Jury Instructions in 12.3 Cases

Defense counsel should be mindful that if the judge finds that a defendant has failed to make out a case that he reasonably believed he was acting under public authority, the judge may refuse to give an instruction to the jury based on this defense. The defense should request such an instruction be given to the jury and, as with the instructions under FRCrP 12.1 governing alibi defenses, defense counsel should be vigilant to object to any instruction that would shift the burden to the defense, including objecting to the term public authority "defense."

Rule 13. Trial Together of Indictments or Informations

The court may order two or more indictments or informations or both to be tried together if the offenses, and the defendants if there is more than one, could have been joined in a single indictment or information. The procedure shall be the same as if the prosecution were under such single indictment or information.

Commentary

By Prof. Inga L. Parsons
New York University School of Law

FRCrP 13 governs the joinder of separate indictments or informations for trial. It should be read in conjunction with FRCrP 8 (Joinder of Offenses and of Defendants) and FRCrP 14 (Relief from Prejudicial Joinder), since the standard for joinder under FRCrP 13 is whether the offenses and defendants could be tried in a single indictment or information. The parties should analyze whether joinder of charges and/or defendants is proper under FRCrP 8: offenses with the same or similar character or part of the same transaction or similar scheme or plan, FRCrP 8(a), and defendants who are part of the same act or transaction or same series of acts or transactions constituting an offense, FRCrP 8(b). If joinder is improper under FRCrP 8, the defense should object to the joinder under FRCrP 12(b)(2).

Joinder Considerations

The prosecution ordinarily moves for joinder for judicial economy reasons, to present witnesses once rather than on many occasions since each testimony provides potential impeachment for subsequent proceedings, and to be able to present an entire illegal operation or scheme. The prosecutor may also add offenses in an attempt to show guilt by cumulative evidence. A jury may think maybe if it were just one count it could be a mistake, but the fourteen times this guy filed his income tax with different social security numbers is surely a crime.

Additional counts in the indictment give the jury the ability to compromise but still convict the defendant of something. It often makes little difference at sentencing whether it is one or more charges, given relevant conduct under § 1B1.3 of the Federal Sentencing Guidelines and inclusion of acquitted conduct in certain cases. *See* the Commentary for FRCrP 32. (There are, however, judges who as a matter of principle will not include acquitted conduct, or will require that such conduct meet a higher standard of proof.) On the other hand, the defense may be able to claim that the prosecution is overcharging, adding a lot of counts, because it does not have the proof on any one count. The argument in this situation might be that the government created numerous offenses to offset the lack of real evidence of a crime on any one count.

The prosecution may try to use joinder to include conduct that it may not otherwise have been able to introduce at a separate trial, *e.g.*, a prior drug offense or a prior conviction in a felon in possession of a firearm charge. Defense counsel obviously should object to such a joinder. *See United States v. Jones*, 16 F.3d 487, 492 (2d. Cir. 1994), where the court reversed conviction when a felon in possession count was joined with a bank robbery charge over objection of the defendant.

There may be times, though rare, when the defense moves to have indictments joined. When the defendant is named in several indictments, the defense may move for joinder to avoid the ordeal of many trials. There may be other advantages to joinder for the defendant. If the codefendants are more culpable it may make the defendant appear less culpable. If the proof against the other defendants is direct, and the proof against the defendant is circumstantial, it may be more difficult for the government to meet its burden of proof for that defendant. In addition, where there are multiple defendants as a result of joinder, the jury has the opportunity to give a compromise verdict by convicting some defendants and acquitting others. Juries typically want someone to pay for the crime; if there is only one defendant the jury may be more likely to convict.

Rule 13. Trial Together of Indictments or Informations

Opposing Joinder

More often joinder poses disadvantages to the defendant. Essentially the same concerns arise in a motion for joinder of indictments as in a motion for severance on the basis of prejudicial joinder under FRCrP 14. However, under FRCrP 13, the opposing party is in a slightly better position because the prosecution has initially proceeded on the case with separate indictments. Thus, the difficult standards to prevail on a motion to sever due to prejudicial joinder under FRCrP 14 should be distinguished since the charges and defendants are already severed in the indictments. Although it is still within the discretion of the judge to grant joinder and judges usually prefer joint trials for judicial economy reasons, the burden of persuasion is on the moving party, *i.e.*, in most cases the prosecution.

The following is a review of some of the concerns of joinder of indictments. *See also* the Commentary for FRCrP 14.

1. *Bruton* issues. There are cases where statements of a codefendant would not be admissible against the defendant at a separate trial as a violation of the defendant's rights under the Confrontation Clause, but would be admissible against the codefendant at a joint trial, a so-called *Bruton* issue, *see Bruton v. United States*, 391 U.S. 123, 20 L. Ed. 2d 476, 88 S.Ct 1620 (1968). The defense should object to joinder of defendants or counts which trigger that conflict. Although the ordinary remedy for introduction of codefendants' statements is redaction of the statements at a joint trial, where the indictments have yet to be joined the defense may be able to argue that the government initially chose to bring separate indictments and the *Bruton* issue should preclude the affirmative act of joinder.

2. Prejudicial spillover. Defense should object to joinder that could result in prejudicial spillover or "guilt by association" for the defendant. A judge may be more receptive to this if the acts of the codefendants are violent or involve other heinous conduct in which the defendant was not involved. For example, if the codefendants are accused of murdering a rival drug dealer but the charge against the defendant is simply for being a "steerer" (sending people to the crack house to buy drugs) the joinder would severely prejudice the defendant. Involvement by the defendant might be assumed by a jury even with a limiting instruction. Similarly, mutually antagonistic defenses, although rarely a basis to

sever, may rise to a level that would preclude joinder where counts and defendants are already separated. If a codefendant's defense, if believed, necessarily excludes the defense of the defendant, the defense should oppose a motion for joinder.

3. Codefendant's testimony. If a codefendant in one indictment would be willing to give exculpatory testimony on behalf of the defendant in a separate trial, the defense should object to joinder. To make such an argument typically requires that the defendant show that the codefendant would be called, that the codefendant would testify (meaning waive his Fifth Amendment privilege against self-incrimination), that the codefendant's testimony would be exculpatory, that the testimony would not be subject to damaging impeachment, and that the testimony would not be cumulative. *See, e.g., United States v. Finkelstein*, 526 F.2d 517, 523–525 (2d. Cir. 1975). The difficulty in this tactic is that the defense basically must show that the codefendant would be willing to testify even if the defendant's trial were held first, since a defendant does not have a right to have a certain order of trials. *See Byrd v. Wainwright*, 428 F.2d 1017, 1022 (5th Cir. 1970). The chances of the codefendant being willing to waive his Fifth Amendment rights in a trial before his own trial is even less likely than winning an appeal on the grounds of mutually antagonistic defenses—a next-to-nothing probability.

4. Untimely joinder. A party moving for joinder under FRCrP 13 should do so in a timely fashion; otherwise the opposing side is in a position to argue prejudice from lack of time to accommodate the additional charges or defendants. The longer the party waits, the more time the other party will have spent preparing the case for those particular charges and codefendants, and the less receptive the judge will be to granting joinder. If there has been a long delay, the moving party should be prepared to provide a sufficient explanation for why the indictments could not be joined earlier. Judges do not like delay, and since the primary purpose of joinder is judicial economy, a judge may deny a joinder motion simply to avoid rescheduling a previously set trial date.

5. Under the Speedy Trial Act, the judge may exclude the time necessary for joinder of offenses or defendants, 18 USCS § 3161(h)(3)(B)(7). If the defense objects to joinder, defense counsel should also object to the exclusion of the time for joinder under the Speedy Trial Act. The judge will still exclude the time, but if

the defendant's trial is significantly delayed, the probability of a successful motion for violation of speedy trial rights increases because the defense objected to joinder and to exclusion of time.

Moving to Sever

If offenses are joined over defense objection, the defense should still request severance under FRCrP 14 on the grounds of prejudicial joinder to ensure that the issue is preserved. Severance motions are made pursuant to FRCrP 12(b)(5). Although the grounds for requesting severance are the same grounds offered in opposition to the joinder of offenses or defendants in the first place, an FRCrP 14 motion gives the defense a second attempt to persuade the judge not to have a joint trial. It also makes it clear that the defense is not waiving any objections to the joinder. Defense counsel should renew the opposition to joinder and the severance motion at the end of trial to preserve the issue (although misjoinder under FRCrP 8 is not necessarily waived since it is a question of law).

Rule 14. Relief From Prejudicial Joinder

If it appears that a defendant or the government is prejudiced by a joinder of offenses or of defendants in an indictment or information or by such joinder for trial together, the court may order an election or separate trials of counts, grant a severance of defendants or provide whatever other relief justice requires. In ruling on a motion by a defendant for severance the court may order the attorney for the government to deliver to the court for inspection in camera any statements or confessions made by the defendants which the government intends to introduce in evidence at the trial.

Commentary

By Prof. Louis M. Natali
Temple University Beasley School of Law

The purpose of this provision is to allow the granting of a motion for relief from prejudicial joinder. This motion is seldom granted but must be made to preserve the issue. There are several classes of cases where a motion should be made.

The first class of case involves the situation where a codefendant has confessed and implicated the defendant. The *Bruton* decision, 391 U.S. 123, 20 L. Ed. 2d 476, 88 S. Ct. 1620 (1968), guarantees that such a confession is inadmissible against the non-confessing defendant. However, the preferred solution is not severance but redaction of the confession to eliminate mention of the defendant both directly and indirectly. Counsel should be careful to ensure that the redaction serves to protect defendant's confrontation rights. Redactions which leave blank space such as "me and blank" have been condemned by the courts, and it has been held that a redaction should not mention the existence of the codefendant. Redactions should be a last resort because it seems inevitable that the jury will add defendant's name.

Another solution that eliminates use of redactions and is preferred is a request for a separate jury for each defendant. The two juries remain in the courtroom for all evidence admissible against all defendants but one is excused when a codefendant's confession is used against him. In this fashion, the jury deciding the non-confessing defendant's case never hears the confession. Opening statements and closing arguments, since the prosecution will always refer to the confession, will have to be done before separate juries. The government and courts are reluctant to use multiple juries because it is expensive and takes longer. Those arguments should not trump a defendant's right to bar hearsay as devastating as a codefendant's confession.

The second class of cases where a severance motion should be made is one where the evidence against a defendant includes or necessitates proof of other crimes to which the second defendant has no connection. For example, defendant A is charged with four bank robberies and defendant B is charged with participation in only one of the four. This motion, while rarely granted, should be argued on the grounds that the evidence will invariably spill over to defendant B and the jury will convict him because of his association with A, a bad person, rather than because of the weight of the evidence. In cases where the other robberies are alleged to have been committed by A and an unknown accomplice, the jury will conclude B is the unknown accomplice. This motion, not surprisingly, is very fact-driven, and counsel should argue that each fact individually and in their totality will prejudice the client.

The final class of cases involves defendants with antagonistic defenses, *e.g.*, A is blaming the crime on B or A seeks to call B as a witness to exculpate A. An early line of cases suggested that upon a proper showing—a showing via affidavits or offer of proof—there was a constitutional right for A to receive a severance. However, use by one codefendant of a defense which admits the crime, *e.g.*, insanity or entrapment, does not per se require a severance but may form the basis for a good argument that acquittal is precluded. More recent circuit court authority has made the threshold showing nearly impossible, *i.e.*, the inconsistent or antagonistic defenses must be mutually exclusive. Another formulation is: does one party's defense preclude acquittal of the other? Moreover the standard of review (abuse of discretion) makes success on appeal virtually impossible. Nevertheless, in an appropriate case, *e.g.*, where a codefendant's confession exculpates a defendant, counsel may successfully urge the court to grant relief. *See, e.g.*, Byrd v. Wainwright, 428 F.2d 1017 (5th Cir. Fla. 1970).

Rule 15. Depositions

(a) When taken. Whenever due to exceptional circumstances of the case it is in the interest of justice that the testimony of a prospective witness of a party be taken and preserved for use at trial, the court may upon motion of such party and notice to the parties order that testimony of such witness be taken by deposition and that any designated book, paper, document, record, recording, or other material not privileged, be produced at the same time and place. If a witness is detained pursuant to section 3144 of title 18, United States Code, the court on written motion of the witness and upon notice to the parties may direct that the witness' deposition be taken. After the deposition has been subscribed the court may discharge the witness.

(b) Notice of taking. The party at whose instance a deposition is to be taken shall give to every party reasonable written notice of the time and place for taking the deposition. The notice shall state the name and address of each person to be examined. On motion of a party upon whom the notice is served, the court for cause shown may extend or shorten the time or change the place for taking the deposition. The officer having custody of a defendant shall be notified of the time and place set for the examination and shall, unless the defendant waives in writing the right to be present, produce the defendant at the examination and keep the defendant in the presence of the witness during the examination, unless, after being warned by the court that disruptive conduct will cause the defendant's removal from the place of the taking of the deposition, the defendant persists in conduct which is such as to justify exclusion from that place. A defendant not in custody shall have the right to be present at the examination upon request subject to such terms as may be fixed by the court, but a failure, absent good cause shown, to appear after notice and tender of expenses in accordance with subdivision (c) of this rule shall constitute a waiver of that right and of any objection to the taking and use of the deposition based upon that right.

(c) Payment of expenses. Whenever a deposition is taken at the instance of the government, or whenever a deposition is taken at the instance of a defendant who is unable to bear the expenses of the taking of the deposition, the court may direct that the expense of travel and subsistence of the defendant and the defendant's attorney for attendance at the examination and the cost of the transcript of the deposition shall be paid by the government.

(d) How taken. Subject to such additional conditions as the court shall provide, a deposition shall be taken and filed in the manner provided in civil actions except as otherwise provided in these rules, provided that (1) in no event shall a deposition be taken of a party defendant without that defendant's consent, and (2) the scope and manner of examination and cross-examination shall be such as would be allowed in the trial itself. The government shall make available to the defendant or the defendant's counsel for examination and use at the taking of the deposition any statement of the witness being deposed which is in the possession of the government and to which the defendant would be entitled at the trial.

(e) Use. At the trial or upon any hearing, a part or all of a deposition, so far as otherwise admissible under the rules of evidence, may be used as substantive evidence if the witness is unavailable, as unavailability is defined in Rule 804(a) of the Federal Rules of Evidence, or the witness gives testimony at the trial or hearing inconsistent with that witness' deposition. Any deposition may also be used by any party for the purpose of contradicting or impeaching the testimony of the deponent as a witness. If only a part of a deposition is offered in evidence by a party, an adverse party may require the offering of all of it which is relevant to the part offered and any party may offer other parts.

(f) Objections to deposition testimony. Objections to deposition testimony or evidence or parts thereof and the grounds for the objection shall be stated at the time of the taking of the deposition.

(g) Deposition by agreement not precluded. Nothing in this rule shall preclude the taking of a deposition, orally or upon written questions, or the use of a deposition, by agreement of the parties with the consent of the court.

Commentary

By Prof. Louis M. Natali
Temple University Beasley School of School

Generally

This rule provides for the preservation of testimony by way of deposition. It is used infrequently and only with leave of court and "in the interest of justice." Its use is important when a witness is ill and may not be available for trial. The rule also references use of depositions when a material witness is being held under 18 USCS § 3144. A defendant must consent to having his or her deposition taken and such use is rare.

Subdivision (b)—Notice of Taking

The Rule requires notice to the parties and the presence of the defendant. Incarcerated defendants may request that the court transport them to the deposition. Under subsection (c) an indigent defendant may apply for funds for him or herself and counsel to be transported to the site of the deposition.

Subdivision (d)—How Taken

The taking of this testimony is for use at trial and not for discovery purposes. The rules of civil procedure apply but there are two important exceptions: all objections to questions and answers must be made at the time the deposition is taken (*see* subdivision (f)), and the scope of cross-examination is limited to the scope at trial (also narrower than that at a civil deposition). For purposes of the deposition, there is also a narrow exception to the Jencks Act (18 USCS § 3500) provision that statements are not discoverable until after the witness' direct. Since for all intents and purposes this is the trial examination of the witness, the government is obliged to furnish a witness' statement at the deposition.

Subdivision (e)—Use

Such deposition testimony may only be used as substantive trial testimony if the witness meets the unavailability requirements of Federal Rule of Evidence 804(a). This generally means that the witness must be exempted from testifying due to the assertion of a privilege, be in contempt, testify to a lack of memory on the subject matter, be unable to be present due to death, physical or mental illness, or finally, be absent from the hearing and unable to be served.

There is, however, a constitutional overlay to Rule 804(a) and it must be read with *California v. Green*, 399 U.S. 149, 26 L. Ed. 2d 489, 90 S. Ct. 1930 (1970), and its progeny. The government must make all efforts to compel witnesses to appear in criminal cases and must use the uniform act to compel their attendance if the witness is in the United States.

If the witness testifies inconsistently, the deposition may of course be used for impeachment purposes.

The rule of completeness stated in Federal Rule of Evidence 106 also applies to deposition testimony and, if only part of the deposition is used, an adverse party may require the reading of additional parts deemed relevant by the court. The adverse party has the option to request such reading then and there while a part of the deposition is being read.

Rule 16. Discovery and Inspection

(a) Governmental disclosure of evidence.

(1) Information subject to disclosure.

(A) Statement of defendant. Upon request of a defendant the government must disclose to the defendant and make available for inspection, copying, or photographing: any relevant written or recorded statements made by the defendant, or copies thereof, within the possession, custody, or control of the government, the existence of which is known, or by the exercise of due diligence may become known, to the attorney for the government; that portion of any written record containing the substance of any relevant oral statement made by the defendant whether before or after arrest in response to interrogation by any person then known to the defendant to be a government agent; and recorded testimony of the defendant before a grand jury which relates to the offense charged. The government must also disclose to the defendant the substance of any other relevant oral statement made by the defendant whether before or after arrest in response to interrogation by any person then known by the defendant to be a government agent if the government intends to use that statement at trial. Upon request of a defendant which is an organization such as a corporation, partnership, association or labor union, the government must disclose to the defendant any of the foregoing statements made by a person who the government contends (1) was, at the time of making the statement, so situated as a director, officer, employee, or agent as to have been able legally to bind the defendant in respect to the subject of the statement, or (2) was, at the time of the offense, personally involved in the alleged conduct constituting the offense and so situated as a director, officer, employee, or agent as to have been able legally to bind the defendant in respect to that alleged conduct in which the person was involved.

(B) Defendant's prior record. Upon request of the defendant, the government shall furnish to the defendant such copy of the defendant's prior criminal record, if any, as is within the possession, custody, or control of the government, the existence of which is known, or by the exercise of due diligence may become known, to the attorney for the government.

(C) Documents and tangible objects. Upon request of the defendant the government shall permit the defendant to inspect and copy or photograph books, papers, documents, photographs, tangible objects, buildings or places, or copies or portions thereof, which are within the possession, custody or control of the government, and which are material to the preparation of the defendant's defense or are intended for use by the government as evidence in chief at the trial, or were obtained from or belong to the defendant.

(D) Reports of examinations and tests. Upon request of a defendant the government shall permit the defendant to inspect and copy or photograph any results or reports of physical or mental examinations, and of scientific tests or experiments, or copies thereof, which are within the possession, custody, or control of the government, the existence of which is known, or by the exercise of due diligence may become known, to the attorney for the government, and which are material to the preparation of the defense or are intended for use by the government as evidence in chief at the trial.

(E) Expert witnesses. At the defendant's request, the government shall disclose to the defendant a written summary of testimony that the government intends to use under Rules 702, 703, or 705 of the Federal Rules of Evidence during its case-in-chief at trial. If the government requests discovery under subdivision (b)(1)(C)(ii) of this rule and the defendant complies, the government shall, at the defendant's request, disclose to the defendant a written summary of testimony the government intends to use under Rules 702, 703, or 705 as evidence at trial on the issue of the defendant's mental condition. The summary provided under this subdivision shall describe the witnesses' opinions, the bases and the reasons for those opinions, and the witnesses' qualifications.

(2) Information not subject to disclosure. Except as provided in paragraphs (A), (B), (D), and (E) of subdivision (a)(1), this rule does not authorize the discovery or inspection of reports, memoranda, or other internal government documents made by the attorney for the government or any other government agent investigating or prosecuting the case. Nor does the rule authorize the discovery or inspection of statements made by government witnesses or prospective government witnesses except as provided in 18 U.S.C. § 3500.

(3) Grand jury transcripts. Except as provided in Rules 6, 12(i) and 26.2, and subdivision (a)(1)(A) of this rule, these rules do not relate to discovery or inspection of recorded proceedings of a grand jury.

Rule 16. Discovery and Inspection

(b) The defendant's disclosure of evidence.

(1) Information subject to disclosure.

(A) Documents and tangible objects. If the defendant requests disclosure under subdivision (a)(1)(C) or (D) of this rule, upon compliance with such request by the government, the defendant, on request of the government, shall permit the government to inspect and copy or photograph books, papers, documents, photographs, tangible objects, or copies or portions thereof, which are within the possession, custody, or control of the defendant and which the defendant intends to introduce as evidence in chief at the trial.

(B) Reports of examinations and tests. If the defendant requests disclosure under subdivision (a)(1)(C) or (D) of this rule, upon compliance with such request by the government, the defendant, on request of the government, shall permit the government to inspect and copy or photograph any results or reports of physical or mental examinations and of scientific tests or experiments made in connection with the particular case, or copies thereof, within the possession or control of the defendant, which the defendant intends to introduce as evidence in chief at the trial or which were prepared by a witness whom the defendant intends to call at the trial when the results or reports relate to that witness' testimony.

(C) Expert witnesses. Under the following circumstances, the defendant shall, at the government's request, disclose to the government a written summary of testimony that the defendant intends to use under Rules 702, 703, or 705 of the Federal Rules of Evidence as evidence at trial: (i) if the defendant requests disclosure under subdivision (a)(1)(E) of this rule and the government complies, or (ii) if the defendant has given notice under Rule 12.2(b) of an intent to present expert testimony on the defendant's mental condition. This summary shall describe the witnesses' opinions, the bases and reasons for those opinions, and the witnesses' qualifications.

(2) Information not subject to disclosure. Except as to scientific or medical reports, this subdivision does not authorize the discovery or inspection of reports, memoranda, or other internal defense documents made by the defendant, or the defendant's attorneys or agents in connection with the investigation or defense of the case, or of statements made by the defendant, or by government or defense witnesses, or by prospective government or defense witnesses, to the defendant, the defendant's agents or attorneys.

(c) Continuing duty to disclose. If, prior to or during trial, a party discovers additional evidence or material previously requested or ordered, which is subject to discovery or inspection under this rule, such party shall promptly notify the other party or that other party's attorney or the court of the existence of the additional evidence or material.

(d) Regulation of discovery.

(1) Protective and modifying orders. Upon a sufficient showing the court may at any time order that the discovery or inspection be denied, restricted, or deferred, or make such other order as is appropriate. Upon motion by a party, the court may permit the party to make such showing, in whole or in part, in the form of a written statement to be inspected by the judge alone. If the court enters an order granting relief following such an ex parte showing, the entire text of the party's statement shall be sealed and preserved in the records of the court to be made available to the appellate court in the event of an appeal.

(2) Failure to comply with a request. If at any time during the course of the proceedings it is brought to the attention of the court that a party has failed to comply with this rule, the court may order such party to permit the discovery or inspection, grant a continuance, or prohibit the party from introducing evidence not disclosed, or it may enter such other order as it deems just under the circumstances. The court may specify the time, place and manner of making the discovery and inspection and may prescribe such terms and conditions as are just.

(e) Alibi witnesses. Discovery of alibi witnesses is governed by Rule 12.1.

Commentary

By Prof. Louis M. Natali
Temple University Beasley School of Law

Generally

This is a major rule that, when read with other rules, enables counsel to understand the complete case, to follow other motions (to suppress, for relief from prejudicial joinder or for a bill of particulars) and is thus a key in preparation and strategy for the entire case. This rule must be read together with Rule 26.2. In multiple defendant cases all clients' statements should also be discoverable under a joint defense agreement.

In many districts there is an open file policy in effect and this should be employed before resorting to formal discovery. A recitation that informal discovery has been attempted is important and useful for federal judges who are not enamored of motions to compel discovery.

Rule 16 is divisible into several parts: information the government must disclose, information the government is privileged to withhold, information the defense must disclose and defense information not subject to disclosure because of privilege.

Information Subject to Disclosure by the Government (Subdivision (a)(1))

This generally will be the nub of what is needed to prepare for trial.

Subdivision (a)(1)(A)—Statement of the Defendant

All statements (written and oral) made by the defendant to any person should be requested. These include statements made pre-arrest, post-arrest, and post-indictment. It also includes grand jury testimony, including statements made to known agents of the government. Case law does not technically provide for the production of statements made to undercover agents or coconspirators (discoverable only at trial after direct pursuant to the Jencks Act (18 USCS § 3500)) but these are usually provided informally. However, tape-recorded statements made by the government have generally been held to be discoverable, especially when they relate to the commission of the crime, *e.g.*, the words of a drug transaction. There is irreconcilable disarray in the cases on this point.

In order to avoid confusion, a discovery request should separately request (a) statements made to known agents, (b) statements made to undercover agents, (c) statements made to coconspirators, (d) statements made to other witnesses who are neither agents or coconspirators which will be used against the defendant at trial, (e) tape-recorded statements or those seized by electronic surveillance, (f) exculpatory statements made by the defendant, and (g) any other statement made by the defendant. *See United States v. Ahmad*, 53 F.R.D. 186 (D. Pa., 1971). In this fashion, the government will be required to answer the discovery requests and to affirm, deny, or avoid providing what is demanded. If the government refuses such a request or takes the position it has no duty to disclose under Rule 16, counsel will be able to seek further relief from the court and will, at the least, learn of the existence of other statements.

Subdivision (a)(1)(B)—Defendant's Prior Record

This device should be utilized because a defendant's recollection of his or her prior record may be incomplete or faulty. After receiving this discovery counsel must consult Federal Rule of Evidence 609 and the applicable law in the circuit concerning use of prior convictions for impeachment purposes. In some circuits certain crimes, *e.g.*, bank robbery, may not be crimes involving "dishonesty or false statement." The ultimate decision about whether a client testifies must not be made without this vital information.

A defendant's criminal record may also be used by the prosecution under Federal Rule of Evidence 404(b) for another evidentiary purpose such as modus operandi or where it forms an element of the new offense, *e.g.*, former felon not to possess firearm. Thus discovery may be the initial step toward a motion in limine under Federal Rule of Evidence Rule 104. Or the prosecution may file such notice under Rule 12(d) that it will seek permission to use such evidence. Counsel should investigate the facts of the prior conviction to determine if they meet the standard under Federal Rule of Evidence 404(b) and the cases. *See Old Chief v. United States*, 519 U.S. 172, 136 L. Ed. 2d 574, 117 S. Ct. 644 (1997), which on one hand, places important limits on how the prosecution may use prior convictions but, on the other, opens the possibility of greater liberality and the ability for the prosecution to refuse stipulations sought by the defense.

Subdivision (a)(1)(C)—Documents and Tangible Objects

All documents, photographs, and other tangible evidence that the government will use should be the subject of a discovery motion. Inspection and copying is provided by the rules and must be used to discover and understand the government's case and case theory. Physical evidence can be far more persuasive then verbal evidence and it is counsel's obligation to obtain all evidence in order to prepare a proper defense. Some time and thought should be given as to how such evidence will be presented and perhaps a Federal Rule of Evidence 403 motion to limit the prejudice of photographs and other graphic evidence should be considered.

Subdivision (a)(1)(D)—Reports of Examinations and Tests

Scientific and expert witnesses may play an important part in the trial. Discovery of such evidence is standard for any federal practitioner. These include drug analyses, psychiatric, psychological and toxicological reports. After discovery, counsel may request permission from the court to conduct his or her own testing and consult his or her own experts. This rule should also be read in conjunction with Rules 12.1 and 12.2 providing for the defense to give notice of alibi and mental health defense.

Information in the Possession of the Government Not Subject to Disclosure

Subdivision (a)(2) protects internal government documents, work product, Jencks material, and jury investigations from disclosure by federal judges. When in doubt about the applicability of this provision, counsel should make the motion and make a record a court will ultimately decide. These items may be obtained through Freedom of Information Act (5 USCS § 552) requests; *see United States v. Bagley*, 473 U.S. 667, 87 L.Ed. 2d 481, 105 S. Ct. 3375 (1985).

Grand Jury Witnesses the Government Will Not Call at Trial

Grand jury testimony and statements of persons the government will not call at trial are not discoverable under this rule. Few courts will order the government to produce such material. Such witnesses should be approached with extreme caution. While the witness may not believe he has given damaging testimony, each factual setting is, of course, quite different and the prior grand jury testimony may serve to impeach the witness on key points.

The best approach is to talk to counsel for the witness and hope that there exists extensive debriefing notes of the grand jury appearance or interview. One must be wary of general statements that the witness did not "hurt" the defendant. The debriefing notes, if accurate, should guide the decision to call the witness.

Disclosure by the Defendant

If the defendant seeks disclosure of the government's documentary, tangible and scientific evidence, and mental examinations under Rule 16(a)(1)(C) or (D), then subparagraph (B) provides for reciprocal discovery. This rule does not permit the disclosure of the statements of defense witnesses. That subject is provided for in Rule 26.2 and such statements are only discoverable after the witness has testified on direct examination.

Information Not Subject to Disclosure

Subdivision (b)(2) makes it clear that the only obligation on defendant to provide discovery is limited to tangible and scientific evidence after defendant has made a reciprocal request. Work product and the statements of witnesses are protected by this rule and will not be disclosed.

Continuing Duty and Sanctions

There is a continuing duty to disclose requested materials and the courts are empowered to sanction discovery violations with limits on testimony, the granting of a continuance, or other order that it "deems just under the circumstances, including the award of a new trial or the dismissal of the prosecution."

Rule 17. Subpoena

(a) For attendance of witnesses; form; issuance. A subpoena shall be issued by the clerk under the seal of the court. It shall state the name of the court and the title, if any, of the proceeding, and shall command each person to whom it is directed to attend and give testimony at the time and place specified therein. The clerk shall issue a subpoena, signed and sealed but otherwise in blank to a party requesting it, who shall fill in the blanks before it is served. A subpoena shall be issued by a United States magistrate judge in a proceeding before that magistrate judge, but it need not be under the seal of the court.

(b) Defendants unable to pay. The court shall order at any time that a subpoena be issued for service on a named witness upon an ex parte application of a defendant upon a satisfactory showing that the defendant is financially unable to pay the fees of the witness and that the presence of the witness is necessary to an adequate defense. If the court orders the subpoena to be issued the costs incurred by the process and the fees of the witness so subpoenaed shall be paid in the same manner in which similar costs and fees are paid in case of a witness subpoenaed in behalf of the government.

(c) For production of documentary evidence and of objects. A subpoena may also command the person to whom it is directed to produce the books, papers, documents or other objects designated therein. The court on motion made promptly may quash or modify the subpoena if compliance would be unreasonable or oppressive. The court may direct that books, papers, documents or objects designated in the subpoena be produced before the court at a time prior to the trial or prior to the time when they are to be offered in evidence and may upon their production permit the books, papers, documents or objects or portions thereof to be inspected by the parties and their attorneys.

(d) Service. A subpoena may be served by the marshal, by a deputy marshal or by any other person who is not a party and who is not less than 18 years of age. Service of a subpoena shall be made by delivering a copy thereof to the person named and by tendering to that person the fee for 1 day's attendance and the mileage allowed by law. Fees and mileage need not be tendered to the witness upon service of a subpoena issued in behalf of the United States or an officer or agency thereof.

(e) Place of service.

(1) In United States. A subpoena requiring the attendance of a witness at a hearing or trial may be served at any place within the United States.

(2) Abroad. A subpoena directed to a witness in a foreign country shall issue under the circumstances and in the manner and be served as provided in Title 28, U.S.C.§ 1783.

(f) For taking deposition; place of examination.

(1) Issuance. An order to take a deposition authorizes the issuance by the clerk of the court for the district in which the deposition is to be taken of subpoenas for the persons named or described therein.

(2) Place. The witness whose deposition is to be taken may be required by subpoena to attend at any place designated by the trial court, taking into account the convenience of the witness and the parties.

(g) Contempt. Failure by any person without adequate excuse to obey a subpoena served upon that person may be deemed a contempt of the court from which the subpoena issued or of the court for the district in which it was issued if it was issued by a United States magistrate judge.

(h) Information not subject to subpoena. Statements made by witnesses or prospective witnesses may not be subpoenaed from the government or the defendant under this rule, but shall be subject to production only in accordance with the provisions of Rule 26.2.

Commentary

By Prof. Louis M. Natali
Temple University Beasley School of Law

Rule 17 deals with subpoenas and is straightforward. Under subdivision (b) the indigent defendant in need of a witness may, upon ex parte application, obtain funds to secure the attendance of witnesses at the trial. This rule should be read together with h provisions in 18 USCS § 3006A which also provide for ex parte applications for funds.

Rule 17.1. Pretrial Conference

At any time after the filing of the indictment or information the court upon motion of any party or upon its own motion may order one or more conferences to consider such matters as will promote a fair and expeditious trial. At the conclusion of a conference the court shall prepare and file a memorandum of the matters agreed upon. No admissions made by the defendant or the defendant's attorney at the conference shall be used against the defendant unless the admissions are reduced to writing and signed by the defendant and the defendant's attorney. This rule shall not be invoked in the case of a defendant who is not represented by counsel.

Commentary

By Prof. Louis M. Natali
Temple University Beasley School of Law

Rule 17.1 deals with pretrial conferences. This procedure has proven to be useful. Stipulations, motions in limine, and advance rulings on exhibits are often discussed and disposed of at these conferences. While many judges are in the practice of recording the conference, the rule does not require it. It is usually very helpful to have a record of the rulings and the conditions for proceeding, and counsel should have a good reason for not wanting to record the meeting. Offers, representations, and concessions of counsel are often made at such meetings. It may be difficult to reconstruct these later.

The rule only prohibits admissions by defendants and defendant's attorney, not admissions by others.

V. Venue

Rule 18. Place of Prosecution and Trial

Except as otherwise permitted by statute or by these rules, the prosecution shall be had in a district in which the offense was committed. The court shall fix the place of trial within the district with due regard to the convenience of the defendant and the witnesses and the prompt administration of justice.

Commentary

By Prof. Louis M. Natali
Temple University Beasley School of Law

Venue will generally be in the judicial district where the offense was committed.

A change of venue may be granted pursuant to Rule 21(a) and this rule must be used together with Rule 21.

Prosecutors have used venue provisions to select extremely remote places to try defendants because one of the conspirators went there or because an overt act, pursuant to the conspiracy, may have taken place in a far-flung district.

The second sentence permits and instructs the court to take the convenience of the defendant into account. Thus the rule embodies a concept of forum non conveniens and courts will balance factors such as the presence of witnesses in a particular district. The court must support an exercise of discretion by findings of record.

Where an offense occurred may be a difficult question and counsel should consider filing a bill of particulars pursuant to Rule 7(f) to understand the prosecution's theory as to what acts took place in the district. That the crime took place in the place alleged in the indictment, usually the district of trial, must be proved by the government beyond a reasonable doubt. A failure to prove venue is grounds for a judgment of acquittal pursuant to Rule 29 or for a motion for arrest of judgment after verdict.

Rule 19. Transfer Within the District

[Rescinded]

Rule 20. Transfer From the District for Plea and Sentence

(a) Indictment or information pending. A defendant arrested, held, or present in a district other than that in which an indictment or information is pending against that defendant may state in writing a wish to plead guilty or nolo contendere, to waive trial in the district in which the indictment or information is pending, and to consent to disposition of the case in the district in which that defendant was arrested, held, or present, subject to the approval of the United States attorney for each district. Upon receipt of the defendant's statement and of the written approval of the United States attorneys, the clerk of the court in which the indictment or information is pending shall transmit the papers in the proceeding or certified copies thereof to the clerk of the court for the district in which the defendant is arrested, held, or present, and the prosecution shall continue in that district.

(b) Indictment or information not pending. A defendant arrested, held, or present, in a district other than the district in which a complaint is pending against that defendant may state in writing a wish to plead guilty or nolo contendere, to waive venue and trial in the district in which the warrant was issued, and to consent to disposition of the case in the district in which that defendant was arrested, held, or present, subject to the approval of the United States attorney for each district. Upon filing the written waiver of venue in the district in which the defendant is present, the prosecution may proceed as if venue were in such district.

(c) Effect of not guilty plea. If after the proceeding has been transferred pursuant to subdivision (a) or (b) of this rule the defendant pleads not guilty, the clerk shall return the papers to the court in which the prosecution was commenced, and the proceeding shall be restored to the docket of that court. The defendant's statement that the defendant wishes to plead guilty or nolo contendere shall not be used against that defendant.

(d) Juveniles. A juvenile (as defined in 18 U.S.C. § 5031) who is arrested, held, or present in a district other than that in which the juvenile is alleged to have committed an act in violation of a law of the United States not punishable by death or life imprisonment may, after having been advised by counsel and with the approval of the court and the United States attorney for each district, consent to be proceeded against as a juvenile delinquent in the district in which the juvenile is arrested, held, or present. The consent shall be given in writing before the court but only after the court has apprised the juvenile of the juvenile's rights, including the right to be returned to the district in which the juvenile is alleged to have committed the act, and of the consequences of such consent.

Commentary

By Prof. Louis M. Natali
Temple University Beasley School of Law

This rule, subject to the approval of the United States attorney at each end, permits transfer of a case for guilty plea and sentence. Such a request by a defendant must be made in writing.

It may be the case that a defendant has been indicted far from his or her home and resources. If, after analysis and consultation with counsel, a guilty plea is appropriate, such a plea may be entered before a local district court. This will be convenient for purposes of the sentencing hearing and may also permit the sentence to be served in an area much closer to the defendant's home. The rule operates if the defendant is arrested, held or, simply present, in any district other than that from which the indictment is issued. Nothing prohibits selection of a venue which a defendant deems to be favorable.

Subdivision (b) permits an uninformed defendant to seek the benefits of Rule 20(a) by submitting a written request for transfer of venue.

A good knowledge of a district's sentencing practices may be key to a client's informed decision to use Rule 20. During the Vietnam era judges in the Northern District of California adopted a policy of sentencing draft resistors to probation.

With the advent of guideline sentencing, it is substantially more difficult to predict how all or any of the judges (drawn at random) will react to a particular offense and PSI sentencing recommendation since both U.S. attorneys must agree. It seems there will be an effective check on an outbreak of sentencing liberality for a particular offense. *But see United States v. Koon*, 518 U.S. 81, 135 L.Ed. 2d 392, 116 S. Ct. 2035 (1996).

Rule 21. Transfer From the District for Trial

(a) For prejudice in the district. The court upon motion of the defendant shall transfer the proceeding as to that defendant to another district whether or not such district is specified in the defendant's motion if the court is satisfied that there exists in the district where the prosecution is pending so great a prejudice against the defendant that the defendant cannot obtain a fair and impartial trial at any place fixed by law for holding court in that district.

(b) Transfer in other cases. For the convenience of parties and witnesses, and in the interest of justice, the court upon motion of the defendant may transfer the proceeding as to that defendant or any one or more of the counts thereof to another district.

(c) Proceedings on transfer. When a transfer is ordered the clerk shall transmit to the clerk of the court to which the proceeding is transferred all papers in the proceeding or duplicates thereof and any bail taken, and the prosecution shall continue in that district.

Commentary

By Prof. Louis M. Natali
Temple University School of Law

Subdivision (a)—For Prejudice in the District

This rule requires the court to grant a change of venue if the court is satisfied there exists "so great a prejudice that the defendant cannot obtain an impartial trial."

The defendant has the burden of showing prejudice and the burden to produce evidence of prejudice. Such a motion is rarely granted. The Oklahoma City bombing trials of McVeigh and Nichols were rare exceptions. In those cases, trial was moved to Denver and a Colorado federal judge presided over the case.

In order to prevail counsel should consider:

(A) news and media accounts,

(B) sampling of potential jurors,

(C) the use of experts in communication and market survey analysis,

(D) opinion polls, and

(E) jury experts.

All factual investigation by witnesses should be presented by affidavit and witnesses should be available for a hearing. Such a motion is often joined with a request for broader voir dire, additional peremptory challenges, and a continuance. Many times the court will deny the change of venue but grant some lesser form of relief, such as a continuance or broader voir dire examination. The motion for change may be repeated during or after jury selection, as it becomes clear that lesser forms of relief have been ineffective.

Subdivision (b)—Transfer in Other Cases

Subdivision (b) permits trial transfer for convenience as discussed in Rule 18 *supra.*

Rule 22. Time of Motion To Transfer

A motion to transfer under these rules may be made at or before arraignment or at such other time as the court or these rules may prescribe.

Commentary

By Prof. Louis M. Natali
Temple University Beasley School of Law

The timing of Rule 19, 20, and 21 motions is generally the arraignment. Rule 12 states the filing of motions is set at arraignment.

The court may permit transfer at a later or earlier time in its discretion or pursuant to Rule 20(b) even where no indictment is pending.

VI. Trial

Rule 23. Trial by Jury or by the Court

(a) Trial by jury. Cases required to be tried by jury shall be so tried unless the defendant waives a jury trial in writing with the approval of the court and the consent of the government.

(b) Jury of less than twelve. Juries shall be of 12 but at any time before verdict the parties may stipulate in writing with the approval of the court that the jury shall consist of any number less than 12 or that a valid verdict may be returned by a jury of less than 12 should the court find it necessary to excuse one or more jurors for any just cause after trial commences. Even absent such stipulation, if the court finds it necessary to excuse a juror for just cause after the jury has retired to consider its verdict, in the discretion of the court a valid verdict may be returned by the remaining 11 jurors.

(c) Trial without a jury. In a case tried without a jury the court shall make a general finding and shall in addition, on request made before the general finding, find the facts specially. Such findings may be oral. If an opinion or memorandum of decision is filed, it will be sufficient if the findings of fact appear therein.

Commentary

By Prof. Louis M. Natali
Temple University Beasley School of Law

Generally

Trial by jury is the rule and a departure from this method of trial must be approved by both the defendant and the government. The government will often quickly agree to such a disposition. This is especially true in those cases where counsel is only going to trial to preserve a legal issue for appeal.

In some instances the government may agree to a bench trial in order not to offend the trial judge. The procedure is cheaper and quicker but should only be considered in the above stated circumstances where:

(1) the case revolves around a legal issue that a jury will not like, *e.g.*, an insanity or other mens rea issue or a mere presence defense which a jury will not abide. In these instances a judge is more likely to understand the issues and follow the law.

(2) the client has no factual issues or evidence to contest the charges (the slow guilty plea) but insists on pleading not guilty.

(3) the judge will resolve the facts in a way a jury will not.

There must be clear, articulable reasons for waiving a jury trial. Hunches will not work. In a jury trial, judges may err in instructing juries and the error can serve as a basis for reversal.

Finally, the decision to waive a jury trial belongs to the defendant not to counsel. Counsel must carefully assess the pros and cons but, at the end of the day, it is the defendant's decision.

Jury of Less Than Twelve

This rule permits counsel to waive, in writing, a twelve person jury. It is difficult to follow why defense counsel would ever make it less difficult to convict the defendant. Even without counsel's agreement the court may permit a verdict by eleven jurors when it becomes necessary to excuse a juror after deliberations have begun. This rule should be challenged as a violation of due process and the right to a jury under the Sixth Amendment.

Rule 24. Trial Jurors

(a) Examination. The court may permit the defendant or the defendant's attorney and the attorney for the government to conduct the examination of prospective jurors or may itself conduct the examination. In the latter event the court shall permit the defendant or the defendant's attorney and the attorney for the government to supplement the examination by such further inquiry as it deems proper or shall itself submit to the prospective jurors such additional questions by the parties or their attorneys as it deems proper.

(b) Peremptory challenges. If the offense charged is punishable by death, each side is entitled to 20 peremptory challenges. If the offense charged is punishable by imprisonment for more than one year, the government is entitled to 6 peremptory challenges and the defendant or defendants jointly to 10 peremptory challenges. If the offense charged is punishable by imprisonment for not more than one year or by fine or both, each side is entitled to 3 peremptory challenges. If there is more than one defendant, the court may allow the defendants additional peremptory challenges and permit them to be exercised separately or jointly.

(c) Alternate jurors.

(1) In general. The court may empanel no more than 6 jurors, in addition to the regular jury, to sit as alternate jurors. An alternate juror, in the order called, shall replace a juror who becomes or is found to be unable or disqualified to perform juror duties. Alternate jurors shall (i) be drawn in the same manner, (ii) have the same qualifications, (iii) be subject to the same examination and challenges, and (iv) take the same oath as regular jurors. An alternate juror has the same functions, powers, facilities and privileges as a regular juror.

(2) Peremptory challenges. In addition to challenges otherwise provided by law, each side is entitled to 1 additional peremptory challenge if 1 or 2 alternate jurors are empaneled, 2 additional peremptory challenges if 3 or 4 alternate jurors are empaneled, and 3 additional peremptory challenges if 5 or 6 alternate jurors are empaneled. The additional peremptory challenges may be used to remove an alternate juror only, and the other peremptory challenges allowed by these rules may not be used to remove an alternate juror.

(3) Retention of alternate jurors. When the jury retires to consider the verdict, the court in its discretion may retain the alternate jurors during deliberations. If the court decides to retain the alternate jurors, it shall ensure that they do not discuss the case with any other person unless and until they replace a regular juror during deliberations. If an alternate replaces a juror after deliberations have begun, the court shall instruct the jury to begin its deliberations anew.

Commentary

By Prof. Louis M. Natali
Temple University Beasley School of Law

Subdivision (a)—Examination

This rule governs the methods for jury selection in federal court. It permits both counsel- and judge-conducted voir dire. It is difficult to conceive of any situation in which the latter would be preferred. In voir dire conducted by defense counsel it is easier to probe bias, prejudice, and true attitudes. It also begins the process of building a rapport. However, many federal judges believe it is a waste of time and that they are better able to pick a fair jury than is counsel. If a motion for change of venue has been made, that may be an additional reason for the need to have counsel-conducted voir dire. *See* the Commentary for FRCrP 21.

It is difficult to persuade judges that counsel must conduct the voir dire but the effort must be made. Every case contains different factual and legal issues that counsel understands far better than the court simply because counsel has lived with them longer than the court. Issues of witness credibility, bias, attitudes towards law enforcement, drug use, witness immunity, the insanity defense, and the like have to be investigated and explored with jurors.

Often, the court will not see the reason for more than the most superficial questions unless the court is persuaded by arguments, sample questions, and expert affidavits that counsel-conducted voir dire is necessary. Jury experts and jury focus groups are often used to persuade courts to expand voir dire.

Much has been written on these subjects and more federal judges are allowing some form of voir dire to be conducted by counsel. Questions must be directed to fixed biases and opinions about the facts or the law and to issues of pretrial publicity or other impermissible knowledge of the case. There is a fine line between asking a hypothetical question, *e.g.*, "Will you believe the prosecution's star witness who has been granted immunity?" (not permitted) and "Would you follow the law and instructions which say that no witness is disqualified from giving testimony because of their participation in the offense?" (permitted). Another example is: "Would you believe the testimony of a law enforcement agent merely because of the position that he (she) holds?" This is permitted. Questions must be tied to instructions and the jurors' ability to follow them.

With respect to pretrial publicity, it is best to begin this topic with a show of hands as to whether anyone has heard or read anything about the case. If there are positive responses, then the court should be asked to listen to these individually and out of the hearing of the other venirepersons. In this fashion the entire panel will be protected against contamination and no one will hear or share in the publicity that one or more has heard.

Each district and each judge within a district conducts voir dire and peremptory challenges a little differently. A request to the judge's clerk should be made to learn exactly how each judge conducts it, including how strikes are handled.

In instances of court-conducted voir dire, counsel should propose and file written questions that the court should ask. These are to be prepared with great care to ensure that all factual and legal issues are covered. Counsel should not fear pushing the envelope to request questions that are considered borderline or are too intrusive. That is the way the law is made. If one judge in the district or, indeed, any district, permits such questions, counsel should cite that as authority or prepare an affidavit in support for such questions. These should, if denied, be made part of the record for appellate purposes.

After the questioning is completed counsel will be allowed an opportunity to make and argue challenges for cause. This should be done at side bar and the venireperson may need to be present for follow up or rehabilitation. The law in most districts will not allow a challenge for cause to be a basis for error on appeal unless all peremptory challenges have been exhausted. Keep this in mind when considering the peremptory challenge.

Subdivision (b)—Peremptory Challenges

Subdivision (b) sets out the rule for peremptory challenges. In a non-capital case the defense has ten and the prosecution has six. In capital cases each side has twenty. Generally the court will bring a panel of thirty-two venirepersons to the courtroom. This will leave twelve jurors and two alternates, assuming each side has used all its challenges. Each side is allowed one peremptory for each alternate. *See* subdivision (c). Some judges put twelve jurors in the jury box and allow the voir dire to take place from there; others seat the entire panel in the first three rows of the audience and the attorneys turn their chairs to face the jury during the voir dire.

Before peremptory challenges are used, the practice is for each side to make their challenges for cause. This should be done at side bar out of the hearing of the other members of the panel who may take offense at the removal of someone they have come to like.

After exhausting peremptory challenges the court has discretion to award additional challenges and an attempt should be made on grounds relating to the motion for change of venue or counsel-conducted voir dire that the defendant's rights have not been protected.

Federal constitutional law does not permit the exercise of peremptory challenges on either racial or gender grounds, *Batson v. Kentucky*, 476 U.S. 79, 90 L. Ed. 2d 69, 106 S. Ct. 1712 (1986). Standing to complain about misuse of challenges is not confined to only those members of affected groups (*e.g.*, racial minorities or women). There is a three-part procedure for preserving and perfecting a *Batson* claim:

1. The prima facie case. Note the prosecutor's use of challenges, *e.g.*, the prosecutor has used three peremptory challenges on African-American venirewomen. This begins the creation of a record on this point.

2. A race- or gender-neutral explanation. The court, if it agrees, will then ask for a race- or gender-neutral explanation. The prosecutor must justify the use of the preempts and satisfy the court that their use was indeed race- or gender-neutral with reasons of record.

3. The opportunity to rebut the race- or gender-neutral explanation. Challenging counsel is given the opportunity to rebut with evidence or argument that the explanation offered was a sham. For example, if a race-neutral explanation is that people from that area don't like the police, a response may be that the prosecutor has chosen other white persons from the same area.

The Remedy: If the court finds that discrimination has occurred, it may discharge the entire venire and begin with a new panel or it may disallow the peremptory and seat the venireperson as a jury.

Batson and its progeny have spawned many decisions and these must be consulted before commencing the selection of a jury in a particular circuit or district.

Rule 25. Judge; Disability

(a) During trial. If by reason of death, sickness or other disability the judge before whom a jury trial has commenced is unable to proceed with the trial, any other judge regularly sitting in or assigned to the court, upon certifying familiarity with the record of the trial, may proceed with and finish the trial.

(b) After verdict or finding of guilt. If by reason of absence, death, sickness or other disability the judge before whom the defendant has been tried is unable to perform the duties to be performed by the court after a verdict or finding of guilt, any other judge regularly sitting in or assigned to the court may perform those duties; but if that judge is satisfied that a judge who did not preside at the trial cannot perform those duties or that it is appropriate for any other reason, that judge may grant a new trial.

Commentary

By Prof. Inga L. Parsons
New York University School of Law

FRCrP 25 governs the situation when a presiding judge dies, becomes disabled, or is absent. Two scenarios are dealt with under the rule: during trial and after verdict.

Disability Before Verdict

If a judge dies or is disabled during trial, FRCrP 25(a) allows essentially any other judge in the court to finish the trial providing he or she certifies familiarity with the trial record. This section of the rule does not provide for substitution during trial simply because the judge is absent.

Disability After Verdict

If there is a verdict in the case, and a judge is unable to perform his or her duties due to death, disability or absence, nearly any other judge in the court may continue with the case (there is no requirement in this section of certifying familiarity with the record), unless the new judge feels the duties cannot be performed by a substitute judge and orders a new trial. FRCrP 25(b).

FRCrP 25(b) does not mention whether the defense or prosecution must consent to a new trial. However, if either party believes that their case is better off with the current trial record rather than a second trial, counsel should object if a new trial is called for.

New Trial Considerations with a Substitute Judge

If a party wants a new trial, FRCrP 25 allows the substitute judge to grant a new trial if appropriate "for any other reason." FRCrP 25(b). If the prosecution objects to a new trial, the defense will have to show that a new judge would be unable to perform his or her duties by not having presided at trial. The cited inability to perform his or her duties is often because the trial was so complex and so complicated that having a substitute judge in such a case would deny the defendant a fair trial. Of course, a complex trial may also compel the court to deny a motion for a new trial because of judicial economy concerns with the expense and delay in retrying a lengthy, complicated case.

Unlike FRCrP 25(b), which provides for the possibility of a new trial when a judge takes over a case after verdict, there is no mention in FRCrP 25(a) of a new trial when a judge takes over during trial. When a judge is substituted at the end of the trial but before verdict, if the defense believes a new trial would be beneficial, counsel should argue that the prejudice to the defense is the equivalent of a post-verdict substitution were there to be a conviction in the case, and that the judge should grant a new trial. In a bench trial, not specifically discussed in FRCrP 25, where the judge is the trier of fact and has to decide the credibility of witnesses, it would be almost impossible for the new judge not to order a retrial if the substitution came before the judge's verdict.

Prejudice to the defendant by virtue of a substitute judge during a jury trial will be difficult to show because the judge is not making determinations of credibility based on demeanor and other factors that are not revealed in a black-and-white record with respect to determining a verdict. The witness credibility issues that arise with a judge taking over during trial, as with a new judge after verdict, relate to sentencing issues in the event of a verdict of guilty (*see* discussion below). If counsel objects to the substitution

Rule 25. Judge; Disability

of a judge during trial, the only available basis under FRCrP 25(a) is that the judge has not fully reviewed the record. Rather than grant a new trial, the more immediate remedy would be to ensure that the judge gets up to speed by reading the record. (At the outset, where there is a possibility that the judge will have to be replaced, counsel should ask the court to have a daily transcript of the proceedings made at court expense so that if the judge is substituted, counsel can expeditiously refer the new judge to previous testimony and rulings in the record.)

In complex cases where the judge physically could not have read the entire record or even skimmed it in time, counsel may be in a position to argue that the judge could not have adequate familiarity with the trial record and thus a new trial is needed. There are obviously some strategic considerations whether to make this argument. Any challenge to the representations of a judge or a judge's competency requires a great deal of sensitivity and diplomacy. The judge is apt to take offense and unlikely to be helpful to that party's case or future cases; institutional players like court-appointed defense attorneys and assistant United States attorneys will no doubt appear before the same judge on other cases.

On the other hand, counsel should not shirk from setting forth such claims clearly, while as tactfully and respectfully as possible, particularly if the objective is to make sure the judge does indeed read the record (although in many cases it may be better for the defendant if the judge does not digest every word of the trial). In any event, it is important for counsel to make a record to preserve the issue in the event of an appeal. The objection should emphasize the inability of any judge to become familiar with the record because of the complexity of the case and short time period, thus necessitating a new trial rather than a personal attack on the judge. Of course, if the new judge's behavior is egregious or unethical, defense counsel will have independent grounds to seek a recusal.

Sentencing Considerations with a Substitute Judge

When a judge presides during a trial and there is a conviction, the judge typically uses the testimony and evidence produced at the trial in making determinations as to enhancements under the Federal Sentencing Guidelines. If the judge is going to rely on the trial transcript in assessing sentencing enhancements, credibility determinations are problematic since demeanor, tone, eye contact, etc., of a witness are not captured in a black-and-white record. In some cases, however, it may be less damaging for defendant to have the court rely on the cold record rather than hear prejudicial testimony from a live witness at a new trial or sentencing hearing.

In most cases, however, since FRCrP 25(b) specifically does not require that the judge certify familiarity with the record, a judge's review of a comprehensive presentence report and a sentencing hearing will be sufficient to allow the court to sentence the defendant including imposition of enhancements.

If an enhancement depends on the credibility of a trial witness who was not observed by the substitute judge, defense counsel should object to the use of the black-and-white transcript. For example, were the government to move for an obstruction of justice enhancement under the Federal Sentencing Guidelines claiming that the jury's conviction was necessarily a determination that the defendant had lied on the stand, defense counsel should object to such an imposition of the enhancement on the grounds that the new judge is not in a position to assess physical demeanor and credibility of the defendant at trial based on the "cold" record of the defendant's testimony. To avoid a new trial on the issue, a judge may be persuaded not to impose the enhancement.

Rearguing Legal Issues

Substitution of the judge is technically not an opportunity for either party to revisit already settled legal issues decided by the previous judge during trial. However, if the rulings were subject to further testimony or argument, or any judge would reasonably review his or her own decision at that time, the parties have a good faith basis to ask the judge to reconsider a ruling. To the extent either counsel can do so without antagonizing the judge, adverse rulings should be revisited when possible. Of course, the other side should object, having prevailed on the first judge's ruling.

Lexis Search Tip
To find a commentary by the author's name, do the following: 1. Click Federal Legal – U.S. 2. Click United States Code Service (USCS) Materials. 3. Click National Institute for Trial Advocacy. Then type the author's last name Parsons in the box and hit enter to find all the commentaries written by Professor Inga L. Parsons. Select FOCUS. Then type in "disability" and you will find the commentary written by Professor Parsons on FRCrP 25. Judge; Disability.

Rule 26. Taking of Testimony

In all trials the testimony of witnesses shall be taken orally in open court, unless otherwise provided by an Act of Congress or by these rules, the Federal Rules of Evidence, or other rules adopted by the Supreme Court.

Commentary

By Prof. Louis M. Natali
Temple University Beasley School of Law

Rule 26 provides for the taking of testimony in open court and defers to the Federal Rules of Evidence and other rules or acts of Congress. These rules must be read with the Federal Rules of Evidence. Two rules bear special mention. Federal Rule of Evidence 501, in particular, is important because it permits the federal court to develop the federal rule of witness privilege according to common law principles and in the light of wisdom and experience. Since there are no Federal Rules of Evidence concerning privileges it is necessary to research the rules by reading cases, some of which may vary from circuit to circuit. From time to time the Supreme Court will define the parameters of the spousal privilege (*see Trammell v. United States*, 445 U.S. 40, 63 L.Ed. 2d 186, 100 S. Ct. 906 (1980)) or the attorney-client privilege (*see United States v. Upjohn*, 449 U.S. 383, 66 L. Ed. 2d 584, 101 S. Ct. 677 (1981)).

Under Federal Rule of Evidence 601, all witnesses are held to be competent. In federal criminal cases state competency rules are inapplicable.

Rule 26.1. Determination of Foreign Law

A party who intends to raise an issue concerning the law of a foreign country shall give reasonable written notice. The court, in determining foreign law, may consider any relevant material or source, including testimony, whether or not submitted by a party or admissible under the Federal Rules of Evidence. The court's determination shall be treated as a ruling on a question of law.

Commentary

By Prof. Inga L. Parsons
New York University School of Law

If a party intends to raise an issue concerning foreign law, the party must provide written notice under FRCrP 26.1. For example, if the prosecution claims that possession of certain artifacts is in violation of foreign law and thus violates the National Stolen Property Act, the prosecution must give notice to the court and to the defendant under FRCrP 26.1. In addition to requiring notice of foreign law, FRCrP 26.1 is an expansive rule allowing the judge to determine foreign law of another country (not a state) based on any relevant material or source. FRCrP 26.1 provides that determination of a foreign law is a question of law. FRCrP 26.1 is essentially identical to its civil sister, FRCP 44.1.

Form of the Notice

Given the amount of research, investigation, time and money that is likely to accompany a foreign law question, it is clear why the rule requires written notice. Failure to give timely notice could preclude a foreign law determination. Although no specific time periods are set forth in FRCrP 26.1, reasonable notice is required, and any counsel needing to make such a motion will gain little in waiting. Once the decision to give notice is made, it must be in writing and should be explicit. Since FRCrP 26.1 is essentially identical to its civil sister FRCP 44.1, the attorneys in a federal criminal case may want to request permission to proceed under civil procedure rules such as exchange of interrogatories or expanded deposition rights, at least with respect to the issues surrounding the application of foreign law.

In the foreign law notice it is a good idea to provide a translated copy of the foreign statute to the judge. It is important that the translation is done by a court-certified interpreter to avoid possible objections. *See* the Commentary for FRCrP 28. A quality interpretation is critical because a good deal of the initial litigation may revolve around the translation of the words in the foreign law, apart from any legal interpretation of those words. Counsel may wish to seek a stipulation from opposing counsel as to the translation being an accurate one to avoid these battles. If opposing counsel is not in a position to take the time and incur the expense needed to make a separate translation, moving counsel may be able to get such a stipulation.

Strategies Whether to Raise a Foreign Law Issue

In deciding whether to raise an issue of foreign law, a party must consider whether foreign law does indeed apply. There may be advantages to the application of American law versus foreign law and counsel should review the effects of both laws before making an application. This review should include the effect of the application of foreign law on the guilt phase as well as sentencing, particularly since the Federal Sentencing Guidelines have enhancements triggered by foreign law elements. For example, the guidelines provide for enhancements if theft of property was from a national cemetery, USSG § 2B1.1(b)(7), or if there was misappropriation of a trade secret to benefit a foreign entity, USSG § 2B1.1(b)(8). If the defendant is from a country where it can be argued that the offense charged is not criminalized, part of the defense may rest on a particular reading of foreign law which may become significant in the defendant's case.

Extradition Cases

Application of foreign law can also arise in extradition cases. Under the doctrine of specialty, the receiving state may have jurisdiction only on those counts on which the surrendering jurisdiction grants extradition. Understanding which counts would be included in the extradition could implicate foreign law, particularly if the failure to specify certain counts is because those counts are contrary to the surrendering jurisdiction's laws, or because the surrendering state's courts are unclear as to which counts were specified.

Once the judge determines that foreign law applies, the next issue is the interpretation of that law. It is very important that the parties seek an in limine ruling well before the trial as to what law will apply. Finding out ten minutes before opening statements what the law governing the case will be is obviously not advised.

Interpreting Foreign Law

The interpretation of foreign law is likely to require a hearing. FRCrP 26 is enormously broad with respect to admission of evidence, allowing for any relevant source of information without regard to admissibility. Both parties should be prepared to call expert witnesses to testify as to what the foreign law means. Ideally these experts will be licensed to practice law or teach in the foreign jurisdiction. Other evidence can include testimony either in court or by deposition, court cases, treatises, academic articles, affidavits, letters, congressional records (either domestic or foreign), etc.

FRCrP 27(b) provides for the manner in which foreign documents are proven as official records and codifies the Hague Public Documents Convention, which abolished the requirement of a final certification. *See* Advisory Committee Notes to FRCP 44. Although the obvious defense argument would be that the inability to cross-examine witnesses where hearsay testimony is admitted through documents violates the defendant's Confrontation Clause rights, the courts have held that because the foreign law issue is essentially one of law and not fact, there is no Sixth Amendment violation. *See*, 1944 Advisory Committee Notes to FRCrP 26.1 *citing Kay v. United States*, 255 F.2d 476, 480 (4th Cir. 1958) et al.

FRCrP 26.1 provides that the court's decision as to the application of foreign law is a question of law. As a result, the ruling is appealable and subject to de novo review by a higher court. Although the question of foreign law is set out as a question of law for the court, FRCrP 26.1 does not mandate that the judge rather than the jury decide all questions of foreign law. Further, it is not reversible error to put the matter to the jury where there is no prejudice to the defendant's substantial trial rights. *See United States v. McClain*, 593 F.2d 658 (5th Cir. 1979) ("... carefully sidestepping the issue of who is to decide the question, was deliberate on the part of the draftsmen" (of FRCrP 26.1)). There may be occasions when the defense may want the issue to be determined by the jury and may be able to show that at the heart of the foreign law issue lies a determination of fact. When issues are to be given to the jury, the parties should prepare extensive comprehensible jury charges on those issues. On the other hand, a foreign law case may be a good candidate to waive a jury and proceed by bench trial, depending on the nature and complexity of the issues.

Even if foreign law is applicable and is ultimately interpreted so that the parties are advised of the foreign law's mandates, counsel should challenge the foreign law on any grounds available under U.S. law. For example, if the foreign law is vague, challenges on that basis should be made. *See, e.g., McClain*, 593 F.2d at 670 (5th Cir. 1979) (view of Mexican law convinced court that defendants "may have suffered the prejudice of being convicted pursuant to laws that were too vague to be a predicate for criminal liability under our jurisprudential standards.")

Rule 26.2. Production of Witness Statements

(a) Motion for production. After a witness other than the defendant has testified on direct examination, the court, on motion of a party who did not call the witness, shall order the attorney for the government or the defendant and the defendant's attorney, as the case may be, to produce, for the examination and use of the moving party, any statement of the witness that is in their possession and that relates to the subject matter concerning which the witness has testified.

(b) Production of entire statement. If the entire contents of the statement relate to the subject matter concerning which the witness has testified, the court shall order that the statement be delivered to the moving party.

(c) Production of excised statement. If the other party claims that the statement contains privileged information or matter that does not relate to the subject matter concerning which the witness has testified, the court shall order that it be delivered to the court in camera. Upon inspection, the court shall excise the portions of the statement that are privileged or that do not relate to the subject matter concerning which the witness has testified, and shall order that the statement, with such material excised, be delivered to the moving party. Any portion of the statement that is withheld from the defendant over the defendant's objection must be preserved by the attorney for the government, and, if the defendant appeals a conviction, must be made available to the appellate court for the purpose of determining the correctness of the decision to excise the portion of the statement.

(d) Recess for examination of statement. Upon delivery of the statement to the moving party, the court, upon application of that party, may recess the proceedings so that counsel may examine the statement and prepare to use it in the proceedings.

(e) Sanction for failure to produce statement. If the other party elects not to comply with an order to deliver a statement to the moving party, the court shall order that the testimony of the witness be stricken from the record and that the trial proceed, or, if it is the attorney for the government who elects not to comply, shall declare a mistrial if required by the interest of justice.

(f) Definition. As used in this rule, a "statement" of a witness means:

(**1**) a written statement made by the witness that is signed or otherwise adopted or approved by the witness;

(**2**) a substantially verbatim recital of an oral statement made by the witness that is recorded contemporaneously with the making of the oral statement and that is contained in a stenographic, mechanical, electrical, or other recording or a transcription thereof; or

(**3**) a statement, however taken or recorded, or a transcription thereof, made by the witness to a grand jury.

(g) Scope of rule. This rule applies at a suppression hearing conducted under Rule 12, at trial under this rule, and to the extent specified:

(**1**) in Rule 32(c)(2) at sentencing;

(**2**) in Rule 32.1(c) at a hearing to revoke or modify probation or supervised release;

(**3**) in Rule 46(i) at a detention hearing;

(**4**) in Rule 8 of the Rules Governing Proceedings under 28 U.S.C. § 2255; and

(**5**) in Rule 5.1 at a preliminary examination.

Commentary

By Prof. Louis M. Natali
Temple University Beasley School of Law

This rule sets out the procedure dictated by the Jencks Act (18 USCS § 3500) for the production at trial of the statements of witnesses who have just completed their direct examination. As previously mentioned, these statements are not discoverable under Rule 16. Subdivision (d) provides for a recess so that the moving party has a real opportunity to read and understand the statement and use it effectively during cross-examination. Many judges will use the threat of a recess to "persuade" the government's attorney to provide Jencks material at an earlier time, *e.g.*, the night before the witness testifies on direct examination. This should be a part of a continuing discovery request.

This rule also applies to the defense and to defense witnesses. Their statements must be surrendered after direct examination is concluded. *See United States v. Nobles*, 422 U.S. 225, 45 L. Ed. 2d 141, 95 S. Ct. 2160 (1975).

Rule 26.3. Mistrial

Before ordering a mistrial, the court shall provide an opportunity for the government and for each defendant to comment on the propriety of the order, including whether each party consents or objects to a mistrial, and to suggest any alternatives.

Commentary

By Prof. Inga L. Parsons
New York University School of Law

FRCrP 26.3 is a relatively recent rule promulgated to avoid situations when a judge orders a mistrial without first hearing from both sides and thus may bar a retrial of the defendant. This rule came in the wake of a number of cases involving such a situation, notably *United States v. Dixon*, 913 F.2d 1305, 1313–1315 (8th Cir. 1990) and *United States v. Bates*, 917 F.2d 388 (9th Cir. 1990), referred to in the Advisory Committee Notes to FRCrP 26.3. In both those cases the district courts, sua sponte, declared a mistrial without hearing from either party. In one of the cases, the defense indicated at the post-mistrial hearing that it would have objected to a mistrial. The circuit courts found each district court's actions to be an abuse of discretion and barred retrial of the defendants. Now, under FRCrP 26.3, the court must give the parties an opportunity to be heard on the issue.

Manifest Necessity and Double Jeopardy

Before deciding whether to seek a mistrial, it is imperative that both sides are aware of the law governing double jeopardy. Several factors can make a difference as to whether the defendant can be retried, including when a mistrial is sought, on what grounds it is sought and whether the defense consents to or seeks a mistrial. Double jeopardy attaches when the jury is sworn in a jury trial, or when the first witness is sworn in a bench trial. After double jeopardy has attached and a mistrial declared, there can be a retrial of a defendant only if there is a "manifest necessity" for the mistrial. *See*, *e.g.*, *Richardson v. United States*, 468 U.S. 317, 82 L.Ed.2d. 242, 250, 104 S.Ct. 3081, 3085 (1984) (*quoting United States v. Perez*, 9 Wheat. 579, 6 L.Ed. 165 (1824). Manifest necessity includes a hung jury, a biased jury, or an unduly influenced jury. It also includes actions on the part of the defendant or defense counsel that trigger a mistrial. However, manifest necessity is not a mechanical standard and depends on the particular issues in the case. Manifest necessity is left to the trial judge's discretion. The government bears the burden of showing manifest necessity on appeal.

Hung Juries and *Allen* Charges

The most common manifest necessity is the declaration of a mistrial on the grounds that the jury is hung or deadlocked. Under FRCrP 26.1, before declaring a mistrial on the basis of a hung jury, the court will hear from the parties. Typically prosecutors request that the court give the jury an *Allen* charge (*see Allen v. United States*, 164 U.S. 492, 41 L.Ed. 528, 17 S.Ct. 154 (1896)). Through this charge, the court directs the minority jurors to reconsider their positions in light of each other's opposition; to consider whether their doubts are reasonable ones, particularly if those doubts have failed to make an impression on others; and to consider the expense and difficulties in retrying the case.

An *Allen* charge is extremely coercive; therefore the defense counsel should almost always object to an *Allen* charge. Also, they should make sure the record is clear as to the judge's tone of voice, what words are emphasized, and any facial expressions or hand gestures used by the judge in giving the charge if they add to the coercive nature of the charge. To avoid an *Allen* charge, the defense should either request that the court declare a mistrial then and there, or continue deliberations where it is perceived to be in the client's best interest. The defense may be successful in delaying the giving of the *Allen* charge if the deliberations have been brief.

A number of courts have recognized the coercive nature of the *Allen* charge and have prohibited or severely restricted its use. *See, e.g., United States v. Eastern Medical Billing, Inc.*, 230 F.3d 600, 605–612 (3d. Cir. 2000) (the efficient judicial administration from verdict can be outweighed by *Allen* charge's potential to distort the workings of the jury system). Counsel should be aware of their circuit's position. In jurisdictions where *Allen* charges have been upheld, counsel should know what instructions have been deemed acceptable under what circumstances, and should object to the charge if it goes beyond a standard *Allen* charge to a more coercive, impermissible strong arming.

When the Defendant Seeks a Mistrial

If the defense seeks or consents to a mistrial, a retrial is not barred. An example from a case arising out of the Southern District of New York is illustrative. A Chinese interpreter was translating at a trial where a number of witnesses testified in Chinese. It was determined that the interpreter, who was an employee of the United States Attorney's Office and was not court certified, had mistranslated the proceedings. Two of the four defendants moved for a mistrial. The other two defendants requested that the proceedings continue and would only move for a mistrial if double jeopardy would bar retrial. The court granted a mistrial across the board, and two of the defendants made clear in the record that they were not joining in the mistrial. A retrial was not barred for the two defendants who moved for a mistrial; however, retrial of the two defendants who objected to the mistrial was barred based on double jeopardy grounds. *See United States v. Huang*, 960 F.2d 1128 (2d. Cir. 1992).

There is one exception to the defense seeking a mistrial resulting in no manifest necessity, and that is when the prosecution acts in bad faith and goads the defendant into making the request for a mistrial. *See Oregon v. Kennedy*, 456 U.S. 667, 674–676, 72

L.Ed.2d. 416, 423–425, 102 S.Ct. 2083, 2088–2089 (1982). This can occur, for example, when the prosecution makes objectionable statements in closing arguments such as shifting the burden of proof onto the defendant or impermissibly commenting on the defendant's right to remain silent, all in an attempt to compel defense counsel to move for a mistrial. Unethical prosecutors who see a case going badly or are unable to obtain an important witness in time have been known to make such comments in an attempt to goad defense counsel into seeking mistrials. Unfortunately, it is very difficult to show that such statements were done intentionally and in bad faith. The prosecutor need only respond that it was inadvertent or unintentional. Judges (generally former prosecutors themselves) are likely to accept the prosecutor's representations even when there would appear to be no other explanation for such behavior.

Defense counsel has a very difficult decision whether to request a mistrial even when it is clear to the defense that the prosecutor's comments were made for the purposes of goading defense counsel into declaring a mistrial. If the trial is going so badly for the prosecution, it may be in the defendant's best interest not to request a mistrial and see the case to verdict despite the prosecutor's conduct, unless the defense can be assured of no retrial. Curative instructions may help to remedy the prosecutor's actions.

Retrial Considerations

The conventional wisdom is that a retrial helps the prosecution. On the other hand, where the jury seems pro-prosecution or a conviction seems inevitable, a mistrial, even with the distinct possibility of a retrial, can be a welcomed resolution of the defendant's case. Moreover, because a retrial means the use of additional resources and subjects witnesses to a second cross-examination, a prosecutor may be more willing to negotiate after the declaration of a mistrial. Comments from a deadlocked jury can influence whether the prosecutor will retry the defendant. If the jury was 10 to 2 for acquittal, this may convince the prosecutor that a retrial is too risky. On the other hand, if the count was 10 to 2 for conviction, the prosecutor may be less likely to bargain, particularly if the jurors reveal that if they had only heard from the second officer, they may have been convinced of the defendant's guilt.

After any trial, counsel on both sides should speak to the jury although some judges and some jurisdictions do not allow counsel to speak to jurors. If attorneys are allowed to speak to jurors, providing the jurors consent, the parties should never pass up this opportunity, particularly when the jury was deadlocked. (Parties should also try to speak to alternates when they are dismissed before the deliberations.) Speaking to jurors is an invaluable opportunity to hear what the jury liked or did not like, discounted, counted, ignored, needed, etc. It is often preferable to send a colleague or supervisor since jurors may be more honest about the attorneys to a third party.

If both sides speak to the jury at the same time, counsel should make sure that the jurors can speak without interruption from opposing counsel. Often opposing counsel may try to retry the case in an attempt to convince the jury of their case. Even worse, the prosecutor may try to "poison" the jurors by telling them about evidence that was not included, such as a prior record or a confession, with the hope that if the jurors sit on another jury, they will be more skeptical and more likely to convict.

Rule 27. Proof of Official Record

An official record or an entry therein or the lack of such a record or entry may be proved in the same manner as in civil actions.

Commentary

By Prof. Inga L. Parsons
New York University School of Law

FRCrP 27 provides for a uniform method for proving an official record in a criminal case in the same manner as a civil case. FRCrP 27 provides little guidance, and counsel must refer to the provisions of FRCP 44, the civil rule regarding Proof of Official Record. FRCP 44 lays out the requirements for authentication of either a domestic or a foreign document.

A domestic official record can be established by an official publication or by a copy with a certificate attached where a records custodian has attested to the custody of the original document. Public officers can certify a document with a seal. Lack of an entry can be certified after a diligent search reveals no record or entry.

Certification of foreign documents is set out in detail in FRCP 44 codifying the Hague Public Documents Convention, which abolished the requirement of a final certification. *See* Advisory Committee Notes to FRCP 44. Moreover, when an issue of foreign law is raised, the Federal Rules of Evidence are suspended. *See* the Commentary for FRCrP 26.1.

If a statute establishes procedures for proof of records, that will trump the procedures in FRCP 44. A lengthy list of statutes that have individual proof requirements follows the annotated version of FRCP 44. Counsel should look through this list if certifying a document from a federal agency such as the post office or INS to see whether governing statutes exist.

Proof of official records is essentially about authenticity: that the document is what it purports to be. Authenticity is not the only hurdle to admissibility. The purpose of FRCrP 27 and FRCP 44 is to avoid having custodians of records and other public officials testify at trial simply to show the document is what it purports to be when this can be shown by an official seal. However, certification of a public document does not necessarily overcome objections to the document on the basis of hearsay, lack of relevance, or undue prejudice, for example. Counsel should still be prepared to object to the admittance of the evidence.

If properly authenticated, the document may meet the public records exception to the rule against hearsay. *See* FRE 803(8). However, the mere fact that a document is a public record does not automatically overcome a hearsay objection. If the proof of the official record sets forth the activities of the office or agency, or matters observed pursuant to a duty to report, the record may establish the necessary foundation for the public records exception without additional testimony. (Under FRE 803(8) availability of the declarant is immaterial. *See* FRE 803.)

There is a significant qualification to the public records exception to the rule against hearsay in a federal criminal case. Matters observed by police officers or other law enforcement officers are excluded from the public records exception when offered against the defendant in a criminal case. *See* FRE 803(8)(B). Defense counsel should be vigilant so that documents which are made by law enforcement, or for law enforcement purposes, are not admitted under this exception, *e.g.*, FBI lab reports on narcotics, police reports, etc. In the rare case the defense wishes to introduce a case agent's report in evidence, such documents are not excluded if they are offered against the government. *See* FRE 803(8)(C).

Rule 28. Interpreters

The court may appoint an interpreter of its own selection and may fix the reasonable compensation of such interpreter. Such compensation shall be paid out of funds provided by law or by the government, as the court may direct.

Commentary

By Prof. Inga L. Parsons
New York University School of Law

FRCrP 28, allowing for the judge to appoint interpreters in federal court, should be read in conjunction with the Court Interpreters Act, 28 USCS § 1827. Under the Court Interpreters Act, interpreters will be appointed if a criminal defendant or witness either only speaks a non-English language or primarily speaks a non-English language which would "inhibit such party's comprehension of the proceedings or communication with counsel or the presiding judicial officer, or so as to inhibit such witness' comprehension of questions and the presentation of such testimony." 28 USCS § 1827(d)(1)(A).

Interpreters are routinely utilized if there is a request by either party, or if the judge, in an abundance of caution, suggests that an interpreter be used. Hearings to determine whether in fact the defendant needs an interpreter are rare, unless the prosecution maintains that the defendant is "pretending" to need an interpreter in order to assert a defense that he did not understand his rights or the nature of a transaction, etc. When an interpreter is used, the interpreter is subject to the rules relating to qualification as an expert (*see* the Commentary for FRE 701 *et seq.*) but, in addition, must take an oath to make a true translation. Use of an interpreter is within the discretion of the judge.

Interpreters in federal court can be either certified interpreters or "otherwise qualified" interpreters. Certified interpreters must pass a performance examination, which is apparently very difficult. Certification is only required for a few languages depending on the needs of a particular district; *e.g.*, Spanish and Navajo in

Arizona. If certified court interpreters are not reasonably available, courts can use otherwise qualified interpreters. The court clerk offices keep a list of certified and otherwise qualified interpreters and are responsible for making sure interpreters are in court when needed.

If defense counsel needs an interpreter, either in court or to meet with the defendant or witness in advance, defense counsel should notify the clerk's office ahead of time. The amount of notice needed depends on the language. A Spanish interpreter is generally available most times while interpreters of less common languages may be more difficult to locate. In addition, it is important to make sure that the interpreter is able to translate any particular dialect needed since many languages, such as Chinese, have a number of distinct dialects.

Using Interpreters to Prepare Witnesses

There is a considerable amount of strategy involved in the use of interpreters in a case, particularly where the defendant or witness will testify at trial through an interpreter. Ideally, the interpreter who will be translating at trial should be used to prepare the witness or defendant in advance. The attorney should consult with the clerk's office to discover which interpreters are slated to interpret at that particular trial. Most of the court-certified interpreters are available as experts outside of court on an hourly basis, and indigent defendants are entitled to appointment of reasonable expert services under 18 USCS § 3006A(e)(1). The benefits of using the same interpreter for preparation as at trial are enormous. Importantly, the witness and interpreter become familiar with one another, including familiarity with the meaning and translation of particular words. This often prevents the disastrous consequence of having the interpreter misinterpret a witness' peculiar phrases and meaning at trial. Although interpreters professionally view themselves as simply conduits, some interpreters are better than others at "interpreting" the defendant's true meaning. If the interpreter comes to know and understand the witness or defendant, the interpreter does a better job of expressing sincerity, surprise, etc.

Like any institutional player, interpreters have reputations. Find out which interpreter best suits your needs. Avoid using an interpreter in preparation for trial who is not court certified or on the court list (that interpreter may not be able to interpret at trial). Know the qualifications of each court interpreter. Know who is certified and who is not. Find out whether the interpreter is used primarily by the U.S. Attorney's Office or whether that office even employs the interpreter. To the extent that counsel has some influence on which interpreters will be appointed to a particular case (often requiring a good working relationship with the court clerk or court interpreter's office), use that influence to get the best interpreters assigned to the case and use those interpreters in preparations.

Make sure that the interpreter is translating fully what is said rather than paraphrasing. Even if counsel does not speak the language, pay attention to the length of the sentences and the subsequent translation. If counsel asks a question twenty-five words long and the translation is three words, it is probably not word-for-word translation. Some interpreters like to paraphrase and even get involved in the legalities of the defendant's case by giving legal advice rather than interpreting. Defense counsel should explain to the interpreter the importance of interpreting every word exactly as it is said.

Use of Interpreters in Court to Translate Witness Testimony

Interpreters are required to translate word for word in court. If the interpreter fails to translate word for word, the defense should seek substitution of the interpreter and object to the translated testimony. The Court Interpreters Act provides that if an interpreter is unable to communicate effectively with the judge or a party (including a defendant in a criminal case), the court shall dismiss the interpreter. 28 USCS § 1827(e)(2). Knowing the reputation of the interpreter will allow the defense or prosecution to move to have the interpreter substituted in advance (ideally without the interpreter knowing he or she has been replaced on the motion of a particular party).

When it is discovered that an interpreter is not fully translating, mistranslating, etc., the parties need to object, but they also need to be thoughtful in what remedy they request. If the defense asks for a mistrial on that basis, a retrial is likely since it is at the request of the defendant. The defense should carefully consider whether the defendant is benefitted by a retrial, particularly where the defendant has already taken the stand. *See* the Commentary for

FRCrP 26.3 (Mistrials). Substitution of the interpreter or reinterpretation, if the proceeding was recorded, by a court-certified, competent interpreter may be better remedies.

In some districts, court proceedings are both transcribed and tape-recorded, *e.g.*, the Central District of California in Los Angeles. In other districts, the proceedings are not ordinarily taped. If there is a case where the translation is essential to the case, counsel should request that the proceeding be taped as well as transcribed in order to capture the actual words used by the witness vis-a-vis the translation. Subsection (d)(2) of 28 USCS § 1827 allows for electronic sound recording when an interpreter is used. This allowance is based on the discretion of the judge who takes into consideration the qualifications of the interpreter, including whether the interpreter is court certified and the length and complexity of the proceeding. Defense counsel or the prosecution should be prepared to explain why this particular case needs to be tape-recorded.

Failure to translate fully or properly at a trial poses an enormous problem for the court and the litigators, especially when a witness requiring an interpreter has taken the stand. A word mistranslated could affect the witness' credibility as well as the final determination of guilt. Moreover, the prior testimony cannot be used for impeachment in many cases because the defendant or witness can simply claim it was an interpreter's error. Challenges to the translation are reviewed by whether it made the trial fundamentally unfair and whether the purposes of the Court Interpreters Act were met. The challenge is subject to a harmless error standard as well. *See*, *e.g.*, *United States v. Gomez*, 908 F.2d 809 (11th Cir. 1990) (although the government conceded that interpreter improperly translated defendant's answer of "disco" as "the Elk's Club," thus corroborating a key witness' testimony, given the overwhelming evidence, the conviction was affirmed).

It is a very good idea to have someone at defense table who is capable of understanding the translation, ideally another court-certified or otherwise qualified interpreter, to ensure that the translation is accurate. If the translation is inaccurate, defense counsel is then in a position to make an immediate objection. Otherwise, the damage is done, since it is often not discovered until the appeal when the tape recording is reviewed against the record. Sometimes the defendant, if he or she is bilingual, can assist in catching those inconsistencies when another witness' testimony is being interpreted.

The U.S. Attorney's Office employs and utilizes interpreters for their witness preparation and will often request that the preparing interpreter be present for the examination in court. This is typical with non-English speaking confidential informants or cooperating witnesses. Defense counsel should object to the use of a special interpreter for confidential informants and government witnesses on the grounds that the interpreters are government employees and therefore, not impartial, or that there is no need for a special interpreter. This request will undoubtedly be denied since under the Court Interpreters Act, the government is required to pay for interpretation for its own witnesses. 28 USCS § 1827(g)(3). Where interpretation is going to be a key issue in the case, it may be necessary for defense counsel to voir dire the government's interpreter with respect to whom she works for and possible bias.

Simultaneous versus Consecutive Translations

There are two methods of interpretation: simultaneous and consecutive. With simultaneous translation, the interpreter translates the speaker's words as they are being said. In this instance, the speaker and the interpreter are usually speaking at the same time. With consecutive translation, the interpreter waits until the speaker has finished a sentence or paragraph and then translates what was said. During consecutive translation, there is only one person speaking at a given time.

The Court Interpreters Act provides for use of the simultaneous method of interpretation for a party; this would include the defendant in a criminal case when he is sitting at the defense table listening to the proceedings. For witnesses (including the defendant when he or she testifies), the act provides for consecutive interpretation, when the witness speaks and then the statement is interpreted after a brief pause. The judge can order simultaneous translation for witnesses if it would "aid in the efficient administration of justice." 28 USCS § 1827(k). As a practical matter, federal judges prefer simultaneous translation because it is much faster.

There are advantages and drawbacks to simultaneous versus consecutive interpretation, and counsel on both sides should consider them as applied to their particular case and witnesses. For example, someone listening to the witness during simultaneous interpretation who does not understand the speaker's language will focus on the interpreter, not the witness. As a result, jurors may end up evaluating the interpreter's credibility, rather than that of the witness.

From the perspective of the party for whom the witness is testifying, it is usually better to have the translation consecutive because the jury can watch the witness while the witness is testifying. Consecutive translation also gives counsel an opportunity to object to a question before the witness answers, because it takes some time to translate. This is true to some extent even when the translation is simultaneous because there is still lag time until full translation. With consecutive translation, the jury is more likely to focus on the witness because they are not hearing the English translation at the same time.

Consecutive versus simultaneous translation can make a difference in cross-examination. Pacing and quick questioning are often used to control a witness. Rapid-fire questioning is much more difficult where there is consecutive interpretation since the examiner has to wait to have his or her question interpreted, then hear the answer in the witness' language and then have it translated back in English. Since in cross-examination ideally the examiner is leading the witness with declarations requiring only a yes or no answer, counsel should consider requesting that the interpretation be simultaneous when cross-examining a witness testifying through an interpreter.

When a witness is speaking through an interpreter, it is essential in most cases to have the witness speak directly to the jury or judge and not to the interpreter. Instead of saying, "tell them I live in my house," the witness should say in his own language, "yo vivo en mi casa", and the interpreter, acting as if he or she were the witness, will say in English, "I live in my house." Because the trier of fact will be tempted to look only at the interpreter, particularly with simultaneous interpretation, the witness must keep eye contact with jurors and use inflections, hand gestures and changes in tone to keep the focus on the witness, rather than the interpreter. Preferably, when the witness should be the focus, counsel should request consecutive interpretation. On the other hand, in some cases it may be better to have the focus on the interpreter who may seem more credible than the witness. In those cases, the witness may want to focus on the interpreter, as well as have counsel request simultaneous interpretation.

There may be cases where it is advisable for the defendant to attempt to speak English rather than speak through an interpreter. In a case where one of the issues is whether the defendant indeed made an inculpatory statement, and the defense is that his language skills are such that he either did not understand his rights or that he did not mean what the officers said he meant because of language difficulties, the jury may get a real sense of how the officer heard the statements by the defendant if the defendant speaks his broken English. Having the essentially non-English speaking defendant speak English should only be attempted when it is clear that the defendant is speaking naturally and not trying to pretend to not speak English well. Defense counsel can advise the judge that if any of the jurors have difficulty understanding the defendant, the juror should raise his or her hand so that the defendant can either repeat the response or have that particular section translated by a court interpreter.

Interpreting the Proceedings for the Defendant

There are also strategic considerations when the proceedings are interpreted for the non-English-speaking defendant. The standard under the Court Interpreters Act is for simultaneous word-for-word translation of what a defendant understanding English would be privy to hear. Often it is the defendant who will notice when an interpreter is paraphrasing or not giving a complete translation, particularly if the defendant also speaks some English. It is important when advancing an argument that the defendant did not understand English and thus his rights, etc., that he not be spoken to by defense counsel or assistants except in his native language or through an interpreter. Otherwise, the jury and the judge will rightly conclude that the defendant does, indeed, understand English.

Defense counsel should ascertain as soon as possible whether an argument that the defendant has limited ability to speak and understand English is going to be advanced and request appointment of an interpreter at every stage including all meetings with the defendant. If there is any doubt as to whether a defendant needs a translator, defense counsel should err on the side of having one at hearings and trials as well as having a paralegal or interpreter who speaks the language at counsel table. A defendant can always waive the right to an interpreter for either all or part of the proceedings if the judge is satisfied the defendant can understand English sufficiently, and the judge explains the effects of the waiver through an interpreter.

When the proceeding is being translated for the benefit of the defendant, attorneys on both sides should keep in mind that some languages take more words to make the same English meaning. Spanish evidently takes 25 percent more words to translate. Therefore, it is considerate to speak slowly and clearly with short sentences so that the interpreters can translate more easily. Interpreters appreciate this, and it is important to have a good working relationship with the interpreters, particularly when they are going to be interpreting for your witness or your client.

Use of Interpreters with Transcripts and Tapes

Interpreters may be called as experts to testify with respect to the translation of a tape or conversation. Counsel for both sides should have a highly qualified expert, court certified if possible, review the tape and the transcripts, both for proper transcription (Were all of the words put down from the tape?) and for what the words mean in English. If the government's version is not accurate, defense counsel should object to admission of the transcript. If it is accurate, defense counsel may or may not want to stipulate to the accuracy of the transcript depending on how it will be presented at trial. Defense counsel may want to present the defense's own transcription based on the defense expert translator.

With many tapes, whether or not in a non-English language, much of the conversation may be unintelligible, and defense counsel may have an independent basis to object to admission of the transcripts regardless of the accuracy if the unintelligible portions are so substantial as to render the entire recording untrustworthy. *See, e.g., United States v. Robinson*, 707 F.2d 872, 875–879 (6th Cir. 1983). The government can usually get around this by offering the transcript as simply an aid to understanding the actual tapes. However, when the tapes are in a non-English language, defense counsel should object that the transcript would be much more than an aid but actually a substitute for the tape itself. Defense counsel may want to have the tape enhanced to get the maximum amount of intelligibility, unless they fear the jury's hearing more will hurt their client. The government usually enhances the tapes as a matter of course.

Even when all of the words are transcribed, the issue may come down to what the words mean in English, since many words have more than one meaning. At the end of the day, if the defense has one transcription and the prosecution another, both may be used. If only the prosecution transcription is admitted, the defense can offer its own expert to impeach that transcription and call into doubt the accuracy of the English. The defense may also want to cross-examine the government's interpreter for possible bias. Interpreters in this role as experts should be treated the same as any expert witness in terms of laying foundations and offering expert testimony pursuant to FRE 701–706.

Miscellaneous Concerns with the Use of an Interpreter

Where the interpreter is placed in the courtroom vis-a-vis the witness has strategic connotations. Placement will depend on the objectives in the individual case. If the witness is more comfortable with the interpreter next to him and the interpreter is good at conveying the witness' meaning, the defense should ask to have the interpreter standing next to the witness. This can also signal credibility and a lack of threat to the jury. With the advent of more sophisticated electronic equipment, more and more courts have the interpreters in a sound booth or at a separate table interpreting the proceedings from afar. Counsel should make sure to know the particular judge's rules and local custom, if any, with respect to placement of interpreters and to consider any strategic benefits.

Some jurors speak the language and must be admonished to listen to the English version and not translate the non-English version. If there is going to be a witness testifying through an interpreter at trial, the judge should be asked to inquire as to the language abilities of jurors during voir dire. If translated testimony is admitted, counsel should request a jury instruction with respect to the use of interpreters and judging credibility, etc. Parties may also want the judge to explain to the jurors at the outset who the interpreter is and what his or her job will be during the course of the trial.

Sometimes a defense counsel may meet with a client out of court, and the only interpreter available is a friend or family member. A third party does not destroy the privilege if the purpose of their participation is to improve the comprehension of the communications between attorney and client. See *United States v. Kovel*, 296 F.2d 918 (2d Cir. 1961). Although having a family member or friend do the translation does not affect the confidentiality of the conversation with the defendant, it is not ideal, particularly when discussing private matters that the defendant may have difficulty discussing openly in front of family or friends. Limit such interpretation to pedigree information, and make every effort to get another interpreter.

Moreover, knowing and speaking a language is different than being a court-certified interpreter, and use of someone fluent in a language is often inadequate translation for the purposes of discussing legal matters. The same is true when the attorney learns the language (less so when it is the attorney's native tongue). Although speaking the client's language can be a terrific way to develop rapport, lawyers should still use a court-certified interpreter when preparing a client or witness to testify. It is the interpreter, not the attorney, who will be translating at a hearing or trial.

Rule 29. Motion for Judgment of Acquittal

(a) Motion before submission to jury. Motions for directed verdict are abolished and motions for judgment of acquittal shall be used in their place. The court on motion of a defendant or of its own motion shall order the entry of judgment of acquittal of one or more offenses charged in the indictment or information after the evidence on either side is closed if the evidence is insufficient to sustain a conviction of such offense or offenses. If a defendant's motion for judgment of acquittal at the close of the evidence offered by the government is not granted, the defendant may offer evidence without having reserved the right.

(b) Reservation of decision on motion. The court may reserve decision on a motion for judgment of acquittal, proceed with the trial (where the motion is made before the close of all the evidence), submit the case to the jury and decide the motion either before the jury returns a verdict or after it returns a verdict of guilty or is discharged without having returned a verdict. If the court reserves decision, it must decide the motion on the basis of the evidence at the time the ruling was reserved.

(c) Motion after discharge of jury. If the jury returns a verdict of guilty or is discharged without having returned a verdict, a motion for judgment of acquittal may be made or renewed within 7 days after the jury is discharged or within such further time as the court may fix during the 7-day period. If a verdict of guilty is returned the court may on such motion set aside the verdict and enter judgment of acquittal. If no verdict is returned the court may enter judgment of acquittal. It shall not be necessary to the making of such a motion that a similar motion has been made prior to the submission of the case to the jury.

(d) Same: conditional ruling on grant of motion. If a motion for judgment of acquittal after verdict of guilty under this Rule is granted, the court shall also determine whether any motion for a new trial should be granted if the judgment of acquittal is thereafter vacated or reversed, specifying the grounds for such determination. If the motion for a new trial is granted conditionally, the order thereon does not affect the finality of the judgment. If the motion for a new trial has been granted conditionally and the judgment is reversed on appeal, the new trial shall proceed unless the appellate court has otherwise ordered. If such motion has been denied conditionally, the appellee on appeal may assert error in that denial, and if the judgment is reversed on appeal, subsequent proceedings shall be in accordance with the order of the appellate court.

Commentary

By Prof. Inga L. Parsons
New York University School of Law

FRCrP 29 governs a motion for judgment of acquittal. The motion is generally referred to as a "Rule 29" motion. The procedure was formerly known as a motion for a directed verdict, but when FRCrP 29 was adopted, the nomenclature became a motion for judgment of acquittal. The name changed because the judge can direct a judgment of acquittal but cannot direct a verdict of guilty no matter how conclusive the evidence against the defendant. A motion for judgment of acquittal is granted where there is insufficient evidence to prove an essential element of the offense.

When to Make a Rule 29 Motion

Typically, the motion for judgment of acquittal is made at the completion of the government's case. It can be made orally—the common practice where there is little issue as to the government's failure to set forth a prima facie case—or in writing. The latter is suggested where sufficiency involves a complicated legal issue such as what constitutes proper venue or the legal elements of larceny. Certain cases lend themselves to Rule 29 arguments. Where the defense has argued entrapment, which involves complex notions of predisposition, etc., the judge is often in a better position to assess whether there is sufficient evidence, and defense counsel should be prepared to make a detailed argument in that kind of case.

There are times, though rare, when the defense might move for a judgment of acquittal after the government's opening statement, if it is clear from the opening that the charge or charges cannot be sustained under any view of the evidence as presented by the prosecution. (The defense should not make such a motion during a bench trial because double jeopardy only attaches after the first witness is sworn—which occurs after the opening statements). Judges are very hesitant to grant such a motion after the opening and before the evidence comes in. Even when the government fails to assert evidence for every element of the offense in the opening statement, the judge is more likely to reserve ruling on the motion until all of the evidence is presented. Moreover, by making the argument before the evidence is offered, defense counsel could very well be tipping the government off to potential weaknesses in their case, which the government may be able to cure during the course of the trial. If the motion is made after the prosecution has rested, it will usually be too late to cure the defects.

When defense counsel has moved for a judgment of acquittal after the opening, counsel must still make a separate motion for judgment of acquittal at the end of the government's case-in-chief and cannot rely on the motion made after openings to preserve the issue.

If defense counsel makes an additional motion for judgment of acquittal based on the prosecution's case-in-chief, likely if the opening statement was so deficient, the defense should make certain that the judge knows that two separate motions for acquittal are being made. If the defense puts on a case, the defense should renew the motion for acquittal after the defense case and any rebuttal case to ensure preservation of the issue.

How to Make a Rule 29 Motion

In many cases the Rule 29 motion is pro forma, and there are judges who do not even ask to hear from counsel but will say for example, "Despite defense counsel's brilliant arguments, I am denying the motion for judgment of acquittal" without a word from either party. Defense counsel may be uncertain whether the issue has been preserved as a result of the judge's dismissive denial, such as "Sit down counsel; you would be wasting your time, I am submitting the case to the jury." In that instance, defense counsel should state for the record, "Your Honor, I wish to make it clear that the defense is moving for entry of a judgment of acquittal pursuant to Rule 29 of the Federal Rules of Criminal Procedure." The judge can bark out "denied," but the issue is preserved. It is essential that the record is clear that a motion for judgment of acquittal has been made by the defense to avoid waiver. The motion should always be made. There is nothing to lose by making it, but much to be lost by not making it. Should defense counsel neglect to do so, sufficiency of the evidence is not reviewable unless plain error is shown—an incredibly difficult standard of review.

Standards for Reviewing the Rule 29 Motion

The same standard is used for considering a motion for judgment of acquittal and in reviewing the denial of such a motion. That standard is whether the evidence is sufficient (when viewed in a light most favorable to the government) such that a reasonably minded jury would have a reasonable doubt as to the existence of any essential element of the crime. *See, e.g., United States v. Galati*, 203 F.3d 254, 258–59 (7th Cir. 2000).

The prosecution's evidence may be purely circumstantial and still be sufficient. Although there is some division in the circuits, most hold that in order to meet sufficiency, the government or the considering judge need not exclude every reasonable hypothesis except guilt. Some circuits set forth stronger language that is helpful to the defense, including requiring "substantial evidence." *See, e.g., United States v. Barfield*, 447 F.2d 85, 88 (5th Cir. 1971) (*citing United States v. Glasser*, 315 U.S. 60, 80, 86 L.Ed. 680, 704, 62 S.Ct. 457 (1944)). Another example of this raised standard is that in a circumstantial case the judge must exclude every reasonable hypothesis but that of guilt. *United States v. Garza*, 426 F.2d 949 (5th Cir. 1970) (*citing Vick v. United States*, 216 F.2d 228, 232 (5th Cir. 1957). Defense counsel should keep the Rule 29 cases of the controlling circuit in their trial notebook and use helpful language when making the argument.

In considering a motion for judgment of acquittal, the judge is not supposed to weigh conflicting testimony or assess the credibility of witnesses unless the conflict in testimony is so great as to render the testimony incredible as a matter of law. Nor is the judge supposed to retry the case or substitute his or her judgment for that of the jury. Counsel making a motion for judgment of acquittal should avoid arguments that use such terms as "credibility," "believability," or "trustworthiness" of a witness. Instead, defense counsel should make any argument couched in terms that the government has "failed to set forth sufficient evidence" as to a particular element. If defense counsel makes the motion dependent upon credibility, the judge will rightly submit the case to the jury.

FRCrP 29 does not require that specific grounds be stated in support of a Rule 29 motion other than that the evidence was insufficient. Prosecutors should insist that the defense provide specific reasons for the claim of insufficiency. If defense counsel sets forth insufficiency as to specified elements such as venue, the defense may be precluded from raising other grounds on appeal. Thus, defense counsel should consider the extent of the motion before making an argument under FRCrP 29. It may be more prudent to make a generalized motion to preserve all issues, particularly where there is not a good chance of winning or the motion is pro forma. However, if there is a chance of convincing the judge, a thorough, detailed argument is more likely to succeed than a general one. Defense counsel should make clear that in detailing certain issues the defense includes all other bases for insufficiency.

Preservation of evidentiary issues and matters at trial can affect the ability to make arguments under FRCrP 29. For example, if there are arguments with respect to relying on certain testimony at trial, the defense may be precluded from raising that issue in consideration of a Rule 29 motion if the testimony was not objected to during the course of the trial. Similarly, where prior convictions have been introduced for limited purposes, if counsel has failed to object to the introduction of the evidence, or a limitation of the evidence with a curative instruction, the defense may be precluded from making that argument to the court when requesting a judgment of acquittal. Defense counsel should ensure that when the judge sustains an objection to testimony that counsel moves to have the objectionable testimony struck if it is in the record so that it cannot be relied upon in reviewing the sufficiency of the evidence.

When the Judge Reserves Ruling

FRCrP 29 provides that the court may reserve ruling on a Rule 29 motion made at the end of the government's case and submit the case to the jury. Previously, FRCrP 29 did not allow the judge to reserve ruling at the close of the government's case, and many circuits held that it was error for the court to reserve ruling on a motion for judgment of acquittal made at the close of the government's case-in-chief. *See, e.g., United States v. Thomas*, 987 F.2d 697, 704 (11th Cir. 1993). The rationale for a ruling at the end of the case was so the defense would know whether it needed to put on a defense case. If the judge failed to rule and the defense proceeded with a defense case, it constituted a waiver of the issue on the part of the defense.

Under the current version of FRCrP 29, it is clear that the judge may reserve ruling at the end of the government's case. However, if the defense presents a case after the judge has reserved ruling at the end of the government's case, the judge must decide the defense's motion based on the evidence at the time of the motion. Defense counsel should request that the judge put on the record, in detail, the basis for the decision in order to assess whether subsequent evidence was relied upon (*e.g.*, the testimony of the defendant). Judges may reserve ruling on close cases with the expectation that the jury will acquit thereby making a ruling from the court unnecessary. The judge can sua sponte grant a judgment of acquittal before the jury's verdict, but after the verdict, the judge can only act on the defendant's motion.

Double Jeopardy Considerations

If the judge grants a motion for judgment of acquittal before the jury returns a verdict, double jeopardy precludes any appeal or retrial of the defendant. *See Smalis v. Pennsylvania*, 476 U.S. 140, 144; 90 L.Ed.2d 116, 121; 106 S.Ct. 1745, 1748 (1986). If the judge grants a motion for judgment of acquittal after the jury has returned a guilty verdict, the prosecution may appeal the verdict since the defendant would not be subject to a retrial but only reinstatement of the jury's verdict of guilt.

In those instances where a judgment of acquittal is granted after a guilty verdict, FRCrP 29 requires the judge to determine whether a motion for a new trial should be granted if the defense requests a new trial. If the appellate court were to reverse, the trial court assesses whether it would grant a new trial on the grounds of judicial efficiency. Judges consider whether the verdict is contrary to the weight of the evidence such that a miscarriage of justice may have resulted. If the court would grant the new trial, a reversal of this conditional judgment of acquittal will result in a new trial unless the appellate court decides otherwise. Where the district court denies the motion for a new trial, should the appellate court reverse the judgment of acquittal, the denial can be challenged for error.

Rule 29 and Bench Trials

In a bench trial, the motion for judgment of acquittal might be considered superfluous because a judge is both the trier of fact and the determiner of law, such that the judge's verdict would appear to constitute a ruling on sufficiency. However, sufficiency of the evidence and proof beyond a reasonable doubt are different concepts with different standards. For strategic purposes, defense counsel should request that the judge make a ruling on a motion for a judgment of acquittal before the defense puts on its case, even in a bench trial. This is particularly important where the defendant is slated to testify. Often the defendant's version is similar to the police officers' but for the denial of guilt and serves to corroborate the officers' version and can very well remove whatever insufficiency existed in the case. In addition, prosecutors will sometimes claim that a verdict of guilty necessarily means the defendant was lying on the stand and seek perjury charges or obstruction of justice sentencing enhancements against the defendant, which can be particularly harsh under the Federal Sentencing Guidelines. *See* the Commentary for FRCrP 32. However, if the judge finds the prosecution case insufficient at the end of the government's case-in-chief, it will not be necessary to put the defendant on the stand.

Rule 29 and Codefendants

Where there is more than one defendant and a judgment of acquittal has been rendered against only one of the defendants, it is crucial that the jury not be advised as to why the codefendant is no longer present. If the jury is told that the case against the other defendant was dismissed because of a judgment of acquittal by the court, the remaining defendants are severely prejudiced because the jury is likely to think the court has determined that the remaining defendants are guilty.

Of course, the jury naturally will be curious as to the fate of the other defendant and will spend much time speculating if something is not said. Defense counsel must make sure that the judge is alerted to the potential prejudice when informing the jury and to give carefully worded instructions on the order that the codefendant's case is the subject of another proceeding and not before the jury any further. It could be problematic for the judge to tell the jury that the codefendant's case has been disposed of or resolved. The jury may be admonished not to speculate on the codefendant's absence or to infer any guilt by the fact that the codefendant is not present. However, there comes a point where the court may "protest too much" and signal to the jury that there is some reason to think it hurts the defendant. The less said of the matter, often the better.

Renewing a Rule 29 Motion

Even after the jury has been discharged following a verdict of guilty or a deadlocked jury, the defense can move for a judgment of acquittal or renew a previous motion provided it does so within seven days. FRCrP 29(c). This is a hard-and-fast rule. On the eighth day the court will lack jurisdiction to hear the motion even when the delay is only one day, there is a claim of innocence, there is no prejudice to the government, the motion is filed before sentence, or the delay was the result of attorney error. *See United States v. Carlisle*, 517 U.S. 416, 132 L.Ed.2d. 921, 16 S.Ct. 40 (1996).

If a Rule 29 motion has previously been made and denied, there is little to be gained and possibly much to be lost by making a formal submission moving for a judgment of acquittal after the verdict. This second review of the motion often gives a judge the opportunity to "clean up" the record and clarify the previous denial so that it is more likely to withstand appellate scrutiny.

If no motion was previously made, then the defense should make the motion within the seven-day period to preserve the issue, and request an extension of the time to file post-trial motions. A thirty-day period is a common extension. It is helpful for the defense to have a verdict checklist when there is a conviction (*e.g.*, poll the jury, etc.). Renewing the FRCrP 29 motion and any reserved or denied pretrial motions when appropriate, and asking for a lengthy extension of all post-trial filings, including extensions under FRCrP 29, 33, and 34, can also be helpful.

Rule 29.1. Closing Argument

After the closing of evidence the prosecution shall open the argument. The defense shall be permitted to reply. The prosecution shall then be permitted to reply in rebuttal.

Commentary

Prof. Inga L. Parsons
New York University School of Law

Although there are certain studies concluding that in many cases the jury makes up its mind how it will vote during the opening statement, lawyers should not discount the power of a strong closing argument. The closing arguments are the last thing the jurors hear from the lawyers before going in to deliberate. Good arguments given to the jurors to fight out points with each other can make a difference in the verdict.

In federal court the government gives the first closing argument ostensibly because the prosecution has the burden of proof. (In many state jurisdictions the defense goes first and the prosecution closes and rebuts in the same argument.) The defense need not give a closing argument because the defendant has no burden of proof, as the judge will explain to the jury, but no defense lawyer should waive the opportunity. The government is allowed to rebut the defense's closing argument in a reply statement. *See* FRCrP 29.1.

There is no set time period for the length of closing arguments. Some judges will limit a lawyer's time to a certain number of minutes or hours. Such limits are clearly within the judge's discretion, however, counsel should object if the amount of time given seems unreasonable given the length of the trial or the complexity of the case. Limiting the amount of time for closing arguments may, in fact, be doing the attorneys a service. Although lawyers love to hear themselves speak, jurors are not always as appreciative. It is difficult to take in information by just hearing it and attorneys should strive for brief closings that avoid repetitive arguments. If the lawyer has laid the groundwork for her theory of the case during the trial examinations, the closing argument need not be lengthy in most cases.

Objectives of the Closing Argument

The objective of the closing argument is to persuade the jury to find for the lawyer's side by arguing how the evidence and exhibits, or lack of evidence, support that conclusion. Ideally it should tie in with the opening statement and be consistent with the theory of the case. The prosecution's closing should describe the proof of the offense and answer the questions the jury may have as to any problems in the government's evidence. Defense arguments usually focus on why the government has failed to meet its burden and point out the reasonable doubts raised by weaknesses in the prosecution's case, affirmative defenses, and any alternative theories. The jury need only have one reasonable doubt as to any element of an offense to acquit on that charge.

For the prosecution, the closing is often in narrative form tracking the events chronologically. It should not, however, simply repeat the opening statement, though it is often effective to remind the jury what was promised in the opening statement and how that promise was met as to the proof shown. The defense format will depend on whether there is an affirmative defense, whether the defendant took the stand, or whether the theory is simply the government did not prove its case. Certain theories may conflict with each other and the defense may be more effective in choosing rather than arguing, "Mr. Jones did not do it, but if you that find that he did, he was entrapped." On the other hand, since the standard is proof beyond a reasonable doubt, in many cases it is better for the defense not to adopt a particular theory of what happened, but argue that the government's witnesses and proof are unreliable and no one can be certain what happened, meaning reasonable doubt.

The closing argument should not be a summation of the evidence despite frequent use of the term "summation" to describe a closing argument. Summarizing the evidence, as opposed to making arguments and inferences from the evidence, is usually less helpful to the jury. The jurors no doubt remember as much of the testimony if not more than the lawyers since the only thing the jury has had to do during the entire trial is listen. What the jury needs to hear from the lawyers is how that evidence fits together to convict or acquit. Similarly, going through the testimony witness by witness is less effective then making an argument and then showing how the various witnesses' testimony supports that conclusion.

The prosecutor gets to rebut the defense closing. It is difficult to write the rebuttal in advance and is usually prepared while the defense is making its closing argument. Some prosecutors prefer to leave one or two bombshells for rebuttal rather than bring out every argument in the closing since the defense will not have an opportunity to respond to the rebuttal. Prosecutors should be careful because sometimes this "sandbagging" is deemed new argument not responsive to the defense and thus improper rebuttal.

In preparing the defense closing argument, the attorney should try to anticipate the prosecutor's rebuttal. Making what appears to be a winning argument that is not only rebutted by the prosecution but turned around and used against the defense is excruciating since the defense does not ordinarily get a chance to reply to the prosecution's rebuttal. In some cases a judge might allow a "sur rebuttal" but the prosecution will always get the last word because it has the burden of proof.

Use of Jury Instructions and Exhibits in the Closing Argument

Ideally the parties will know what the judge is going to charge the jury before the end of the case so that the lawyers can incorporate the judge's charges into their closing arguments. Most judges hold charging conferences during the course of the trial and lawyers should seek such conferences as early as possible. *See* FRCrP 30. Jurors are impressed when a lawyer makes reference to the law verbatim to what the judge thereafter advises them. Having said this, lawyers should be very careful not to instruct the jurors themselves. Reference to the charges is one thing, reciting the judge's charges is another. In some cases the judge may charge the jury before the closing argument and the parties may want to request that the judge do so depending on the case.

As to the use of exhibits, it is surprising how infrequently lawyers use exhibits during their closing arguments. If the exhibits are not relevant to the closing argument, it is questionable why the party wanted them admitted in evidence in the first place. Incorporating the pictures and physical evidence from the case will make the party's position more believable—the argument being witnesses may lie but this kilo of cocaine found in the defendant's apartment cannot. Our society is highly influenced by visual stimuli. Demonstrative aids such as graphs and diagrams and computer-generated simulations can be extremely effective. Attorneys should obtain the court's permission to use any demonstrative aid prior to the closing arguments to avoid unnecessary objections from opposing counsel during the argument itself.

Objections During Closing Arguments

There is an unspoken rule that a certain courtesy is afforded lawyers during closing argument and thus objections should be rare. Courtesy is one thing, but an attorney must protect the record for a possible appeal. Without a contemporaneous objection the standard for review is plain error. *See United States v. Young*, 470 U.S. 1, 14, 105 S.Ct. 1038. 1045, 84 L.Ed.2d 1, 9 (1985). When one side misstates the law, the other side should object. When one side relies on facts not introduced at trial or stricken from the record, opposing counsel should object. When one side misstates the facts, objecting is often a strategic means of pointing the error out to the jury immediately, however, the judge will advise that it is the jury's recollection that controls. Misstatement of fact is not usually a viable ground for appeal. Typically the judge will give a curative instruction to counter any misstatement or error in an effort to avoid reversal.

If the prosecutor makes comments during the closing argument tending to shift the burden of proof to the defense by remarking on the absence of defense witnesses, for example, the defense should object. The standard for getting a reversal on such grounds is high in that it must "infect" the trial with such unfairness as to result in a denial of due process, and even then if the evidence is overwhelming, the conviction may be upheld. *See Darden v.*

Wainwright, 477 U.S. 168, 179, 106 S.Ct. 2464, 2470, 91 L.Ed.2d 144 (1986). Nevertheless, defense counsel must object to preserve the issue for any appeal. Similarly, if the prosecutor says anything about the defendant not testifying or invoking a Fifth Amendment privilege, *e.g.*, "You heard from the government's witnesses who took the stand under oath subject to cross-examination. The defendant did not subject himself to cross-examination," the defense should object. The test is whether the comment is such that a jury would "naturally and necessarily" take the comment to be a failure of a defendant to testify. *See, e.g., Knowles v. United States,* 224 F.2d 168, 169 (10th Cir. 1955). The defense should avoid inviting such responses from the prosecution about potential defense witnesses by not opening the door to these issues during the defense's closing argument.

It is improper for a lawyer to vouch for the credibility of a witness. An example of vouching is telling the jury, "Mr. Jones is telling the truth. I am an officer of this court and I would not put Mr. Jones on the stand if he were lying." Another form of vouching is to state outright that "I believe Mr. Jones, you should too." If the thrust of an attorney's statement is that the witness can be believed because the lawyer personally believes the witness is telling the truth, it is considered vouching and is objectionable. An attorney may, however, argue why a particular witness should be believed based on inferences and deductions from the evidence.

If evidence has been suppressed or excluded during the course of the trial, each side should be vigilant not to open the door to the introduction of the evidence with statements made during closing arguments. When a party does open the door, the other side should take advantage of the opportunity to get the evidence before the jury. For example, if the judge kept out the defendant's 1987 conviction for possession of marijuana in a cocaine distribution case on the grounds that the probative value of the evidence was outweighed by its prejudice, the defense should not get up in closing argument and claim that the defendant has never dealt with drugs before. Although the defense can argue that "dealt" means to distribute, the government may very well convince the judge that due to the false impression made by the defense argument the government should be allowed to tell the jury that the defendant has a prior drug conviction.

With respect to the rebuttal, defense counsel should listen carefully for statements from the prosecution that are not rebuttal but instead new arguments or points the prosecutor forgot in her closing argument or deliberately withheld. If the government's reply goes beyond the scope of rebutting the defense's closing argument, the defense should object. The defense should also object if the prosecutor asks for a conviction to further some social goal rather than based on the specific evidence against the defendant such as a plea for a conviction to send a message to drug dealers so society can win the war on drugs.

Rule 30. Instructions

At the close of the evidence or at such earlier time during the trial as the court reasonably directs, any party may file written requests that the court instruct the jury on the law as set forth in the requests. At the same time copies of such requests shall be furnished to all parties. The court shall inform counsel of its proposed action upon the requests prior to their arguments to the jury. The court may instruct the jury before or after the arguments are completed or at both times. No party may assign as error any portion of the charge or omission therefrom unless that party objects thereto before the jury retires to consider its verdict, stating distinctly the matter to which that party objects and the grounds of the objection. Opportunity shall be given to make the objection out of the hearing of the jury and, on request of any party, out of the presence of the jury.

Commentary

By Prof. Louis M. Natali
Temple University Beasley School of Law

This rule sets out the procedure for the court to rule on points for charge. The requests for instructions must be made before closing arguments. After the court rules on the instructions, the lawyers will know which instructions they may refer to in closing argument. Often an instruction will form the building blocks for an effective factual argument. For example, in a homicide trial, if anger may serve as the grounds for provocation, the facts showing anger may be marshaled and provided to the jury in closing argument.

The court has the option to instruct the jury before or after the arguments of counsel. This is a matter of local practice. Given the choice, counsel should opt to speak to the jury after the court's instructions because counsel's arguments will be the last thing the jury hears.

The submitted points which are denied will also form the basis for a motion for new trial and for appellate review.

Rule 31. Verdict

(a) Return. The verdict shall be unanimous. It shall be returned by the jury to the judge in open court.

(b) Several defendants. If there are two or more defendants, the jury at any time during its deliberations may return a verdict or verdicts with respect to a defendant or defendants as to whom it has agreed; if the jury cannot agree with respect to all, the defendant or defendants as to whom it does not agree may be tried again.

(c) Conviction of less offense. The defendant may be found guilty of an offense necessarily included in the offense charged or of an attempt to commit either the offense charged or an offense necessarily included therein if the attempt is an offense.

(d) Poll of jury. After a verdict is returned but before the jury is discharged, the court shall, on a party's request, or may on its own motion, poll the jurors individually. If the poll reveals a lack of unanimity, the court may direct the jury to deliberate further or may declare a mistrial and discharge the jury.

(e) Criminal forfeiture. (Abrogated)

Commentary

By Prof. Louis M. Natali
Temple University Beasley School of Law

This rule makes the procedure for taking verdicts clear.

If there are two or more defendants, counsel must be aware that a verdict for one may be taken according to subdivision (b) even though the jury may be hung as to one or more defendants.

Rule 31. Verdict

Subdivision (c) sets out the general rule as to lesser-included offenses. This general language must, of course, be read with the particular statute and applicable case law. It is not necessary that the lesser-included offense be cited in the indictment.

Under subdivision (d) defense counsel, in the event of guilty verdict, should poll the jury to ensure there is unanimous concurrence. It frequently occurs that at least one juror may not be in agreement but may fear stating such in the deliberation room. The exact language used by the clerk in the poll should be agreed to by counsel and the court and usually will include an open question as to the individual juror's verdict on each count.

Subdivision (e) also specifies the need for a special verdict in forfeiture cases. Counsel should work with the court to draft a clear special verdict form.

VII. Judgment

Rule 32. Sentence and Judgment

(a) In general; time for sentencing. When a presentence investigation and report are made under subdivision (b)(1), sentence should be imposed without unnecessary delay following completion of the process prescribed by subdivision (b)(6). The time limits prescribed in subdivision (b)(6) may be either shortened or lengthened for good cause.

(b) Presentence investigation and report.

(1) When made. The probation officer must make a presentence investigation and submit a report to the court before the sentence is imposed, unless:

(A) the court finds that the information in the record enables it to exercise its sentencing authority meaningfully under 18 U.S.C. § 3553; and

(B) the court explains this finding on the record. Notwithstanding the preceding sentence, a presentence investigation and report, or other report containing information sufficient for the court to enter an order of restitution, as the court may direct, shall be required in any case in which restitution is required to be ordered.

(2) Presence of counsel. On request, the defendant's counsel is entitled to notice and a reasonable opportunity to attend any interview of the defendant by a probation officer in the course of a presentence investigation.

(3) Nondisclosure. The report must not be submitted to the court or its contents disclosed to anyone unless the defendant has consented in writing, has pleaded guilty or nolo contendere, or has been found guilty.

(4) Contents of the presentence report. The presentence report must contain—

(A) information about the defendant's history and characteristics, including any prior criminal record, financial condition, and any circumstances that, because they affect the defendant's behavior, may be helpful in imposing sentence or in correctional treatment;

(B) the classification of the offense and of the defendant under the categories established by the Sentencing Commission under 28 U.S.C. § 994(a), as the probation officer believes to be applicable to the defendant's case; the kinds of sentence and the sentencing range suggested for such a category of offense committed by such a category of defendant as set forth in the guidelines issued by the Sentencing Commission under 28 U.S.C. § 994(a)(1); and the probation officer's explanation of any factors that may suggest a different sentence—within or without the applicable guideline—that would be more appropriate, given all the circumstances;

(C) a reference to any pertinent policy statement issued by the Sentencing Commission under 28 U.S.C. § 994(a)(2);

(D) verified information, stated in a nonargumentative style, containing an assessment of the financial, social, psychological, and medical impact on any individual against whom the offense has been committed;

(E) in appropriate cases, information about the nature and extent of nonprison programs and resources available for the defendant;

(F) in appropriate cases, information sufficient for the court to enter an order of restitution;

(G) any report and recommendation resulting from a study ordered by the court under 18 U.S.C. § 3552(b); and

(H) any other information required by the court.

(5) Exclusions. The presentence report must exclude:

(A) any diagnostic opinions that, if disclosed, might seriously disrupt a program of rehabilitation;

(B) sources of information obtained upon a promise of confidentiality; or

(C) any other information that, if disclosed, might result in harm, physical or otherwise, to the defendant or other persons.

(6) Disclosure and objections.

(A) Not less than 35 days before the sentencing hearing —unless the defendant waives this minimum period—the probation officer must furnish the presentence report to the defendant, the defendant's counsel, and the attorney for the Government. The court may, by local rule or in individual cases, direct that the probation officer not disclose the probation officer's recommendation, if any, on the sentence.

(B) Within 14 days after receiving the presentence report, the parties shall communicate in writing to the probation officer, and to each other, any objections to any material information, sentencing classifications, sentencing guideline ranges, and policy statements contained in or omitted from the presentence report. After receiving objections, the probation officer may meet with the defendant, the defendant's counsel, and the attorney for the Government to discuss those objections. The probation officer may also conduct a further investigation and revise the presentence report as appropriate.

(C) Not later than 7 days before the sentencing hearing, the probation officer must submit the presentence report to the court, together with an addendum setting forth any unresolved objections, the grounds for those objections, and the probation officer's comments on the objections. At the same time, the probation officer must furnish the revisions of the presentence report and the addendum to the defendant, the defendant's counsel, and the attorney for the Government.

(D) Except for any unresolved objection under subdivision (b)(6)(B), the court may, at the hearing, accept the presentence report as its findings of fact. For good cause shown, the court may allow a new objection to be raised at any time before imposing sentence.

(c) Sentence.

(1) Sentencing hearing. At the sentencing hearing, the court must afford counsel for the defendant and for the Government an opportunity to comment on the probation officer's determinations and on other matters relating to the appropriate sentence, and must rule on any unresolved objections to the presentence report. The court may, in its discretion, permit the parties to introduce testimony or other evidence on the objections. For each matter controverted, the court must make either a finding on the allegation or a determination that no finding is necessary because the controverted matter will not be taken into account in, or will not affect, sentencing. A written record of these findings and determinations must be appended to any copy of the presentence report made available to the Bureau of Prisons.

(2) Production of statements at sentencing hearing. Rule 26.2(a)–(d) and (f) applies at a sentencing hearing under this rule. If a party elects not to comply with an order under Rule 26.2(a) to deliver a statement to the movant, the court may not consider the affidavit or testimony of the witness whose statement is withheld.

(3) Imposition of sentence. Before imposing sentence, the court must:

(A) verify that the defendant and defendant's counsel have read and discussed the presentence report made available under subdivision (b)(6)(A). If the court has received information excluded from the presentence report under subdivision (b)(5) the court—in lieu of making that information available—must summarize it in writing, if the information will be relied on in determining sentence. The court must also give the defendant and the defendant's counsel a reasonable opportunity to comment on that information;

(B) afford defendant's counsel an opportunity to speak on behalf of the defendant;

(C) address the defendant personally and determine whether the defendant wishes to make a statement and to present any information in mitigation of the sentence;

(D) afford the attorney for the Government an opportunity equivalent to that of the defendant's counsel to speak to the court; and

(E) if sentence is to be imposed for a crime of violence or sexual abuse, address the victim personally if the victim is present at the sentencing hearing and determine if the victim wishes to make a statement or present any information in relation to the sentence.

(4) In camera proceedings. The court's summary of information under subdivision (c)(3)(A) may be in camera. Upon joint motion by the defendant and by the attorney for the Government, the court may hear in camera the statements—made under subdivision (c)(3)(B), (C), (D), and (E)—by the defendant, the defendant's counsel, the victim, or the attorney for the Government.

(5) Notification of right to appeal. After imposing sentence in a case which has gone to trial on a plea of not guilty, the court must advise the defendant of the right to appeal. After imposing sentence in any case, the court must advise the defendant of any right to appeal the sentence, and of the right of a person who is unable to pay the cost of an appeal to apply for leave to appeal in forma pauperis. If the defendant so requests, the clerk of the court must immediately prepare and file a notice of appeal on behalf of the defendant.

(d) Judgment.

(1) In general. A judgment of conviction must set forth the plea, the verdict or findings, the adjudication, and the sentence. If the defendant is found not guilty or for any other reason is entitled to be discharged, judgment must be entered accordingly. The judgment must be signed by the judge and entered by the clerk.

(2) Criminal Forfeiture. Forfeiture procedures are governed by Rule 32.2.

(e) Plea withdrawal. If a motion to withdraw a plea of guilty or nolo contendere is made before sentence is imposed, the court may permit the plea to be withdrawn if the defendant shows any fair and just reason. At any later time, a plea may be set aside only on direct appeal or by motion under 28 U.S.C. § 2255.

(f) Definitions. For purposes of this rule—

(1) "victim" means any individual against whom an offense has been committed for which a sentence is to be imposed, but the right of allocution under subdivision (c)(3)(E) may be exercised instead by—

(A) a parent or legal guardian if the victim is below the age of eighteen years or incompetent; or

(B) one or more family members or relatives designated by the court if the victim is deceased or incapacitated; if such person or persons are present at the sentencing hearing, regardless of whether the victim is present; and

(2) "crime of violence or sexual abuse" means a crime that involved the use or attempted or threatened use of physical force against the person or property of another, or a crime under chapter 109A of title 18, United States Code [18 USCS §§ 2241 et seq.].

Commentary

By Prof. Inga L. Parsons
New York University School of Law

FRCrP 32 covers a substantial area of federal criminal law: sentencing. As an indication of the breadth of this topic, there are over 750 categories of annotations to FRCrP 32 alone. Voluminous treatises have been written on the subject. This is largely the result of the 1984 Sentencing Reform Act that ushered in a number of significant changes including establishing the Federal Sentencing Guidelines that govern all federal offenses (other than petty offenses) occurring after November 1, 1987. Some of the changes from the guidelines include abolishing federal parole, reducing federal good time, and imposing mandatory minimums for certain drug offenses.

Of the criminal cases litigated in federal court, only about 10 percent proceed to trial. Nearly 90 percent of all federal criminal cases are disposed of by guilty plea, and in some districts it is as high as 95 percent. (*See* U.S. Sentencing Commission, Federal Sentencing Statistics, Fiscal Year 1999.) As a result, the federal criminal practitioner is by and large a sentencing litigator. For most federal defendants, this litigation is carried out under the Federal

Sentencing Guidelines scheme. Federal criminal attorneys must thoroughly understand the Federal Sentencing Guidelines law in order to practice effectively in the federal criminal justice system. The following is a brief review of the federal sentencing scheme that provides a context for considerations of the provisions of FRCrP 32.

Federal Sentencing Guidelines Scheme

The Federal Sentencing Guidelines are not particularly complex or conceptually difficult, especially when compared to such areas of federal law as securities regulation or the federal tax code. Although the guidelines are rightly criticized for the length of many of the sentences mandated, divining a sentencing range under the guidelines is formulaic. It is true that some of the terms for enhancements and adjustments in determining an offense level are not well defined, but at the end of the day calculating a sentence under the guidelines is a bit like following a recipe: ingredients are ultimately added or subtracted to produce the sentence, but adding or subtracting the ingredients is not in itself particularly complicated.

If an attorney is unfamiliar with the Federal Sentencing Guidelines, there is no substitute for reading the Federal Sentencing Guidelines Manual—the cookbook, if you will—for a federal sentence. Each section includes Commentary and Application Notes, which are provided to define and clarify the various provisions, and the provisions should be applied in order of the chapters. Chapter 1, Part B is particularly useful as a starting point because it sets out the general application principles. Chapters 2 through 4 provide for the offense conduct, adjustments, and criminal history calculations. Chapter 5 guides the determination of the final sentence, including departures. Chapter 6 covers sentencing procedures and plea agreements. Chapter 7 governs violations of supervised releases and probation, and Chapter 8 deals with organizations as defendants.

In its most basic form the guideline range under which a defendant is sentenced in federal court is the result of a fact-generated assessment of the defendant's offense characteristics gridded against the defendant's criminal history. The intersection of the offense level (the y-axis) with the criminal history level (the x-axis) on the sentencing table results in a sentencing range expressed in months. The judge is supposed to sentence the defendant within that range (the range itself has a top of end no more than 25 percent greater than the lower end). There are occasions where the judge can depart upward from that range (appealable by the defense) or depart downward from that range (appealable by the prosecution). There are specific departures set out in the guidelines, including departures for cooperating with the government, departures when a factor exists to an extraordinary degree taking it out of the "heartland" of the guidelines, or departures where there exists "an aggravating or mitigating circumstance of a kind, or to a degree, not adequately taken into consideration by the Sentencing Commission in formulating the guidelines . . ." *See* USSG Ch. 1 Pt. A (4)(b).

Although the guideline is a range, the final sentence imposed by the court is a determinate sentence. For example, if the defendant's final guideline range is 108–135 months and there are no departures, the judge will impose a sentence of no less than 108 months, but no greater than 135 months, such as 115 months. High-level drug offenses carry statutory mandatory minimums that trump a guideline range. *See* 21 USCS § 841(b). With a ten-year mandatory minimum, a guideline of 108–135 months becomes a sentencing range of 120–135 months where the judge could not sentence the defendant to anything below 120 months, absent two special departures: if the defendant cooperates under USSG § 5K1.1 (*see* discussion below) or the defendant falls under a safety valve exception under USSG § 5C1.2 where the defendant is a low-level, nonviolent first offender who has informed the government of all evidence and information she has concerning the offense and any relevant conduct. There is no longer parole in the federal system, and the most a defendant can get off for good time in prison is 15 percent of her sentence. As a result, if a judge imposes a ten-year federal sentence, the defendant will serve a minimum of eight and one-half years in jail, providing she earns all of her good time.

Chapter 1: General Application Principles and Relevant Conduct

Chapter 1 includes a very important provision that must be understood in order to apply the guidelines accurately, and that is the definition of "relevant conduct" in USSG § 1B1.3. The base offense level for a particular offense, specific offense characteristics and adjustments—the main ingredients in a sentence—are calculated on all relevant conduct, meaning all acts by the defendant in the commission of the offense and reasonably foreseeable acts in furtherance of jointly undertaken criminal activity. USSG § 1B1.3(1)(A) & (B). Relevant conduct may include uncharged conduct and even acquitted conduct. *See, e.g., United States v. Watts*, 519 U.S. 148, 136 L.Ed.2d 554, 117 S.Ct. 633 (1997). The Commentary to section 1B1.3 sets forth specific examples describing when conduct is reasonably foreseeable. Counsel for both sides should be familiar with those examples and whether they apply to the facts of the case. For example, if the defendant was the codefendant's girlfriend and had known about her boyfriend's ongoing drug trafficking for the past two years but agrees to carry drugs for him on one occasion, how much of the entire conspiracy should be included in her offense level? See USSG § 1B1.3 comment. (n. 2(c)(5)).

Chapter 2: Offense Conduct

Chapter 2 sets forth what goes into the sentence for a particular offense. Each offense starts with a base offense level and then points are added (sometimes subtracted) based on various conduct. For example, drug offense levels start out based on the amount of drugs involved, with enhancements for such things as possessing a dangerous weapon, distributing drugs within 1000 feet of a school, or selling to a pregnant woman. *See* USSG § 2D1.1. Financial crime offense levels start out based on the amount of money taken or the loss involved, with enhancements for such things as whether the offense involved more than minimal planning, was committed through mass-marketing, or involved misrepresentation of a charitable institution. *See* USSG § 2B1.1. Much of counsel's litigation will revolve around whether these enhancements apply, and if so, to what extent.

Since the Federal Sentencing Guidelines have been in effect for over a decade, many of the terms used to calculate a sentence have been subject to extensive litigation, *e.g.*, what is meant by more than minimal planning or loss. Despite hundreds of cases on these issues, defense counsel should attempt to distinguish those cases with the particular facts of the case when necessary to avoid an enhancement. Sometimes the government may be willing not to seek a certain enhancement, such as the two-point enhancement for more than minimal planning, in exchange for an early plea.

Chapter 3: Adjustments Including Obstruction of Justice

Chapter 3 sets forth adjustments that are not offense specific, including victim-related adjustments such as hate crime motivation, and aggravating and mitigating role—whether the defendant was a minimal or minor participant or a supervisor or manager of an organization. See USSG §§ 3A1.1, 3B1.1 & 2. There are also enhancements for use of a special skill, like being a pilot and transporting drugs, and abuse of a position of trust—both fertile areas for litigation. See USSG § 3B1.3. For example, if an everyday teller does not ordinarily get an enhancement for abuse of a position of trust, should a supervisor of a teller who committed the offense while acting in the capacity of an ordinary teller get the enhancement?

Obstruction of justice, also a Chapter 3 enhancement, is a particularly draconian adjustment and merits its own discussion. Obstruction of justice is ordinarily a two-point enhancement that can be assessed for conduct before or during the offense—for example, intimidating potential witnesses—as well as for conduct after the offense—escaping or providing false information to a probation officer for example. See USSG § 3C1.1. Significantly, if the court assesses a two-point obstruction of justice enhancement, the defendant will not ordinarily be entitled to the two- or three-point reduction for acceptance of responsibility, except in extraordinary circumstances. See USSG § 3E1.1 comment. (n. 4). As a result, obstruction of justice in fact may be the equivalent of a five-point enhancement and should be avoided assiduously.

Prosecutors might ask for an obstruction of justice enhancement if the defendant took the stand at trial and was found guilty, arguing that the jury necessarily found the defendant untruthful. If the court finds by a preponderance of the evidence that the defendant perjured himself at trial or during the course of the case, in some circuits the court must impose the enhancement. See, e.g., United States v. Shonubi, 998 F.2d 84, 88 (2d. Cir. 1993). The prosecutor may argue that when the defendant submits a declaration in support of a motion to suppress, which the court then denies, the defendant necessarily perjured himself. In making the assessment, the judge is advised by the commentary to the guidelines to be cognizant that inaccurate testimony may result from "confusion, mistake or faulty memory" and not necessarily a "willful attempt to obstruct justice." USSG § 3C1.1, comment.

(n.2). Indeed, in some circuits the judge must find a specific intent to obstruct justice. *See, e.g., United States v. Thomas-Hamilton,* 907 F.2d 282, 285 (2d Cir.1990). Moreover, the enhancement is not to punish a defendant for exercising a constitutional right. USSG § 3C1.1, comment. (n.2). Defense counsel can argue that the judge's decision may simply be based on lack of legal merit rather than the defendant lied. The obstruction of justice enhancement provides additional incentive for defense counsel to be very cautious about what is included in client affidavits. As a precaution, it is advised to include a clause that the affidavit has been prepared by the attorney, that only certain facts are relevant to the motion, and the assertions are carefully couched in such terms as "I don't recall being advised of my rights," etc.

Chapter 3 also provides the formula for determining an offense level on multiple counts, which depends on the relative seriousness of each count. There is a point allotment and a table that counsel can consult to determine the combined offense level. *See* USSG §§ 3D1.1–1.4. A defendant may also be entitled to a reduction of two or three points for acceptance of responsibility under Chapter 3, which generally means the defendant has pleaded guilty. *See* USSG § 3E1.1. The third point is available for offense levels higher than sixteen when the defendant saves the government from having to prepare for trial as a result of an early plea. USSG § 3E1.1(b). The timing of the defendant's plea can make a difference whether the defendant receives acceptance of responsibility deductions, and counsel should know the customary deadlines in their particular jurisdiction. For example, at one time the U.S. Attorney's Office in the Southern District of New York would ordinarily not oppose a two-point reduction for acceptance of responsibility if the defendant pleaded guilty two weeks before trial, and would ordinarily not oppose a three-point reduction if the plea took place at least three weeks before trial.

In rare situations the defendant may receive acceptance of responsibility even after trial. USSG § 3E1.1 comment. (n. 2). The guidelines suggest such a situation when the defendant does not contest factual issues but goes to trial to preserve issues. *Id.* In other cases, defense counsel will have an uphill battle after trial unless there are preconviction statements or conduct evincing acceptance of responsibility.

Rule 32. Sentence and Judgment

Chapter 4: Criminal History and Career Offenders

Chapter 4 sets forth the formula for determining a defendant's criminal history by providing for various points for prior convictions depending largely on the length of the sentence imposed and whether the offense was committed while on parole or probation. Offense levels are significantly increased if the defendant is deemed to be a career offender: basically a three strikes and you are out, where the defendant is eighteen years old at the time of the current offense, the current offense is a drug offense or crime of violence, and the defendant has two prior felony convictions for a crime of violence or a controlled substance offense. USSG § 4B1.1. As a result of the Supreme Court's decision in *United States v. Custis*, 511 U.S. 485, 128 L.Ed.2d 517, 114 S.Ct. 1732 (1994) counsel can arguably no longer make collateral challenges to state offenses unless the defendant was not represented by counsel. However, defense counsel can argue that the criminal history category seriously overstates the seriousness of the defendant's prior record and can ask for a downward departure; alternatively, the prosecution can argue that the defendant's criminal history category understates the seriousness of the defendant's prior record and can ask for an upward departure.

Chapter 5: Determining the Sentence and Noncooperation Downward Departures

Chapter 5 sets forth the type of sentence that can be imposed at a specific range (probation, imprisonment, etc.). The judge can consider certain relevant factors in imposing a sentence such as role in the offense and prior record. *See* USSG §§ 5H1.7–1.8. Some factors are not considered relevant and cannot be used in imposing a sentence, such as race, sex, national origin, religion, and socioeconomic status. *See* USSG § 5H1.10 & 12. Some factors are not ordinarily relevant, including most individual offender characteristics like age, employment, mental health, family ties, military service, or charitable contributions. *See* USSG §§ 5H1.1–1.3, 5H1.5–1.6, and 5H1.11.

Chapter 5, Part K, governs departures under the guidelines. Section 5K2.0 provides for specific departures, many of them upward departures, such as where the victim suffered death or physical or psychological injury. *See* USSG §§ 5K2.1–2.3. The guidelines allow for downward departures on such grounds as coercion, diminished capacity, or voluntary disclosure, although a number of these provisions are rarely invoked because they require nearly impossible criteria. For example, even though the defendant may have voluntarily disclosed information that increased his guideline calculation, he is not entitled to a downward departure under USSG § 5K2.16 if the motivating factor to disclose the information to the government was because the defendant knew that discovery of the offense was imminent or the disclosure occurs in connection with the investigation of the defendant for related conduct. See USSG § 5K2.16. There is very little information that a defendant would give that would not be part of the investigation or likely to be disclosed. A downward departure for diminished capacity is only applicable to nonviolent offenders, and the reduced mental capacity has to be significant and not from drug use. USSG § 5K2.13. Similarly, coercion of the defendant as grounds for departure does not include economic hardship or personal financial difficulties; the threat must be one of physical injury or substantial damage to property. USSG § 5K2.12.

Many defense arguments involve taking "not ordinarily relevant" factors under Chapter 5, Part H, like age, family ties, employment, and showing that they exist to a degree not adequately considered by the guidelines or are present in an unusual or exceptional way that merit a downward departure. In short, defense counsel must individualize the client in a sentencing scheme that contrives to minimize or eliminate individualization. Other arguments for departure include extraordinary post-arrest rehabilitation, *see United States v. Bryson*, 163 F.3d 742, 747 (2d Cir.1998) and aberrant act, *see Zecevic v. United States Parole Comm'n*, 163 F.3d 731, 734 (2d Cir.1998). An aggregate of factors also may warrant a downward departure even though each factor on its own would be insufficient to justify a departure. *See* USSG § 5K2.0, comment.

Downward departures are a powerful weapon in defense counsel's sentencing arsenal as shown by the fact that approximately one in three defendants in federal court is sentenced with some kind of downward departure; in some districts it is as high as 50 percent. *See* U.S. Sentencing Commission, Federal Sentencing Statistics, Fiscal Year 1999. Some jurisdictions (and judges) are more receptive to departures than others, and counsel should be familiar with their circuit's cases, as well as the Supreme Court's decision in *United States v. Koon*, 518 U.S. 81, 135 L.Ed.2d 392,

116 S.Ct. 2035 (1996), discussing forbidden, discouraged, and encouraged factors in terms of downward departures under the Federal Sentencing Guidelines.

5K1.1 Cooperation under the Federal Sentencing Guidelines

The most common downward departure under the guidelines is cooperation pursuant to USSG § 5K1.1 when the defendant substantially assists in the investigation or prosecution of another person. A downward departure for the defendant's cooperation is made on the government's motion (it cannot be made by the court or the defense) through what is called a "5K1.1 letter." This letter is written by the prosecution detailing the timing, nature, and extent of the defendant's cooperation plus any risk the defendant or his family faced as a result of the cooperation. A cooperation letter is the key to the sentencing city. This letter allows the court to downwardly depart from both the defendant's guideline range and any mandatory minimum sentence. With a 5K1.1 letter, the court can depart to the lowest sentence of probation or time served no matter how long the original sentence the defendant faced.

Perhaps one of the most significant changes in federal criminal defense practice since the advent of the guidelines and mandatory minimums is the extraordinary increase in the number of defendants cooperating with the government. Over 30 percent of all drug defendants were sentenced in 1999 pursuant to a 5K1.1 cooperation departure. *See* U.S. Sentencing Commission, Federal Sentencing Statistics, Fiscal Year 1999. There are some attorneys who refuse to represent so-called snitches. Institutional defenders do not have a choice, and, practically speaking, any federal practitioner failing to consider cooperation as an option may very well be ineffective. In the Federal Sentencing Guidelines era it is often in the defendant's best interest and may be the only option when facing a mandatory minimum.

Defense counsel needs to consider whether the defendant should cooperate at the earliest opportunity. Cooperation should be an automatic consideration when the defendant is facing a mandatory minimum drug sentence and does not fit into the nonviolent, low-level first offender category that is eligible for a safety valve departure under 5C1.2. The earlier the defendant decides to cooperate, the better. Judges consider the timing of the cooperation as well as the nature and extent of the assistance in imposing a sentence. *See* USSG § 5K1.1(a)(1)–(5). Moreover, if a defendant waits too long, there may be no one left to cooperate against since his codefendants may very well be cooperating against him.

Cooperating with the authorities involves its own risks and difficulties. In order to cooperate, a defendant must go in for a proffer session with the U.S. Attorneys' Office. The purpose of the session is for the defendant to "proffer" his information for consideration by the government in deciding whether to sign him up as a cooperator. It is like an audition for a part. Before going into a proffer session, defense counsel must debrief the defendant thoroughly, including all prior arrests and convictions, prior bad acts even if not arrested or convicted, associations with other people, and the defendant's entire personal background, along with drug or alcohol use. The defendant should be cross-examined and probed for inconsistencies. All questions the prosecution might ask should be asked by the defense counsel in advance and investigated to the extent possible; it is better to hear the bad facts beforehand and assess the advisability of proffering rather than hear it for the first time in front of the prosecution.

At the proffer session the defendant must tell the prosecution and case agent (often it is the case agent asking the questions) everything about himself, the offense, and what he knows about other people. The defendant should be advised always to tell the complete truth; this means not to understate or overstate anyone's involvement, including the defendant's own. In giving information, the defendant should assume that the prosecutor and agents know everything and have met with the codefendants, the informants, family members, grade school classmates, etc. If the defendant lies, it is worse than no proffer since technically the defendant could be prosecuted for making false statements. Without a 5K1.1 letter, the defendant is facing a mandatory minimum with no other means to avoid a draconian sentence.

The defendant typically signs a "queen for a day" agreement that protects the defendant from the use of the information against him at trial. However, that agreement does not protect him from the use of the information by the prosecution to investigate the case, and it does not protect the defendant from being impeached by the information should he take the stand and say something different or for perjury charges if he lies. Some "queen for a day" agreements even provide that the government can introduce the statements made by the defendant in the proffer session if the defense attorney suggests a defense at trial that contradicts the defendant's statements at the proffer session—this last clause should be assiduously avoided. If possible, the defense should seek to have the defendant proffer under the protections of FRCrP 11(e)(6), a broader protection from the use of information by the government. Most government attorneys will require the signing of the office's own agreement and will not agree to proceed under FRCrP 11.

Most prosecutors or agents who ask the questions at the proffer know much more than the defendant about the case, particularly if the codefendants are cooperating or there is a confidential informant. The government will often ask misleading questions just to test the defendant's truth telling. Defense counsel should avoid stopping the proffer session when a topic or answer comes out unexpectedly. The more pre-proffer preparation, the less likely that will be necessary. When defense lawyers interrupt questioning at the proffer session to speak to their client, prosecutors see a red flag and assume that defense counsel did not know the answer because the defendant had been less than forthright with his counsel. If it is imperative that defense counsel speak to the client during a proffer session, it is better to stop the proceedings for counsel's own reasons—to make a phone call or to use the restroom, and then use the break to discuss matters with the client. Defense counsel should be present for an initial proffer session and ordinarily should keep verbatim notes of what was said in case there is any dispute later on about what the defendant disclosed. Prosecutors and agents should seldom take notes since they would have to be turned over to opposing counsel as Jencks material under 18 USCS § 3500 and FRCrP 26.2 if the defendant were called as the government's witness at a hearing or trial. *See* the Commentary for FRCrP 26.2.

Once the defendant signs a cooperation agreement ("gets the part"), the standard policy in most districts is that he must eventually plead to all the charges or at least the top count—this is usually much worse than what the defendant would ordinarily be required to do under a straight plea agreement. The rationale for requiring the heaviest plea is that the defendant will make a better witness if he is subject to prosecution on everything and can only get a reduction if he tells the truth. The expectation is that the defendant will receive a lower sentence, in some cases significantly lower, due to his cooperation. The defendant needs to understand the importance of being truthful and continuing to be truthful, because if he lies after he has signed a cooperation agreement, the agreement is ripped up and the defendant is stuck with all of the charges to which he has pled.

Under the Federal Sentencing Guidelines, information given by the defendant during the course of cooperation is not to be used in determining the applicable guideline range except as agreed by the government. *See* USSG § 1B1.8. As a practical matter, most plea agreements provide that the prosecutor will make such information known to the probation officer and the court. Indeed, making such information count toward a sentence makes the defendant a better witness for the prosecution since it will be more difficult to show on cross-examination that the cooperating defendant is getting off for free on the other offenses or conduct. Although the expectation is that the cooperating defendant will receive a lower sentence, it will depend on the prosecution filing a 5K1.1 letter and moving for a departure under the guidelines and the mandatory minimums. The 5K1.1 letter is not ordinarily filed until after cooperation is complete and the government has determined that the defendant has been truthful and that his assistance has been substantial. When the defendant is sentenced, the judge will take into consideration the strength of the 5K1.1 letter and can give as low of a sentence as the judge wants. The judge can also reduce a sentence already imposed for substantial assistance. *See* FRCrP 35(b).

Presentence Investigation and Report

Prior to the imposition of sentence, FRCrP 32 provides for a presentence investigation and report to be completed by the probation officer assigned to the defendant's case. *See also* 18 USCS § 3552 and 6A1.1–13. A presentence report, referred to either as a "PSI" or a "PSR," is required unless the court finds that the information in the record would allow the court to impose a sentence without a report. Typically, the only time a report is not requested is when the case is a petty offense (B misdemeanor or lower) since the Federal Sentencing Guidelines do not apply to these offenses. USSG § 1B1.9. If the judge is going to order restitution, a report must be submitted. FRCrP 32(b)(1).

The PSR is an extremely important document. The report details information in a number of areas set forth in FRCrP 32, most significantly the offense conduct, the defendant's personal history and characteristics, criminal record, and financial condition. The PSR also includes determination of factors under the Sentencing Guidelines categories discussed above and a recommended sentence from the probation officer. The report is used by the judge to impose a sentence. The report is included in the case record for any appeal. In addition, the PSR is used by the Bureau of Prisons to assign the defendant to a particular facility or to place the defendant in a treatment program.

Because of the importance of the PSR, the probation officer's role has become much more significant and problematic for the defense attorney with the advent of the Federal Sentencing Guidelines. Before the sentencing guidelines came into being, counsel's general view of the probation officer was that of a social worker who was interested in assisting the defendant in rehabilitation; the probation officer was typically viewed as a defense ally. Today that is much less the role of the probation officer, who is now seen in more of a law enforcement role and who investigates conduct and factors often with the aim of achieving the highest possible sentence.

Strategies When the Defendant Is Interviewed by the Probation Officer

The defendant is interviewed for the PSR during the course of the probation officer's investigation. This is a critical interview. FRCrP 32 was recently amended to provide notice of the interview to defense counsel and give counsel a reasonable opportunity to attend. FRCrP 32(b)(2). Defense counsel or a representative must be present to protect the defendant from a probing interview that could result in a higher guideline range. Counsel should make a request to be present at the interview on the record at the time of the guilty plea or guilty verdict, when ordinarily a sentencing date is set.

There is considerable tension between the need for the defendant to make a good impression with the probation officer by showing remorse and cooperativeness in order to assure acceptance of responsibility, weighed against the real fear of increasing a defendant's sentence or collateral punishment from statements made at the interview. Defense counsel must protect the defendant, while still considering the probation officer an important player to persuade since judges often give great deference to probation officer recommendations. A helpful solution is to have a trustworthy paralegal attend the interview with clear ground rules as to what will and what will not be discussed. The paralegal can always explain that because the defense counsel could not attend the interview, the defense's position on those issues will be included in a letter. The Supreme Court recently held that a defendant does not waive the Fifth Amendment privilege in entering a plea of guilty and that no negative inferences can be drawn when a defendant invokes a Fifth Amendment privilege against incrimination even after a guilty plea, *i.e.*, at a probation interview. *Mitchell v. United States*, 526 U.S. 314, 143 L.Ed.2d 424, 119 S.Ct. 1307 (1999).

Usually it is not a good idea for the defendant to discuss the offense conduct at the interview. The defendant's version can be provided to the probation officer in a letter written by defense counsel who can control what is said to avoid alerting the probation officer to information that could be interpreted as relevant conduct and increasing a guidelines range. Of course, when the client is a first offender, has no skeletons in his closet, and may be more persuasive in person to detail why the crime occurred, counsel may want the defendant to speak directly to the officer. The defendant's in-person statement should only be made with defense counsel or a paralegal present.

It is wise not to have the defendant discuss criminal history. The defendant might disclose an offense that the probation officer was not aware of because it did not show up on the federal rap sheet. It is also problematic if the defendant discusses criminal history but forgets a conviction that shows up on the rap sheet. The probation officer may view the defendant as having misled or lied to the officer and assess obstruction of justice points. The probation officer is going to get the rap sheet anyway, and the prior criminal history points are imposed by formula, so there is virtually no discretion on the part of the probation officer in calculating the criminal history category of the defendant. If there is a particular offense that needs explanation, that can be provided in a written submission. When the probation officer complains that the defendant is not being forthcoming, the simple explanation is that it is the policy of the office to rely on the rap sheet. Counsel can also explain when the defendant clearly has a record that the state systems are so crazy that defendants often do not know what they pled to or whether the case was dismissed; therefore, it is more accurate to rely on the rap sheet. If it is absolutely certain that the defendant has no prior record, the defendant can say so; however, counsel should be extremely cautious to have inquired about any misdemeanor convictions or any type of arrest to confirm that this is, indeed, the defendant's first brush with the law.

The defendant usually should not discuss drug use at the presentence interview. A statement regarding drug use and need for treatment can be included in the defendant's written version of the offense to the probation officer. Should the defendant talk fully about his heroin habit, for example, the probation officer may discern that it would be impossible to support the defendant's habit on his legitimate and illegitimate income based on the amount of drugs he claimed he has sold. The probation officer may conclude that the defendant must have been selling more drugs than was set forth in the charges and include that additional amount as relevant conduct, which may possibly increase the defendant's guideline range. On the other hand, completion of certain Bureau of Prison programs for drug treatment can reduce a sentence, but such programs may only be available for defendants with documented drug problems, or the defense may intend to argue that the defendant has exhibited extraordinary drug rehabilitation that merits a downward departure. In such cases, drug use may need to be discussed at the interview in an attempt to have the probation officer on the defendant's side; however, the defendant should speak only about the type of drug and length of use in general terms rather than specific quantities.

The defendant usually should not talk about immigration status particularly in the wake of the extremely harsh deportation laws under the Antiterrorism and Effective Death Penalty Act (AEDPA), where even minor offenses can lead to automatic deportation. Again, if the probation officer complains, the answer can be that it is the standard policy of counsel's office for any client not to discuss the issue in light of AEDPA. However, if counsel intends on making a downward departure argument based on circumstances related to immigration status, it may be necessary for the defendant to speak to the probation officer directly in order to be most effective. Counsel must weigh carefully the risks and benefits given the extremely draconian deportation laws.

When there are going to be disputes with respect to guideline calculations—*e.g.*, whether the defendant was a minor player or abused a position of trust, or whether the defendant is entitled to a downward departure—defense counsel may consider letting the defendant discuss that aspect of the offense at the interview. At a minimum, it should be included in the defense's statement. Ideally, the downward departure will be recommended by the probation officer and possibly acquiesced to by the prosecutor. The defense statement should be provided to the probation officer immediately after the interview so that it can be incorporated into the probation officer's initial report.

Review of the PSR

Before the PSR is submitted to the judge, the probation officer must furnish a copy to both defense counsel and the prosecutor at least thirty-five days before sentencing. FRCrP 32(b)(6)(A). Providing the report to counsel in advance of sentencing gives the parties time to add information, make comments, and voice objections in writing before the final report is submitted to the judge. The parties must return the report fourteen days after receiving it from the probation officer. FRCrP 32(b)(6)(B). Counsel should read every word of the report. Even minor discrepancies can make a difference in final guideline calculations. Do the math. Probation officers do make mistakes and may err in an individual assessment or the total offense points. To ensure that objections are included in the final report, counsel must provide objections to the probation officer in a timely manner, noting that the probation officer must submit the report to the judge seven days before sentencing. (Any of these time limits may be changed for good cause. *See* FRCrP 32(b)(6)(C) & (D)).

In the past, many districts did not allow disclosure of probation officer recommendations, and it was difficult to litigate for or against the recommendation, even if they were paraphrased by the court. Now the trend seems to be disclosure of the probation officer's recommendation as a matter of due process and more directed arguments at sentencing. Both defense counsel and the prosecution should request a copy of the probation officer's final recommendation to the judge in advance in order to prepare for sentencing.

Imposition of Sentence

At the sentencing, the judge will ask whether the defendant has received a copy of the presentence report, had an opportunity to review the report and discuss it with counsel, and whether the defendant has any objections to the report, other than those already submitted to the court. If there are factors that remain unresolved, the court must rule on those objections unless those factors will not be taken into account or will not affect sentencing. The parties may be entitled to a hearing to resolve disputed factors. If witnesses are going to testify, defense counsel is entitled to prior statements under FRCrP 26.2.

The standard the judge uses in determining sentencing factors is preponderance of the evidence. *See* USSG § 6A1.3 (policy statement), comment. Formerly, the judge determined not only the enhancement and adjustments under the sentencing guidelines by a preponderance of the evidence, but also the amount of drugs involved and other enhancements that could trigger mandatory minimums and increase maximum penalties. *See, e.g.*, 21 USCS § 841(b). However, the Supreme Court's recent decision in *Apprendi v. New Jersey*, 530 U.S. 466, 147 L.Ed.2d 435, 120 S.Ct. 2348 (2000) has dramatically changed the burden of proof in sentencing enhancements. Enhancements that increase the statutory maximum penalty must be charged in the indictment, submitted to the jury, and proven beyond a reasonable doubt. When the jury does not make a finding of an enhancement factor like drug quantities, the defendant cannot be subject to the enhancement that increases maximum penalties. Counsel for both sides should make an initial assessment as to which penalty enhancements are subject to Apprendi standards, and they must be set forth in the indictment and proven to the finder of fact beyond a reasonable doubt. Knowledge of the effect of Apprendi is critical in any drug case, but it is also considered for other offenses that increase maximum and even minimum penalties, such as penalty enhancements under the mail and wire fraud statutes for telemarketing or crimes affecting a financial institution. *See* 18 USCS §§ 1341 and 1343.

Prior to the sentencing, it is advisable in most cases to provide a detailed sentencing memorandum to the judge with attachments of important documents such as drug treatment completion forms, letters from clergy, family, and friends, etc. Counsel should review the submissions for accuracy and authenticity. If the defense has requested a downward departure due to extraordinary family circumstances because all of the defendant's children were killed in a fire, the five letters from the defendant's children describing how important it is for him to be home to care for them should not be submitted (true story).

At the actual proceeding to impose the sentence, defense counsel is afforded an opportunity to speak, as is the defendant. It is important for defense counsel to prepare the defendant for the opportunity. This is not the time for the defendant to offer excuses. Judges are looking for remorse and acceptance of responsibility. The defendant is not required to give a statement and often it may be in the defendant's best interest to rely on the Presentence Report. Defense counsel should make a critical assessment of the advantages and disadvantages of the defendant making a personal statement. If there is concern the defendant will provide harmful information or argue the case again so that the judge may not give the defendant acceptance of responsibility, it may be wise to have the defendant write down what he or she intends to say and review it in advance. At the end of the day, a defendant is unlikely to get into trouble by telling the court he or she is sorry.

The prosecution is also afforded an opportunity to make a recommendation. FRCrP 32(c)(3)(D). It is important for defense counsel to learn in advance what the prosecution's position will be. Many prosecutors will agree to take no position and either remain silent or rely on the probation officer's recommendation. If a defense attorney can persuade a prosecutor to join in recommending a downward departure or lowest range sentence, that is ideal. If the prosecution is going to recommend a high sentence or oppose a downward departure, defense counsel should learn the basis for the prosecution's position and be prepared to counter it at sentencing. In some cases the prosecution will file a sentencing memorandum that details the prosecution's position on contested issues.

Victims may be allowed to speak in sexual abuse and violent crime cases. *See* FRCrP 32(c)(3)(E). Prosecutors should encourage their attendance at sentencing hearings for these offenses because victim allocutions could significantly impact the judge's decision. Defense counsel must be vigilant that victims (or their guardians or family members as defined in FRCrP 32(f)(1)) of only the

Rule 32. Sentence and Judgment

specific crimes defined in FRCrP 32(f)(2) are given such an opportunity.

Even if the parties agree on a guideline range, the judge is not bound by the plea agreement, especially if that range is disputed by the probation officer, which can happen where there has been a plea agreement between the parties to not seek certain enhancements. *See* USSG § 6B1.2. The judge is supposed to ensure that the guidelines are not subverted by a plea agreement that fails to take into account all of the egregious conduct by its sentencing recommendation or dismissal of charges. *Id.* As a matter of practice, most judges pat the probation officer on the head for the good work and then go with the guideline calculations provided by the parties' plea agreement. District judges, often former prosecutors, usually recognize that these plea agreements frequently include an assessment by the prosecutor of the strength of the government's case, the weakness of any witnesses, and strategic considerations of not wanting to expose confidential informants on certain cases.

Sentencing Ranges

Under the Federal Sentencing Guidelines, if a guideline range is in Zone A of the sentencing table (ranges of 0–6 months), the judge can impose a sentence of straight probation because a sentence of imprisonment is not required. USSG § 5C1.1(b). If the guideline range is in Zone B of the sentencing table (1–7 up to 6–12 months), the judge may impose a straight sentence of imprisonment (generally not imposed at these lower levels unless the defendant has a substantial criminal record). This sentence of imprisonment may include a term of supervised release instead of confinement, provided at least one month is by imprisonment, or a sentence of probation that includes substitute confinement for imprisonment. *See* USSG § 5C1.1(c) & (e). In most first offender or minor offender cases, judges impose home confinement for Zone B cases. Where the guideline range is in Zone C of the sentencing table (8–14 up to 10–16 months), the judge can impose a straight sentence of imprisonment or a split sentence where at least half the minimum term is served in prison and half is served in alternative confinement like home detention or confinement in a halfway house. USSG § 5C1.1(d). For Zone D offenses (12–18 months and higher) the judge must impose a term of imprisonment. USSG § 5C1.1(f). If the offense is a Class A or Class B felony, probation may not be imposed. 18 USCS § 3561(a)(1).

The judge is required to consider a number of listed factors in imposing a sentence. These include nature and circumstances of the offense, history and characteristics of the defendant, the need for the imposed sentence to reflect the seriousness of the offense and respect for law, deterrence, rehabilitative services for the defendant, as well as to avoid unwarranted sentencing disparities, and the need to provide restitution for victims. *See* 18 USCS § 3553(a). The judge can impose an order requiring the defendant to give notice of a fraud or deceptive practices conviction to victims. *See* 18 USCS § 3555. Before imposing such an order, the defendant and prosecution are entitled to submit affidavits and address the court on the appropriateness of such an order. 18 USCS § 3551(d).

The judge will impose a determinate sentence and may require a fine and/or restitution in addition to a mandatory special assessment fee. Indigent clients are rarely required to pay a fine since one of the considerations is the defendant's ability to pay, which is demonstrated by whether the defendant could afford his own counsel. *See* 18 USCS § 3572(a)(2). The court is required to state in open court the reasons for the imposition of a particular sentence. 18 USCS § 3553(c). If the guideline range exceeds twenty-four months, the judge must detail the reason for imposing a sentence within a particular range or the reasons for imposing a sentence outside the range. *Id.* The prosecution should also ensure that the defendant is advised of his right to appeal the judgment if the case went to trial and his right to appeal a sentence. FRCrP 32(c)(5).

The sentence will be set forth in a judgment and commitment order (referred to as a "J&C"). *See* FRCrP 32(d). It is important for both parties to review the judgment to ensure that the correct sentence is documented, including the amount of any fine or restitution. If the defendant wishes to be incarcerated in a particular area or facility in order to be closer to family, defense counsel should make such a request at the time of sentencing and ensure that the court's recommendation is included in the judgment and commitment order. Although a judge's recommendation to that effect is not binding on the Bureau of Prisons, it is often persuasive.

Rule 32.1. Revocation or Modification of Probation or Supervised Release

(a) Revocation of probation or supervised release.

(1) Preliminary hearing. Whenever a person is held in custody on the ground that the person has violated a condition of probation or supervised release, the person shall be afforded a prompt hearing before any judge, or a United States magistrate[1] who has been given the authority pursuant to 28 U.S.C. § 636 to conduct such hearings, in order to determine whether there is probably[2] cause to hold the person for a revocation hearing. The person shall be given

(A) notice of the preliminary hearing and its purpose and of the alleged violation;

(B) an opportunity to appear at the hearing and present evidence in the person's own behalf;

(C) upon request, the opportunity to question witnesses against the person unless, for good cause, the federal magistrate decides that justice does not require the appearance of the witness; and

(D) notice of the person's right to be represented by counsel.

The proceedings shall be recorded stenographically or by an electronic recording device. If probable cause is found to exist, the person shall be held for a revocation hearing. The person may be released pursuant to Rule 46(c) pending the revocation hearing. If probable cause is not found to exist, the proceeding shall be dismissed.

(2) Revocation Hearing. The revocation hearing, unless waived by the person, shall be held within a reasonable time in the district of jurisdiction. The person shall be given

(A) written notice of the alleged violation;

(B) disclosure of the evidence against the person;

---

1. So in original. Probably should be "magistrate judge".
2. So in original. Probably should be "probable".

(C) an opportunity to appear and to present evidence in the person's own behalf;

(D) the opportunity to question adverse witnesses; and

(E) notice of the person's right to be represented by counsel.

(b) Modification of probation or supervised release. A hearing and assistance of counsel are required before the terms or conditions of probation or supervised release can be modified, unless the relief to be granted to the person on probation or supervised release upon the person's request or the court's own motion is favorable to the person, and the attorney for the government, after having been given notice of the proposed relief and a reasonable opportunity to object, has not objected. An extension of the term of probation or supervised release is not favorable to the person for the purposes of this rule.

(c) Production of statements.

(1) In general. Rule 26.2(a)–(d) and (f) applies at any hearing under this rule.

(2) Sanctions for failure to produce statement. If a party elects not to comply with an order under Rule 26.2(a) to deliver a statement to the moving party, the court may not consider the testimony of a witness whose statement is withheld.

Commentary

By Prof. Inga L. Parsons
New York University School of Law

Probation and Supervised Release Generally

A defendant may be sentenced to a term of probation except for certain higher-level felonies. See 18 USCS §§ 3561(a) and 3561(c). The Federal Sentencing Guidelines (USSG) (18 USCS Appx) provide for terms of probation for the various sentencing zones. See 18 USCS Appx §§ 5B1.2 and 5C1.1 (USSG). Parole was abolished in the federal system for offenses occurring after November 1, 1987. Under the Federal Sentencing Guidelines scheme, the court imposes a term of supervised release to follow a prison term. 18 USCS 3583(a). Supervised release is not parole, as it does not replace a part of the jail term; instead, supervised release is imposed consecutively to the jail term. Violation of the terms of supervised release can subject the defendant to additional imprisonment, even though the defendants have served out their initial federal prison term.

Maximum terms of supervised release are set out in USCS, Title 18. *See* 18 USCS § 3583(b). Some offenses, like certain drug charges, mandate imposition of a specific or minimum term of supervised release. *See, e.g.*, 21 USCS § 841(b)(1)(A) (mandating a minimum of five years supervised release). The judge is not required under Title 18 to impose a sentence of supervised release except where specifically mandated by the statute of conviction or in certain domestic violence convictions. However, the Sentencing Guidelines mandate imposition of a term of supervised release in cases where more than one year of imprisonment is imposed or where required by statute. See 18 USCS Appx § 5D1.1(a) (USSG).

Imposition and Conditions of Probation and Supervised Release

The court is required to consider a number of factors in determining whether to impose probation or supervised release and the length and conditions of those terms. These factors (the same for both probation and supervised release) are the standard sentencing factors set forth in 18 USCS § 3553(a), *e.g.*, nature of the offense, background of the defendant, purposes of sentencing, etc. There are special provisions for first-time domestic violence offenders, and attorneys should consult USCS §§ 3561(b) and 3563(a)(4) in those cases.

When probation and supervised release are imposed, there are mandatory conditions that the court must impose and discretionary conditions that the court may impose. Mandatory conditions include not committing another crime while on probation and not possessing a controlled substance. 18 USCS § 3563(a). Discretionary conditions include supporting dependents, making restitution, being gainfully employed, undergoing treatment, residing in a specified place, not possessing a firearm, notifying the probation officer if arrested, etc. 18 USCS § 3563(b). The court can modify, reduce, or enlarge the conditions of probation and supervised release prior to the expiration of a term as set out in 18 USCS §§ 3563(c) and 3583(e).

The judge must impose conditions of supervised release or probation reasonably related to the purposes of sentencing. *See* 18 USCS § 3553(a). Defense counsel should object to any condition that fails to relate to the objectives of the sentencing factors. For example, if the offense was a nonviolent misdemeanor, prohibitions on the possession of a firearm may not be sufficiently related to the sentencing goals. Similarly, defense counsel should object to mandatory drug testing if the underlying offense was not drug related and there is little risk of substance abuse. Defense counsel should object to any conditions that are too onerous or likely to become so. At a minimum, defense counsel should set up the reasons why the conditions may be difficult to meet in anticipation of a potential breach of the terms. For example, suppose the court imposes a condition that the defendant must find gainful employment. The defense should object to such a condition if the defendant does not have the skills to get a job, has never held a job for any significant length of time, or suffers from serious mental and physical disorders. However, objections based on constitutional grounds, such as challenges to prohibitions on associations with certain people, have consistently been rejected. *See, e.g., United States v. Bortels*, 962 F.2d 558, 559 (6th Cir. 1992) (upholding condition prohibiting offender from associating with her fiancé).

It is important that defense counsel go through the court-ordered conditions carefully with the clients to insure they understand their obligations. It is also essential to impress upon the defendants the value in establishing a good, trusting relationship with the supervising probation officer who can truly make the defendants' lives easy or miserable. In larger districts the probation officer who prepared the presentence investigation is often different than the supervising officer, so even if the defendants established a good relationship with the first officer, they must connect with a new officer. If the defendants have been cooperative and forthcoming, should they engage in behavior that subjects them to a possible violation of probation or supervised release, the probation officer may be less likely to recommend revocation.

After imposition of sentence, many defense lawyers dust off their hands and file away the case assuming their troubles are over when in fact the client's troubles may have just begun. Many probation and supervised release conditions require monitoring well past the sentencing date. If the defendant is required to find gainful employment, counsel should make sure that is happening, and perhaps assist the defendant to obtain a job through various service organizations. If the defendants' financial situation changes and they are no longer able to meet court-ordered commitments, the probation officer should be brought in to effect a joint solution and perhaps even a modification of the terms of probation or supervised release to accommodate a change in circumstances. If the probationers are having personality conflicts with their supervising probation officers, counsel can often act as a mediator and in some cases get their clients reassigned to different officers.

Violations of Probation or Supervised Release

There are three different grades of violations of probation and supervised release under the guidelines set out in 18 USCS Appx § 7B1.1 (USSG). Grade A violations constitute crimes of violence, drug and firearm felonies, or any offense punishable by more than twenty years. Revocation is mandatory with a Grade A violation. Grade B violations include any felony not classified as a Grade A violation and revocation is also mandatory. Grade C violations are misdemeanors and any other violation of conditions. Revocation for a Grade C violation is discretionary.

A violation does not have to be established by a conviction; it can be established by evidence of conduct that would constitute an offense. 18 USCS Appx § 7B1.1 (USSG) comment. n. 1. In cases where the prohibited conduct does not result in an actual conviction, much of the litigation will revolve around the quality of the government's evidence to prove the conduct. No burden of proof is specified for determination of violations of probation, although courts have held it is a lower standard of proof than at trial, and the facts need only be such as will "reasonably satisfy" the judge. *See, e.g., United States v. Guadrrama*, 742 F.2d 487, 489 (9th Cir. 1984). However, in order for the judge to revoke supervised release, which would result in additional jail time, the judge must find proof of the allegations by a preponderance of the evidence. 18 USCS § 3583(e)(3).

There are policy statements in the guidelines that require the probation officer to report promptly any new criminal conduct that constitutes a Grade A or B violation. 18 USCS Appx § 7B1.2(a)

(USSG). Any other violation is to be reported to the judge unless the probation officer determines that the violation is minor and not a part of a pattern, and that non-reporting will not present an undue risk. 18 USCS Appx § 7B1.2(b) (USSG). Thus, the probation officer has significant discretion to decide whether minor conduct should be reported to the judge and whether to recommend that supervision be revoked.

Even some of the mandatory reporting requirements are open to interpretation. For example, the court is bound by statute to revoke the sentence of probation and resentence the defendant to some term of imprisonment if the probationer commits a controlled substance offense, *see* 18 USCS §§ 3565(b), 3583(d). However, many probation officers will not view a single dirty urine as "possession" of a controlled substance for purposes of revocation and will give the probationer another chance to test negative for narcotics.

The ability of the probationer and defense counsel to develop a good working relationship can affect the probation officer's decision to notify the court in discretionary situations. Where there is a good working relationship between counsel and the probation officer, the officer will often call counsel to notify them of problems beforehand to give counsel some time to assist the probationer in improving. At a minimum, a probation officer who has a good relationship with defense counsel will usually advise counsel in advance when the officer is seeking revocation and will permit the probationer to come to court voluntarily.

A frequent but avoidable problem arises when the probation officer is the last to know about violative behavior such as a new arrest or conviction. If the defendant has been rearrested, it is usually good advice to have the defendant tell the probation officer as soon as possible. Waiting until there is a conviction—or sentence—to notify the probation officer is usually a disaster. In addition to acting on the news of the recent criminal behavior, the officer is likely to view the defendant in a very bad light for having failed to give notice of the arrest at the outset. On the other hand, where the probation officer is notified of the arrest, the probation officer may be able to tell defense counsel whether a particular disposition in the new case will result in a violation. This can be helpful in negotiating a disposition, and can ultimately affect whether the

Rule 32.1. Revocation or Modification of Probation or Supervised Release

probation officer notifies the court of the conviction on an offense where the officer has the discretion not to report it.

Revocation Hearings

Many probationers are given notices or summons to appear voluntarily for a hearing. Under FRCrP 32.1, if the probationer has been arrested and is held in custody on the basis of a violation of probation, the probationer must be afforded a prompt hearing before a judge who will determine whether there is probable cause to hold a revocation hearing. As a practical matter, the preliminary hearings almost never occur because the defendant appears voluntarily for the hearing, is released on bail, or the revocation hearing is held immediately and no preliminary hearing is required. However, if a revocation hearing is put off for some time and no bail is granted, the defense should insist on a preliminary hearing in order to hear the evidence, cross-examine witnesses, etc. In determining bail for revocation of supervised release, the court uses the statutory standards for release pending sentence and appeal—a higher standard than general bail standards. *See* the Commentary to FRCrP 46.

However, a revocation hearing is not always held. The probationer may waive the hearing and agree to plead to one or more of the violations. In cases where the court's relief would be favorable to the probationer, a hearing need not be held. Under FRCrP 32.1, extending a term of probation or supervised release is not considered favorable to the probationer. *See* FRCrP 32.1(b). Thus, if the judge says, "We don't need a hearing because I am going to restore the probationer to probation and simply extend the term," the defense could insist on a hearing in an effort to convince the judge that the term should not be extended but simply restored. Of course there may be strategic reasons for not objecting to the judge's proposal if there is little chance of convincing the judge to restore the defendant to the original term of probation, or the hearing may provide a basis for the judge to revoke the probation rather than simply extend the term.

When the revocation hearing is held, the probationer is entitled to an attorney, to written notice of the allegations, disclosure of the evidence, an opportunity to appear and present evidence, and the opportunity to question witnesses. FRCrP 32.1(2)(A)–(E). The right to counsel is statutory, not constitutional. Defense counsel should review the violation findings carefully to make sure that they are sustainable and to assess whether there are viable defenses. For example, it may be restitution was made, but the payments were late. Counsel should investigate and secure whatever supporting documents may be needed. Since the hearing is not a trial, the rules of evidence do not apply. *See* FRE 1101(d)(3). Hearsay is admissible, although it may not be sufficiently reliable to sustain the government's burden of proof.

Under FRCrP 32.1 the magistrate judge may not require the appearance of a witness at a revocation hearing if the judge finds justice does not require it. If the defense believes the appearance of a witness is necessary, the defense should ask the judge to have the witness testify. In many cases it will be detrimental to the probationer to have a probation officer take the stand and detail all of the probationer's transgressions. In other cases, where defense counsel knows that there are a lot of good things about the probationer that can be brought out, it may be advantageous to have the officer or other witnesses take the stand. FRCrP 26.2, regarding production of witness statements, applies to revocation hearings.

Even if the court finds sufficient evidence in support of the violative conduct, the defense should argue mitigating circumstances that warrant the continuation of probation or supervised release. In some cases the best result may be convincing a judge to terminate probation unfavorably. Although the defendant has a type of "dishonorable discharge," there is no jail time or continued probation that could lead to future violations. Some judges will consider terminating probation unfavorably where the defendant may seem unable to comply with conditions but the judge is not persuaded that the defendant will benefit from a term of imprisonment. Counsel should also consider creative alternatives to revocation and incarceration such as drug treatment or community service. In determining what sentence to impose, the guidelines set forth a revocation table with sentencing ranges for classes of violations gridded against the defendant's criminal history category (the criminal history category is the original level used at sentencing and does not include the present charge). These guidelines are termed nonbinding, although 18 USCS § 3553(a)(4) requires the courts to consider them.

An issue arises as to whether the court can impose an additional term of supervised release where the judge has revoked the supervised release and imposed a new term of imprisonment. Before the 1994 Crime Bill went into effect, most jurisdictions did not allow the imposition of an additional term of supervised release after the defendant's supervised release was revoked and the defendant was sentenced to an additional term of imprisonment. The 1994 Crime Bill now allows for imposition of a new term of supervised release after revocation and imprisonment as a result of the first supervised release term. 18 USCS § 3583(h). If the defendant's case occurred before September 13, 1994, in a jurisdiction where an additional term of supervised release was not allowed, counsel should object to the imposition of the new term of supervised release as a violation of the Ex Post Facto Clause. When a sentence of imprisonment is imposed, the defendants receive no credit against that prison term for the time they were on supervised release or probation. *See* 18 USCS Appx § 7B1.5 (USSG).

Rule 32.2. Criminal Forfeiture

(a) Notice to the defendant. A court shall not enter a judgment of forfeiture in a criminal proceeding unless the indictment or information contains notice to the defendant that the government will seek the forfeiture of property as part of any sentence in accordance with the applicable statute.

(b) Entry of preliminary order of forfeiture; post verdict hearing.

(1) As soon as practicable after entering a guilty verdict or accepting a plea of guilty or nolo contendere on any count in an indictment or information with regard to which criminal forfeiture is sought, the court shall determine what property is subject to forfeiture under the applicable statute. If forfeiture of specific property is sought, the court shall determine whether the government has established the requisite nexus between the property and the offense. If the government seeks a personal money judgment against the defendant, the court shall determine the amount of money that the defendant will be ordered to pay. The court's determination may be based on evidence already in the record, including any written plea agreement or, if the forfeiture is contested, on evidence or information presented by the parties at a hearing after the verdict or finding of guilt.

(2) If the court finds that property is subject to forfeiture, it shall promptly enter a preliminary order of forfeiture setting forth the amount of any money judgment or directing the forfeiture of specific property without regard to any third party's interest in all or part of it. Determining whether a third party has such an interest shall be deferred until any third party files a claim in an ancillary proceeding under Rule 32.2(c).

(3) The entry of a preliminary order of forfeiture authorizes the Attorney General (or a designee) to seize the specific property subject to forfeiture; to conduct any discovery the court considers proper in identifying, locating, or disposing of the property; and to commence proceedings that comply with any statutes governing third-party rights. At sentencing—or at any time before sentencing if the defendant consents—the order of forfeiture becomes final as to the defendant and shall be made a part of the sentence and included in the judgment. The court may include in the order of forfeiture conditions reasonably necessary to preserve the property's value pending any appeal.

(4) Upon a party's request in a case in which a jury returns a verdict of guilty, the jury shall determine whether the government has established the requisite nexus between the property and the offense committed by the defendant.

(c) Ancillary proceeding; final order of forfeiture.

(1) If, as prescribed by statute, a third party files a petition asserting an interest in the property to be forfeited, the court shall conduct an ancillary proceeding but no ancillary proceeding is required to the extent that the forfeiture consists of a money judgment.

(A) In the ancillary proceeding, the court may, on motion, dismiss the petition for lack of standing, for failure to state a claim, or for any other lawful reason. For purposes of the motion, the facts set forth in the petition are assumed to be true.

(B) After disposing of any motion filed under Rule 32.2(c)(1)(A) and before conducting a hearing on the petition, the court may permit the parties to conduct discovery in accordance with the Federal Rules of Civil Procedure if the court determines that discovery is necessary or desirable to resolve factual issues. When discovery ends, a party may move for summary judgment under Rule 56 of the Federal Rules of Civil Procedure.

(2) When the ancillary proceeding ends, the court shall enter a final order of forfeiture by amending the preliminary order as necessary to account for any third-party rights. If no third party files a timely claim, the preliminary order becomes the final order of forfeiture, if the court finds that the defendant (or any combination of defendants convicted in the case) had an interest in the property that is forfeitable under the applicable statute. The defendant may not object to the entry of the final order of forfeiture on the ground that the property belongs, in whole or in part, to a codefendant or third party, nor may a third party object to the final order on the ground that the third party had an interest in the property.

(3) If multiple third-party petitions are filed in the same case, an order dismissing or granting one petition is not appealable until rulings are made on all petitions, unless the court determines that there is no just reason for delay.

(4) An ancillary proceeding is not part of sentencing.

(d) Stay pending appeal. If a defendant appeals from a conviction or order of forfeiture, the court may stay the order of forfeiture on terms appropriate to ensure that the property remains available pending appellate review. A stay does not delay the ancillary proceeding or the determination of a third party's rights or interests. If the court rules in favor of any third party while an appeal is pending, the court may amend the order of forfeiture but shall not transfer any property interest to a third party until the decision on appeal becomes final, unless the defendant consents in writing or on the record.

(e) Subsequently located property; substitute property.

(1) On the government's motion, the court may at any time enter an order of forfeiture or amend an existing order of forfeiture to include property that:

(A) is subject to forfeiture under an existing order of forfeiture but was located and identified after that order was entered; or

(B) is substitute property that qualifies for forfeiture under an applicable statute.

(2) If the government shows that the property is subject to forfeiture under Rule 32.2(e)(1), the court shall:

(A) enter an order forfeiting that property, or amend an existing preliminary or final order to include it; and

(B) if a third party files a petition claiming an interest in the property, conduct an ancillary proceeding under Rule 32.2(c).

(3) There is no right to trial by jury under Rule 32.2(e).

Commentary

By Susan C. Wolfe
Hoffman Pollok & Pickholz

FRCrP 32.2 is a recently enacted and fairly straightforward summary of the criminal forfeiture procedures that apply during and after a trial or guilty plea. The goal of this commentary is to place these rules in context by sensitizing the practitioner to the numerous forfeiture-related issues that arise long before the trial or guilty plea phase.

There are three basic criminal forfeiture statutes: the general criminal forfeiture statute, 18 USCS § 982, which sets forth the crimes to which it is applicable, including most of the fraud statutes; 21 USCS §§ 853 and 848, applicable to narcotics offenses; and 18 USCS § 1963, applicable in RICO cases. Practitioners should keep in mind that the RICO and narcotics forfeiture statutes include extensive procedural rules, including provisions for a pretrial restraining order. Section 982 of Title 18 incorporates some of the provisions of 21 USCS § 853.

Although an analysis of these three laws is beyond the scope of this commentary, it is important to keep in mind, especially in narcotics and RICO cases, that the prospect of forfeiture should be addressed even before counsel signs onto the case because it affects the client's ability to pay legal fees. Under 21 USCS § 853(e) and 18 USCS § 1963, the government may obtain an ex parte order restraining the defendant's assets. If counsel learns that her client is the target of a RICO investigation, it is a good idea to discuss legal fees with the client as soon as possible, because the client's assets may be unavailable at the crucial time of arrest.

As FRCrP 32.2(a) states, forfeiture allegations must be contained in the indictment or information. Typically, the government alleges that a certain, usually substantial sum, is the proceeds of, or was involved in, the alleged offenses. In addition, the forfeiture count usually alleges that specific property, real and personal, including specified bank accounts, are the proceeds of the alleged unlawful activity and that the defendant's right, title, and interest in the property are forfeitable to the government. The count also typically includes notice that, if the specified property cannot be located or otherwise obtained by the government, the government will seek to forfeit any other property of the defendant ("substitute assets"), up to the value of the alleged forfeitable property.

If the government has obtained an ex parte restraining order and the defendant needs funds to retain counsel of choice, the defendant is entitled to a post-restraint, pretrial hearing at which the government must establish probable cause that the defendant committed the crimes underlying the forfeiture allegations, and that the properties specified as forfeitable are the proceeds of illegal activity. Even if the defendant has been indicted, the defendant is entitled to a judicial determination of probable cause at this hearing. *See United States v. Monsanto*, 924 F.2d 1186, 1195, 1199 (2nd Cir.).

One of the benefits of this hearing is that the government is motivated to avoid it. As a result, defense counsel is in a good position to negotiate for payment of her legal fees and the posting of money or property for bail out of the restrained assets. The government may also be willing to negotiate an agreement providing for the payment of the defendant's living expenses. In RICO cases where a legitimate business is involved, the parties often enter into a monitoring agreement whereby the business is able to continue running so long as the government is able to conduct periodic audits to make sure that its assets are not being diverted or squandered.

In the course of negotiating an agreement for counsel fees and payment of defendant's living expenses from the restrained assets, counsel must give serious thought to the best way of handling legal fees under these circumstances. Options include having a sum of money placed in counsel's escrow account against which she will bill hours, or a flat fee, or a flat fee with the right to make an application for additional fees. Counsel must also be prepared to make cogent and specific arguments to the government about the financial needs of the defendant and his family during the pendency of the case.

A defendant is entitled, upon request, to a jury determination of the forfeiture allegations. Typically, this is accomplished through a bifurcated proceeding at which the jury first renders a verdict of guilty or not guilty on each count in the indictment. In the event of a guilty verdict, the jury reconvenes to hear additional evidence on the forfeiture count. Counsel should specifically request bifurcation prior to trial, as well as a special verdict or special interrogatories regarding each forfeiture allegation.

The standard of proof at the bifurcated forfeiture phase of the trial is a somewhat thorny issue. Counsel should press for the beyond a reasonable doubt standard because that is the appropriate standard in criminal cases, keeping in mind, however, that most circuits have adopted the preponderance of the evidence standard for criminal forfeiture. *See, e.g., United States v. Ida*, 176 F.3d 580, 595 (2d Cir. 1999); *United States v. Rogers*, 102 F.3d 641, 647–48 (1st Cir. 1996); *United States v. Tanner*, 61 F.3d 231, 234–35 (4th Cir. 1995). The Supreme Court has not yet squarely addressed this issue.

Counsel should also keep in mind that the language of the RICO forfeiture statute, 18 USCS § 1963(a), is different than that of the narcotics and general criminal forfeiture provisions of 21 USCS § 853 and 18 USCS § 982, respectively. Unlike the RICO statute, section 853(d) of Title 21 specifically provides a preponderance of the evidence standard for criminal forfeiture in narcotics cases. The Third Circuit has held that, while the preponderance standard applies to 21 USCS § 853 and 18 USCS § 982, the beyond a reasonable doubt standard applies to RICO forfeiture. *United States v. Pellulo*, 14 F.3d 881, 904–05 (3rd Cir. 1994), *United States v. Voigt*, 89 F.3d 1050, 1082–83 (3rd Cir. 1996).

If there is a guilty verdict, counsel may feel inclined to reach a stipulation with the government regarding forfeiture rather than proceeding to the forfeiture phase, on the theory that the jury has already found your client guilty and is therefore likely to give the government what it asks for on the forfeiture. While counsel should certainly take the opportunity to negotiate "a good deal" for her client on the forfeiture count, I urge counsel to consider the

Rule 32.2. Criminal Forfeiture

possibility that juries are often naturally inclined to compromise or "split the baby," if you will. Any doubts your arguments may have engendered during the trial proper may ultimately accrue to your client's benefit during the forfeiture phase. The jurors may have a latent feeling that a guilty verdict is punishment enough, and the defendant's family should not be rendered destitute as well. This could result in the jury rendering a forfeiture verdict in an amount far less than the government asked or in the jurors sparing the marital residence, for example, even where the standard of proof is less rigorous. For these reasons, counsel should consider being a little more hard-nosed in their post-verdict negotiations with the government on forfeiture. In other words, you may not be in as vulnerable a position vis-a-vis forfeiture as you think you are.

The remaining subdivisions of FRCrP 32.2 deal with the technical requirements for entry of a preliminary and final order of forfeiture. Following a guilty verdict that includes a jury determination that property is the proceeds of criminal activity, third parties have an opportunity to assert their right to the property in an ancillary proceeding. For example, a spouse may claim that certain property ordered forfeited is his or hers, rather than the defendant's, and that the property was the proceeds of legitimate activity and not used in connection with any criminal activity.

Counsel representing a third party claimant should refer to the forfeiture statute at issue to ensure that the relevant, time-sensitive procedures are followed. Because the ancillary proceedings are civil in nature, the Federal Rules of Civil Procedure apply. This means that, under FRCrP 32.2(c)(1)(B), the third party claimant may be entitled to conduct certain discovery procedures, such as depositions, that are unavailable to a defendant in a criminal case. The third party, however, is not entitled to a jury trial. The defendant has no standing in connection with third party proceedings, because his interest in the property has already been adjudicated. (Note: The conduct of third-party proceedings is beyond the scope of this commentary.)

If the defendant appeals his conviction, he should request a stay of the order of forfeiture pending appeal. The stay does not delay the third-party ancillary proceedings, but it ensures that no final transfer of the property, either to the government or a third-party, may occur unless and until the conviction and the forfeiture verdict are affirmed on appeal.

> **Lexis Search Tip**
>
> To use the Lexis Search Advisor to find detailed concepts in broader issues, do the following:
>
> 1. Click Search Advisor tab.
> 2. Click Criminal Law & Procedure.
> 3. Click Sentencing.
> 4. Click Forfeiture.
>
> Click on NITA and review Susan C. Wolfe's commentary on FRCrP 32.2 Criminal Forfeiture.

Rule 33. New Trial

On a defendant's motion, the court may grant a new trial to that defendant if the interests of justice so require. If trial was by the court without a jury, the court may—on defendant's motion for new trial—vacate the judgment, take additional testimony, and direct the entry of a new judgment. A motion for new trial based on newly discovered evidence may be made only within three years after the verdict or finding of guilty. But if an appeal is pending, the court may grant the motion only on remand of the case. A motion for a new trial based on any other grounds may be made only within 7 days after the verdict or finding of guilty or within such further time as the court may fix during the 7-day period.

Commentary

By Steven M. Statsinger
The Legal Aid Society, Federal Defender Division
Southern District of New York

FRCrP 33 sets the parameters for motions for a new trial in the district court. While the particular standard for granting an FRCrP 33 motion depends on the issue raised, in general the court can only grant a new trial if the "interests of justice so require."

Motions Based on Newly Discovered Evidence

FRCrP 33 motions based on newly discovered evidence must be filed within three years of the verdict. This time period is jurisdictional and cannot be extended. It is generally a good idea to plead a newly discovered evidence motion in the alternative, seeking either a new trial or an evidentiary hearing on the motion. Substantively, the motion must satisfy a five-part test: (1) the evidence must be newly discovered and not available at the time of trial; (2) the failure to learn of it cannot be due to a lack of diligence on the part of the defense; (3) the newly discovered evidence must be material; (4) it cannot be cumulative or merely impeaching; and (5) its impact must be such that there is a reasonable probability of an acquittal at a retrial.

(a) Standards for a Rule 33 motion.

The first requirement, that the evidence be newly discovered, is relatively straightforward. Information possessed by counsel but not presented at the trial, or possessed by the defendant but not disclosed to counsel, will fail this test.

Second, the failure to learn of the new evidence cannot be the result of a lack of diligence on the part of the defense in investigating the case and preparing for trial. Only ordinary diligence is required, however. This is readily satisfied if the evidence that serves as the basis for the motion did not exist or was deliberately withheld from the defense at the time of trial. Diligence is measured by the cumulative knowledge of both the defendant and counsel, as well as by the steps taken in preparing the case for trial.

Third, a successful motion must show that the newly discovered evidence is material, which means that it is relevant to substantial issues in dispute in the case, or would tend to influence the decision of the case. The motion must also show that the newly discovered evidence would be admissible at a new trial because inadmissible evidence will be deemed immaterial.

The fourth prong requires a showing that the newly discovered evidence is noncumulative and not merely impeachment evidence. To show that the new evidence is noncumulative, the motion must demonstrate that the particular point raised by the evidence was not adequately made at the trial, or that the damage it might have caused to the prosecution's case did not occur in some other way. A motion based on new impeachment material that would have further discredited a witness who was cross-examined with vigor at the trial will be denied because the new evidence does not go to the defendant's guilt. This particular hurdle can be overcome in cases where the newly discovered evidence is so powerful that it would thoroughly discredit an important prosecution witness and there is insufficient remaining evidence to support the conviction.

The fifth and final component is, in essence, a showing of prejudice. The new evidence must be so strong that there is a reasonable probability of an acquittal at a retrial. To sustain this burden, the motion should do more than demonstrate the strength of the new evidence; it should analyze the new evidence in light of the entire record, and particularly in light of the strength of the evidence adduced at trial.

(b) Motions based on a claim of perjured testimony.

If the FRCrP 33 motion is based on a claim that a government witness gave false testimony, or has since recanted, some courts apply the ordinary "reasonable probability of acquittal" standard if the government did not know of the perjury. Others apply a somewhat relaxed prejudice standard in this situation, so you should look carefully into the rule for your particular court. Courts are unanimous, however, in concluding that if the government solicits testimony that it knew or should have known was false, or permits unsolicited false testimony to go uncorrected, the prejudice standard is significantly relaxed. A new trial will be granted if there is any reasonable likelihood that the false testimony could have affected the judgment of the jury.

(c) Motions based on *Brady* violations.

FRCrP 33 motions are frequently based on the government's nondisclosure of information favorable to the defense under *Brady v. Maryland*, 373 U.S. 83, 10 L.Ed.2d 215, 83 S.Ct. 1194 (1963) and its progeny. In *United States v. Bagley*, 473 U.S. 667, 87 L.E.2d 481, 105 S.Ct. 3375 (1985), the United States Supreme Court announced a single prejudice standard covering all such cases, regardless of whether the exculpatory materials were specifically requested by the defense, responsive to a general defense request, or not requested by the defense at all. There must be a "reasonable probability that, had the evidence been disclosed to the defense, the result of the proceeding would have been different." *Bagley*, 473 U.S. at 682, 87 L.E.2d 494, 105 S.Ct. at 3383. The Court recognized that a more serious impairment to the adversary process occurs when the government withholds material responsive to a specific defense request, and thereby misleads the defense, but concluded that the standard was flexible enough to account for it, because "the reviewing court may consider directly any adverse effect that the prosecutor's failure to respond might have had on the preparation or presentation of the defendant's case." *Id.*

(D) Other grounds.

FRCrP 33 motions can also be based on newly discovered evidence that goes to an issue other than the defendant's guilt. For example, a motion could be based on new evidence affecting the court's resolution of a dispositive suppression or other pretrial motion. If the motion is based on one of these claims, the prejudice prong is satisfied by showing a reasonable probability that the outcome of the pretrial litigation would have been different if the newly discovered evidence had been considered.

FRCrP 33 motions can raise claims about conduct of the jury, but such claims are restricted by FRE 606(b), which prohibits a juror from impeaching the verdict by testifying about "any matter or statement occurring during the course of the jury's deliberations" other than any "extraneous prejudicial information" or "outside influence." To show prejudice, the motion must demonstrate that an improper outside influence affected the jury's decision. A motion may also be based on newly discovered evidence that a juror failed to disclose material information, or gave untruthful answers, during voir dire. Prejudice exists if the newly discovered information reveals actual bias on the part of the juror.

(e) Interaction with the direct appeal.

The district court lacks the authority to grant a motion based on newly discovered evidence if it is filed when an appeal is pending, unless the court of appeals remands the case to the district court. Some circuits will entertain a motion to remand a pending case to the district court for the purpose of ruling on an FRCrP 33 motion while in others it might be better to withdraw the appeal by stipulation without prejudice to reinstatement after the court decides the motion. If the FRCrP 33 motion is filed after the appeal has been decided, or if no notice of appeal was filed, there is no bar to the district court's jurisdiction other than the three-year time limit.

Motions Alleging Trial Error

Motions for a new trial based on any ground other than newly discovered evidence must be made within seven calendar days of the verdict unless, within the seven-day period, the court grants an extension of time. Typically such motions are based on an error that occurred in the trial court.

Before a court can grant such a motion it must find prejudice under the same standards that an appellate court would apply under FRCrP 52. Tactical considerations must be taken into account to a much greater extent than with motions based on newly discovered evidence. Since it is unlikely that the court will conclude that it has committed an error so serious as to require a new trial, there is often little to gain by filing an FRCrP 33 motion if the issue was fully litigated and is going to be pursued on appeal. Indeed, it may be disadvantageous to do so, since the motion will give the government advance notice of the issues to be raised on appeal and additional time to formulate its response.

A motion based on a trial error is more likely to be successful if based on changed circumstances, *e.g.*, if the court admitted evidence subject to connection but the connection never materialized; or if the government's theory of culpability was other than anticipated or if it changed during the trial.

An FRCrP 33 motion can sometimes be tactically advantageous. It can be used to amplify the factual record for the appeal by including information that would not otherwise appear in the trial transcript: the content of off-the-record or ex parte communications, omissions by defense counsel that constitute ineffectiveness; or information suggesting government misconduct, such as tampering with defense witnesses, withholding discoverable material, or violating a pretrial agreement. It is also possible that a motion raising an error that was not objected to at trial will preserve the issue for appeal.

Another advantage to FRCrP 33 motions is that, for certain claims, the defendant benefits from a standard of review that is more favorable than that available in an appellate court. The court of appeals has no power to vacate a conviction based on the weight of the evidence; it is limited to determining whether the evidence was legally sufficient, and in making this determination it views the evidence in a light most favorable to the government. But a district court can grant a new trial under the "interests of justice" standard by finding that there was a miscarriage of justice based on an issue that a court of appeals could not reach. For example, the trial judge can find that the evidence preponderates against the jury's guilty verdict, and it is not required to view the evidence in the government's favor in making this finding.

Finally, an FRCrP 33 motion cannot be used to seek the withdrawal of a guilty plea, an issue that is governed by FRCrP 32(e). Nor can it be used to seek a resentencing or the correction of sentencing error. The preference in the federal system is that sentencing errors be corrected through the appellate process. A tightly circumscribed procedure for correcting a sentence in the district court is set out in FRCrP 35(c).

Rule 34. Arrest of Judgment

The court on motion of a defendant shall arrest judgment if the indictment or information does not charge an offense or if the court was without jurisdiction of the offense charged. The motion in arrest of judgment shall be made within 7 days after verdict or finding of guilty, or after plea of guilty or nolo contendere, or within such further time as the court may fix during the 7-day period.

Commentary

By Prof. Inga L. Parsons
New York University School of Law

An arrest of judgment motion is a post-verdict challenge on either of two grounds: (1) the indictment or information fails to charge an offense; or (2) the court is without jurisdiction. It is determined on the face of what is called "the record alone," meaning the indictment, plea, and verdict—and sometimes sentence (although in federal court a felony or Class A misdemeanor sentence necessarily takes place more than thirty-five days after the verdict or plea because of Federal Sentencing Guidelines time periods, and it would not be part of the record at the time an arrest of judgment motion is filed).

When to Use an Arrest of Judgment

An arrest of judgment motion is not often employed by the defense because jurisdictional and indictment defects are usually litigated before the verdict as pretrial motions under FRCrP 12. Conceptually an arrest of judgment exists to challenge defects in the indictment based upon knowledge obtained during or after the conclusion of the trial; otherwise, a pretrial motion would be filed.

Indeed, if the defect was known prior to trial, failure to make such pretrial challenges to charges, etc., may result in a denial of an arrest of judgment motion due to a liberal reading of the indictment and a higher standard of review. "[C]ourts of the United States long ago withdrew their hospitality toward technical claims of invalidity of an indictment first raised after trial, absent a clear showing of substantial prejudice to the accused—such as a showing that the indictment is 'so obviously defective that by no reasonable construction can it be said to charge the offense for which conviction was had.'" *United States v. Wydermeyer*, 51 F.3d 319 (2d. Cir. 1995).

If an FRCrP 12 motion challenging the indictment or jurisdiction is made and is either reserved or denied, defense counsel should renew the FRCrP 12 motion, as well as file a formal written motion to arrest judgment under FRCrP 34. Even if the court finds the defense has waived the issue for failing to raise it earlier or defense counsel neglected to make an FRCrP 34 motion at all, it may still amount to plain error.

To avoid such waivers or litigation under a higher standard, it is essential that in every case defense counsel review the indictment thoroughly, as an initial matter, to ascertain whether it makes out an offense and whether the court has jurisdiction. Defense counsel should grid out the elements of the offense and how the case law defines those elements. The mind-set of defense counsel should not be, "Is my client guilty?" Rather, "Can the government make out a prima facie case given the elements and alleged facts?"

Jurisdiction Considerations

A few areas to pay particular attention involve jurisdiction. Some offenses are federal because of their occurrence on federal property. This is particularly true where an otherwise state offense is assimilated under the Assimilated Crimes Act because it has occurred on federal property. *See* 18 USCS § 13. The buzzwords are "within the special maritime and territorial jurisdiction of the United States." 18 USCS § 7. Defense counsel should assure themselves that indeed the property where the offense is alleged to have occurred is federal. Nothing should be assumed. Some property appearing to be federal is actually state land, and the extent of the federal government's right or authority over that property may need to be determined by a lease contract or easement rights. Some property abutting federal property is still state property and not federal property; for example, the sidewalks in New York are owned by the city, even those directly in front of the federal courthouse.

Federal jurisdiction may hinge on statutory interpretation. For example, with respect to an otherwise state offense, such as robbery, being brought under the Hobbs Act makes it a federal crime. A violation of the Hobbs Act requires that the offense affect interstate commerce, etc. Some offenses, particularly those set forth in the Code of Federal Regulations, may require that there be conspicuous notice posted by the federal government in order to prosecute.

The defense counsel will often be in a stronger position to request a motion to arrest judgment where they have asked for a bill of particulars under FRCrP 7(f) to ascertain the nature of the charges. Many of these requests are routinely denied, and there are some U.S. Attorney's Offices which refuse to answer bills of particulars as a matter of policy. Where there is an issue as to the elements and clarity is required, the defense should make such a request if there is nothing else to bolster a motion to dismiss or a motion to arrest judgment later on.

The conventional wisdom (and the explicit rule of most circuits) is that consideration of a motion to arrest judgment should not be based on a review of the evidence of the case. However, in making arguments to arrest judgment, defense counsel should incorporate the evidence presented, or not presented, at trial to support the motion. Indeed, the defense may need to show how the defect was raised as a result of evidence during the trial to explain why there was no motion to dismiss under FRCrP 12. In addition, as with any argument to the court, the weaker the prosecution's case, the more likely the court will grant such a motion. (Just as the more drugs found in the trunk, the more likely the court will deny a motion to suppress.) Judges simply are not immune to the ends justifying the means, providing there is a legal hook.

Prosecutors, on the other hand, should be vigilant in constraining defense counsel's argument to the face of the indictment and verdict. An FRCrP 34 motion is not considered an appropriate challenge for errors in the admission of evidence, double jeopardy challenges, or procedural improprieties—only the two grounds listed above. Prosecutors should object to any other challenges that are the basis for a defense motion to arrest judgment.

Using a Rule 29 Motion Instead of an Arrest of Judgment

If, however, the true nature of the motion is insufficiency of evidence, the defense should make such arguments in a motion for a judgment of acquittal under FRCrP 29. A motion for a judgment of acquittal is much better for the defense than an arrest of judgment. A motion for judgment of acquittal that is granted before the jury's verdict is unappealable and double jeopardy precludes a retrial. (The government can appeal a judgment of acquittal granted after a guilty verdict. See the Commentary for FRCrP 29.) A motion for arrest of judgment under FRCrP 34 is appealable, and retrial is not barred. There may be times when both an FRCrP 29 motion and an FRCrP 34 motion will be made in the same case.

Time Limits on Rule 34 Motions

An arrest of judgment motion must be made within seven days from the verdict. Like the time periods in FRCrP 29 requesting a directed verdict after discharge of the jury and FRCrP 33 requesting a new trial, the time periods control jurisdiction. If the defense fails to make the motion within seven days or the court fails to extend the period within those seven days, the court will lack jurisdiction to hear the motion. There are no exceptions, even for excusable neglect by the defense lawyer or bad information from the court clerk. Defense counsel should automatically ask for suitably lengthy extensions—ideally at the time the verdict is entered. It is helpful for the defense attorney to have a verdict checklist when there is a conviction: poll the jury, renew FRCrP 29 motion and any reserved or denied motions, ask for extensions of all post-trial filings, including extensions under FRCrP 29, 33, and 34.

FRCrP 12(b)(2) allows the court to notice a lack of jurisdiction or failure to charge an offense at any time during the pendency of the proceedings. Thus, FRCrP 34 seems to narrow FRCrP 12(b)(2) as to the timing of a motion to challenge jurisdiction or the indictment for failure to charge an offense. If the seven-day time period has expired but the court has not imposed a sentence, the defense can attempt to argue that the case is still pending and the court should hear the motion to dismiss for lack of jurisdiction or failure to charge an offense under FRCrP 12(b)(2) despite the seven-day restriction under FRCrP 34. There is at least a thirty-five day delay between a verdict and the imposition of the sentence in federal cases to allow for the preparation of a presentence report, *see* FRCrP 32(6)(A), so the argument for dismissal under FRCrP 12(b)(2) would effectively extend the seven-day time period under FRCrP 34 an additional twenty-eight days or until the date fixed for sentencing.

The prosecution should argue against application of FRCrP 12 when defense counsel has missed the seven-day cutoff by arguing that FRCrP 34 specifically sets forth the triggering of the time period from the verdict or plea and not the sentencing; otherwise FRCrP 12(b)(2) would eviscerate FRCrP 34. In fact, FRCrP 34 was amended to specifically overrule the Supreme Court's decision in *Lott v. United States*, 367 U.S. 421, 6 L. Ed. 2d 940, 81 S. Ct. 1563 (1961) where the Court held that a plea was not a determination of guilt until after the sentence. The defense counsel are unlikely to prevail under FRCrP 12 unless they can make a showing that the information needed to make the determination only became available to the defense at that time. Filing of a motion under FRCrP 34 tolls the time within which an appeal needs to be taken.

Rule 35. Correction or Reduction of Sentence

(a) Correction of a sentence on remand. The court shall correct a sentence that is determined on appeal under 18 U.S.C. 3742 to have been imposed in violation of law, to have been imposed as a result of an incorrect application of the sentencing guidelines, or to be unreasonable, upon remand of the case to the court—

(1) for imposition of a sentence in accord with the findings of the court of appeals; or

(2) for further sentencing proceedings if, after such proceedings, the court determines that the original sentence was incorrect.

(b) Reduction of sentence for substantial assistance. If the Government so moves within one year after the sentence is imposed, the court may reduce a sentence to reflect a defendant's subsequent substantial assistance in investigating or prosecuting another person, in accordance with the guidelines and policy statements issued by the Sentencing Commission under 28 U.S.C. § 994. The court may consider a government motion to reduce a sentence made one year or more after the sentence is imposed if the defendant's substantial assistance involves information or evidence not known by the defendant until one year or more after sentence is imposed. In evaluating whether substantial assistance has been rendered, the court may consider the defendant's presentence assistance. In applying this subdivision, the court may reduce the sentence to a level below that established by statute as a minimum sentence.

(c) Correction of sentence by sentencing court. The court, acting within 7 days after the imposition of sentence, may correct a sentence that was imposed as a result of arithmetical, technical, or other clear error.

Commentary

By Prof. Inga L. Parsons
New York University School of Law

FRCrP 35, detailing the procedures for correcting and reducing federal sentences, was substantially amended to reflect changes brought on by the implementation of the Federal Sentencing Guidelines as part of the Sentencing Reform Act of 1984. *See* the Commentary for FRCrP 32. Under the original FRCrP 35, the district judge had a great deal of discretion to reduce a sentence he or she imposed providing the judge acted within 120 days from imposition of the original sentence. The judge could amend a sentence based on a number of considerations including the discovery of new information as well as reduce a sentence from incarceration to probation. Any sentence imposed in an illegal manner could be corrected within the 120-day period and an illegal sentence could be corrected at any time. The objective of the old FRCrP 35 was to "give every convicted defendant a second round before the sentencing judge, and [afford] the judge an opportunity to reconsider the sentence in the light of any further information about the defendant . . ." *See* Advisory Committee Notes *citing United States v. Ellenbogan*, 390 F.2d 537, 543 (2nd Cir. 1968).

Grounds for a Rule 35 Motion

Today, in the era of the Federal Sentencing Guidelines where federal sentences are subject to formulaic calculations and substantial appellate scrutiny, FRCrP 35 provides a much more narrow basis on which a district judge is able to correct or reduce a sentence. The paramount legislative objective of the present reincarnation of FRCrP 35 appears to be finality in sentencing. The sentence ordinarily must be appealed and the appellate court must find that the sentence was: (1) imposed in violation of law; (2) the result of an incorrect application of the sentencing guidelines; or (3) unreasonable. FRCrP 35(a). The case is then remanded to the sentencing judge for either resentencing pursuant to the appellate court's ruling or additional sentencing proceedings if the original sentence was incorrect. FRCrP 35(a)(1), (2).

Under the current version of FRCrP 35, the district judge is no longer authorized to reduce a sentence from incarceration to probation or to reduce a sentence on its own motion or a party's motion, except when the defendant cooperates (*see* discussion below). The amendments to FRCrP 35 also eliminated the judge's ability to resentence a defendant based on new factual information not known at the time of sentencing. Elimination of newly discovered information as a basis for resentencing places a premium on the parties to anticipate possible changes and to investigate thoroughly a case in advance so that all of the relevant information is before the judge at the time of the sentencing.

Avoiding Sentencing Errors

Despite counsel's best efforts to have accurate information before the judge at the time of the sentencing, there are times when a factor relied on in sentencing turns out to be erroneous. For example, the parties and the judge may have expected the defendant's pending state offense to run concurrently with the federal offense in fashioning a federal sentence, yet the state offense ultimately is to run consecutively. Under the present version of FRCrP 35 there is no provision to allow the judge to reduce the sentence to reflect the court's original intentions unless the mistake can be categorized as an "arithmetical, technical or other clear error" under FRCrP 35(c). Judges who have categorized an original sentence as erroneous under FRCrP 35(c) in order to reduce a sentence have been overturned. See, e.g., United States v. Abreu-Cabrera, 64 F.3d 67 (2nd Cir. 1995) (Second Circuit reversed where district judge declared assessment of sixteen-point enhancement for aggravated felony a mistake in the original sentence under FRCrP 35 and imposed a lower sentence).

Moreover, the district judge can only correct a sentence imposed as a result of an arithmetical, technical, or other clear error within seven days from the imposition of the sentence. The seven days runs from the oral pronouncement of the sentence, not from the date the judgment is filed. See United States v. Abreu-Cabrera, 64 F.3d 67, 73 (2d Cir. 1995). Like the seven-day time periods in FRCrP 29, 33, and 34, the time period under FRCrP 35(c) is jurisdictional. However, unlike FRCrP 29, 33, and 34, there is no provision in FRCrP 35 for a court-ordered extension made within the seven-day period. If the seven-day period has elapsed under FRCrP 35(c), the court will lack jurisdiction to correct even obvious errors, and must await the outcome of any appeal, although the defendant might have a remedy for a plainly illegal sentence under 28 USCS § 2255.

Counsel should be particularly cautious when the judge is fashioning a sentence relying on a subsequent event such as a Bureau of Prisons determination to credit a defendant's pretrial detention toward his federal sentence or imposition of a state sentence to run concurrently with the federal sentence. Before the judge imposes such a sentence, counsel should be confident that the contingency would take place. When possible, the sentencing hearing should be adjourned to a date less than seven days from the expected event, so that errors can be corrected within the seven-day time period under FRCrP 35(c).

Both parties should take verbatim notes on the court's oral pronouncement of sentence and subsequently read the written judgment and commitment order very carefully for any errors. If there is ambiguity in the court's pronouncement of the sentence, the prosecution should endeavor to make the judge clarify the sentence on the record at the time of sentencing. It may or may not be in the defendant's best interest to have the court clarify the sentence, since ambiguity that results in a more lenient sentence would, of course, be preferable to the defendant.

The defense lawyer has an obligation to represent the client zealously within the bounds of the law. *See, e.g.*, Model Code of Professional Responsibility Canon 7. Failing to notify the court of a favorable ambiguity or error would ordinarily be within the bounds of the law as opposed to presenting or facilitating perjured testimony, the sine qua non of the unethical defense lawyer. Defense counsel should be cautious not to mislead the court and should also be mindful that there is an affirmative obligation to notify the court when a defense lawyer is aware of legal authority in the controlling jurisdiction directly adverse to the defense's position. *See* Model Rules of Professional Responsibility DR 3.3(a)(3).

When the written judgment and commitment order does not match the oral pronouncement, the judge's oral pronouncement will control. However, it is the written judgment and commitment order that is given to the Bureau of Prisons to carry out the sentence and defense counsel should ensure that it does not indicate a higher sentence than ordered by the court and includes the appropriate fine, special assessment, and supervised release term. If the errors in the sentence or judgment are purely clerical they may be corrected at any time pursuant to FRCrP 36. *See* the Commentary for FRCrP 36.

Strategies to Reduce a Sentence

Conceptually, FRCrP 35(c) exists for the sentencing judge to correct obvious or clear errors before an appeal must be filed rather than require the case to be reviewed by the appellate court and then handed back down. FRCrP 35(c) corrections are supposedly not an opportunity for the court to reconsider the guidelines or simply change its mind. However, given the current state of FRCrP 35, there is no other provision available to modify a sentence in a noncooperation case. As a result, defense counsel must become extremely creative (and diplomatic) to have a sentence modified or corrected at the trial level.

Defense counsel should try to couch the request for a reduction in sentence as a technical error, *e.g.*, miscalculation of the amount of drugs that compelled the guideline range for the offense or a mistake in the reading of state sentencing laws on concurrent sentences. Even so, a technical correction must be made within seven days from sentencing under FRCrP 35. If the new information is discovered after seven days, defense counsel can try to convince the prosecutor and the judge that the new information should be treated as a clerical error that may be corrected at any time under FRCrP 36. Such a correction under FRCrP 36 would have to be with the consent of opposing counsel because it would not withstand appellate scrutiny. *See, e.g., United States v. Weber*, 51 F.3d 342 (2nd Cir. 1995) (FRCrP 36 did not allow the district court to amend sentence imposed months earlier even though judge had mistakenly assumed that defendants would get credit for federal pretrial detention and would have downwardly departed to reduce sentence for lack of pretrial detention credit at initial sentencing).

Defense counsel can make the pitch to the prosecution and judge that a corrected sentence would further "honesty in sentencing"—one of the main principles underlying the implementation of the Federal Sentencing Guidelines. *See* USSG Ch. 1, Pt. A.

Cooperation Under Rule 35

Cooperation is the one area where FRCrP 35 has expanded the district court's authority to reduce a sentence, although such a motion can only be made by the prosecution. The government now has within one year after sentence to move for a downward departure under 28 USCS § 994 (*see* 28 USCS § 994(n), authorizing substantial assistance departures under the Federal Sentencing Guidelines where the defendant substantially assists in the investigation or prosecution of another person). Moreover, there is no longer a requirement that the court rule on a post-sentencing substantial assistance motion within that same one-year time limit, further expanding the time in which the parties can demonstrate substantial assistance. Indeed, the court may even consider a motion for reduction of sentence filed more than one year from the imposition of the sentence if the substantial assistance involved information not known by the defendant until that time. FRCrP 35(b). Under the new FRCrP 35, the court may aggregate presentencing cooperation with post-sentencing cooperation, where presentencing cooperation did not previously result in a reduced sentence.

In sum, the only viable reduction in sentence available without prevailing on an appeal (an extremely unlikely event) is cooperation.

Defense counsel thus should explore the possibility of the defendant cooperating as a means to effect a just sentence in light of newly discovered evidence or other sentencing error not available for reduction under FRCrP 35(c). If the prosecutor is sympathetic to the change in circumstances, or new evidence, they may be willing to move for a reduction in sentence under FRCrP 35(b) on the basis of some cooperative efforts by the defendant. A prosecutor's motion for reduction of sentence based on this cooperation would give the judge a means not only to correct the sentence to reflect the cooperation but also to accommodate the new information and go below any mandatory minimum. For a more detailed discussion on cooperation, *see* the Commentary for FRCrP 32.

Rule 36. Clerical Mistakes

Clerical mistakes in judgments, orders, or other parts of the record and errors in the record arising from oversight or omission may be corrected by the court at any time and after such notice, if any, as the court orders.

Commentary

By Prof. Inga L. Parsons
New York University School of Law

FRCrP 36 is a short but important rule regarding the correction of clerical mistakes in judgments, orders and other parts of the record. Mistakes arising from "oversight or omission" may be corrected "at any time" and without notice to the parties unless ordered by the court. FRCrP 36. Much of the litigation surrounding the rule is what constitutes a clerical error. The strictest interpretations of this rule do not allow for any corrections that are not clearly errors of the clerk, as opposed to errors of the judge. Other interpretations consider it the court's duty and power to correct its own errors and offer broader considerations. Counsel should be aware of the decisions in their circuit and how clerical error has been defined.

Errors in Dates

Errors in dates are usually the least controversial use of the rule. Defense counsel should be vigilant when the dates can affect the substance of the case or provide a strategic opportunity. If the prosecution claims that an erroneous date listed in an affidavit accompanying a search warrant application was a clerical error, this may be an opportunity for the defense to request a hearing on the matter if timing of the warrant is important. A hearing would allow the defense an opportunity to cross-examine the case agent or other officers in advance of trial. Similarly, if the prosecution claims that the dates in the indictment are clerical errors, the defense may wish to demand that the case be re-presented before the grand jury (resulting in additional sworn testimony by case agents and officers) if the date would result in a variance in the charges, or, at a minimum, the opportunity to review the ordinarily unavailable grand jury testimony to ascertain that the error is, indeed, clerical. If the error occurred with the officer, rather than the typist or the court clerk, this may be grounds to show that the officer is sloppy and unreliable. Defense counsel should then object simply to correcting the document since it is not strictly a clerical error and evidence of the error may be helpful in impeaching the officer.

Indictment Errors

If there are indictment errors where the proof at trial differs from the date or other information in the indictment, it may rise to a level of impermissible variance. In cases where impermissible variance is alleged, the defense should identify the variance and request a motion for a judgment of acquittal at the end of the government's case-in-chief arguing that the government has failed to make out a prima facie case on the charges in the indictment. If the motion is denied, defense counsel should ensure that the jury is properly instructed on what must be found in order to convict the defendant of the charges set out in the indictment, and object to any instructions which allow for conviction based on the varied information.

Sentencing Errors

A common use of FRCrP 36 is to correct sentences. The type of errors that arise in judgments are plentiful including times when the oral sentence does not match the written judgment, numbers stating the offense or sentence are transposed, or the wrong section of the law is listed. FRCrP 35(c) provides for correction of a sentence that was imposed as a result of "arithmetical, technical, or other clear error" but the court must make the correction within seven days after sentencing. Conceptually FRCrP 35(c) is available to correct the original sentence where there is a clear or

Rule 36. Clerical Mistakes

obvious error in sentencing. FRCrP 36 is available to correct the judgment and commitment order that incorporated the original sentence. Most courts hold that it is the transcription of the sentence that can be corrected by FRCrP 36, otherwise FRCrP 36 would eviscerate the time deadline of FRCrP 35(c), since an FRCrP 36 correction can be made at any time but a correction under FRCrP 35(c) has a seven-day limit that cannot be extended. Given the restrictions of FRCrP 35 in terms of correcting sentences, defense counsel may have to be creative in the use of FRCrP 36 to modify an imposed sentence. *See* the Commentary for FRCrP 35.

When the written judgment is inaccurate and does not reflect the oral sentence, a correction under FRCrP 36 is appropriate. When the judge's sentence is in itself ambiguous or inaccurate, an FRCrP 36 correction may or may not be proper depending on the circuit and the nature of the ambiguity or error. If the correction requires in essence substituting the right number for the wrong number, FRCrP 36 may be used. However, if the order changes the structure of the sentence, even if the length of the sentence is the same, that has been determined to go beyond a clerical correction under FRCrP 36. *See, e.g., United States v. Burd*, 86 F.3d 285 (2nd Cir. 1996) (change in sentence from twelve concurrent seventy-eight-month sentences to six concurrent sixty-month sentences to be followed by six concurrent eighteen-month sentences was not correction of a clerical error under FRCrP 36; thus, court lacked jurisdiction to correct sentence).

Transcript Errors

An FRCrP 36 issue may arise when the transcript of the proceedings does not reflect accurately what transpired. If the error is undisputed, *e.g.*, whether the defendant was present, whether defense counsel appeared, etc., the correction is easily made. It gets trickier when parties' recollections differ from the court reporter's transcript. Counsel for both sides should review the transcript of the proceedings as soon as possible and request correction of any errors immediately. To assist in evaluating the record, it is advisable for counsel or a paralegal to take excellent notes at a hearing or trial that can be compared to the transcript. The district court settles any differences and will conform the record to its findings. *See* FRAP 10(e). Resolution of the discrepancies may require a hearing. In some districts, notably the Southern District of New

York, it is the practice for judges to be given a transcription of their jury instructions before a final transcript is made in order for the judge to review the jury charges and make corrections. If this is the practice in your district, counsel for both sides should ask to be notified of any changes that have been made to the record by the judge.

Counsel on both sides should review motions for correction of clerical errors critically to ensure that what is being requested is truly correction of a clerical error rather than a request to have the court reconsider a ruling or sentence disguised as a motion to correct a clerical error under FRCrP 36. For example, in *United States v. Jones*, 608 F.2d 386 (9th Cir. 1979) the government requested the district court vacate its suppression order as a correction of a clerical error under FRCrP 36, when the practical effect was asking the district court to reconsider its ruling. The fact that a motion is entitled, "Correction of Clerical Error," is certainly not dispositive, and opposing counsel should object to any motion that is in reality a request for rehearing or reconsideration.

VIII. Appeal

Rule 37. Taking Appeal; and Petition for Writ of Certiorari

[Abrogated]

Rule 38. Stay of Execution

(a) **Death.** A sentence of death shall be stayed if an appeal is taken from the conviction or sentence.

(b) **Imprisonment.** A sentence of imprisonment shall be stayed if an appeal is taken from the conviction or sentence and the defendant is released pending disposition of appeal pursuant to Rule 9(b) of the Federal Rules of Appellate Procedure. If not stayed, the court may recommend to the Attorney General that the defendant be retained at, or transferred to, a place of confinement near the place of trial or the place where an appeal is to be heard, for a period reasonably necessary to permit the defendant to assist in the preparation of an appeal to the court of appeals.

(c) **Fine.** A sentence to pay a fine or a fine and costs, if an appeal is taken, may be stayed by the district court or by the court of appeals upon such terms as the court deems proper. The court may require the defendant pending appeal to deposit the whole or any part of the fine and costs in the registry of the district court, or to give bond for the payment thereof, or to submit to an examination of assets, and it may make any appropriate order to restrain the defendant from dissipating such defendant's assets.

(d) **Probation.** A sentence of probation may be stayed if an appeal from the conviction or sentence is taken. If the sentence is stayed, the court shall fix the terms of the stay.

(e) **Notice to victims and restitution.** A sanction imposed as part of the sentence pursuant to 18 U.S.C. 3555 or 3556 may, if an appeal of the conviction or sentence is taken, be stayed by the district court or by the court of appeals upon such terms as the court finds appropriate. The court may issue such orders as may be reasonably necessary to ensure compliance with the sanction upon disposition of the appeal, including the entering of a restraining order or an injunction or requiring a deposit in whole or in part of the monetary amount involved into the registry of the district court or execution of a performance bond.

(f) Disabilities. A civil or employment disability arising under a Federal statute by reason of the defendant's conviction or sentence, may, if an appeal is taken, be stayed by the district court or by the court of appeals upon such terms as the court finds appropriate. The court may enter a restraining order or an injunction, or take any other action that may be reasonably necessary to protect the interest represented by the disability pending disposition of the appeal.

Commentary

By Steven M. Statsinger
The Legal Aid Society, Federal Defender Division
Southern District of New York

This rule authorizes stays pending appeal for most, but not all, aspects of the sentence imposed.

(a) Death sentence.

Under FRCrP 38(a), a death sentence is automatically stayed if an appeal is taken, either of the conviction or the sentence.

(b) Sentence of imprisonment.

Under FRCrP 38(b), a sentence of imprisonment is stayed if the defendant is released on bail pending appeal. Defendants convicted of crimes of violence, offenses for which the maximum sentence is life imprisonment or death, or narcotics offenses for which the maximum authorized penalty is ten years or more are categorically precluded from bail pending appeal. *See* 18 USCS §§ 3142(f)(1), 3143(b)(2).

For the remaining defendants, bail pending appeal may be set if the defendant can show that: (1) there is clear and convincing evidence that he is not a flight risk or a danger to the community; (2) the appeal is not for the purpose of delay; and (3) the appeal raises a "substantial question of law or fact" that is likely to result in a reversal, a new trial, a noncustodial sentence, or a sentence that will be shorter than the appellate process. 18 USCS § 3143(b)(1).

Rule 38. Stay of Execution

If the trial court denies the application for bail pending appeal, counsel can make a motion for bail in the court of appeals under FRAP 9(b). If the conviction and/or sentence are affirmed, the district court will set a surrender date, and any application for bail pending certiorari would have to be made at that time. The statutory standard for bail pending certiorari is the same as those for bail pending appeal.

In light of the strict standard, bail pending appeal is not often granted. A common alternative is a stay pending execution of the sentence, better known as a "voluntary surrender." While voluntary surrenders are not addressed in the Federal Rules of Criminal Procedure, the Bail Reform Act authorizes them. *See, e.g.*, 18 USCS § 3143(a) (discussing release pending "imposition or execution" of sentence). If the defendant has been on release pending the imposition of sentence, the court can continue release until a date certain, on which the defendant is expected to surrender to the authorities to begin serving the sentence. The court can permit a surrender directly to the designated facility or can order that the defendant surrender to the local United States Marshal on the appointed date. Because the statutory standard for bail pending execution of the sentence is more relaxed than that for release pending appeal, many judges will permit a voluntary surrender even after denying a motion for bail pending appeal.

(c) Fines, restitution, and costs.

Where a stay pending appeal is denied, but the sentence imposed was short and the case presents substantial sentencing issues, counsel should consider moving in the court of appeals for an expedited appeal so the appeal can be heard before the sentence runs. In the rare case where there are substantial appellate issues relating both to a short sentence and the trial, counsel can ask the court of appeals to bifurcate the appeal, so that the sentencing appeal can be heard on an expedited basis, and the appeal of the trial can be heard later.

Under FRCrP 38(c) and (e), fines and restitution orders can be stayed pending appeal. In these cases, the court is free to condition the stay with any terms thought necessary to ensure the payment of the penalty if it is ultimately upheld on appeal. These could include: requiring the defendant to deposit some or all of the money with the court; requiring the defendant to post a bond; requiring the defendant to submit to an examination of assets; or entering an order restraining the defendant from disposing of any assets pending appeal. Since, under 18 USCS § 3612(f), fines and restitution accrue interest, any stay should make clear that the accrual of interest is stayed as well.

Two rarely invoked statutes, 28 USCS § 1918(b) and 26 USCS § 7201, authorize the court to order the defendant to pay the costs of prosecution. FRCrP 38(c) permits a stay pending appeal of an order imposing costs, subject to the same terms as the stay of a fine.

Financial penalties work a hardship on wealthy and indigent defendants alike, and counsel should consider seeking a stay even if representing a client who has no immediate source of funds to pay the penalty. Increasingly, courts are ordering incarcerated defendants to make fine and/or restitution payments from their rather insignificant prison earnings, or from their inmate commissary accounts. It is advisable, in the first instance, to ask the sentencing court to exercise its authority in fixing a payment schedule (*see* 18 USCS § 3572(d) (fines); 18 USCS § 3664(f)(2) (restitution)) and order that payments not commence until a reasonable period after the defendant is released from custody. If the court declines, and there are appellate issues surrounding the financial penalty, then a stay should be sought under FRCrP 38(c) or (e).

(d) Probation.

FRCrP 38(d) authorizes a stay of a sentence of probation pending appeal. The statute enumerating the conditions of probation, 18 USCS § 3563, makes clear that probation involves a significant deprivation of liberty. This is particularly true in light of USSG § 5C1.1, which often requires a period of home detention or confinement in a halfway house as a condition of probation. Accordingly, if there are significant appellate issues likely either to result in a reversal of the conviction or a reduction in the period of probation, counsel should not hesitate to seek a stay of probation pending appeal.

(e) Civil disabilities.

A number of federal statutes impose civil or employment disabilities as a result of the defendant's conviction or sentence. *See, e.g.*, 12 USCS § 1829(a) (restricting bank employment after conviction of certain financial offenses); 21 USCS §§ 862 and 862a (denial of federal benefits on conviction of a narcotics offense). Under FRCrP 38(f) the court can stay any such disability pending appeal, but can also enter any order, including a restraining order or injunction, necessary to protect the interest represented by the disability pending appeal.

(f) Other components of the sentence.

There are two commonly imposed components of a federal sentence not mentioned in FRCrP 38. The first is supervised release. While ordinarily supervised release follows a sentence of imprisonment, which can itself be stayed under FRCrP 38(b), occasionally a defendant will be sentenced to time served or zero days' imprisonment, to be followed by supervised release. This will occur where the defendant has served the entire incarceration portion of the sentence awaiting trial and sentencing, or where there is no other lawful way to fashion a noncustodial sentence because the defendant was convicted of one of the offenses for which probation is illegal. *See* 18 USCS § 3561(a)(enumerating offenses for which probation is not authorized). Since supervised release represents as great a restriction of liberty as probation, counsel should vigorously argue for a stay of a sentence of supervised release by analogy to FRCrP 38(d). The rule is also silent on the mandatory special assessment required by 18 USCS § 3013. But since the special assessment is similar to a fine, counsel could argue for a stay of the special assessment by analogy to FRCrP 38(c).

Lexis Search Tip

To do a word search of the Federal Rules – Federal Rules of Criminal Procedure, do the following:

1. Click Federal Legal – U.S.

2. Click United States Code Service (USCS) Materials.

3. Click USCS – Federal Rules Annotated.

Type in the search: death w/3 stayed w/3 appeal. Select the first of the two retrieved documents displaying FRCrP 38. Sentence and Judgment. Click on "Review expert commentary from The National Institute for Trial Advocacy", which appears just before Rule 38, and view the commentary on Rule 38 Stay of Execution written by Steven M. Statsinger.

Rule 39. Supervision of Appeal

[Abrogated]

IX. Supplementary and Special Proceedings

Rule 40. Commitment to Another District

(a) Appearance before Federal Magistrate Judge. If a person is arrested in a district other than that in which the offense is alleged to have been committed, that person shall be taken without unnecessary delay before the nearest available federal magistrate judge, in accordance with the provisions of Rule 5. Preliminary proceedings concerning the defendant shall be conducted in accordance with Rules 5 and 5.1, except that if no preliminary examination is held because an indictment has been returned or an information filed or because the defendant elects to have the preliminary examination conducted in the district in which the prosecution is pending, the person shall be held to answer upon a finding that such person is the person named in the indictment, information or warrant. If held to answer, the defendant shall be held to answer in the district court in which the prosecution is pending—provided that a warrant is issued in that district if the arrest was made without a warrant—upon production of the warrant or a certified copy thereof. The warrant or certified copy may be produced by facsimile transmission.

(b) Statement by Federal Magistrate Judge. In addition to the statements required by Rule 5, the federal magistrate judge shall inform the defendant of the provisions of Rule 20.

(c) Papers. If a defendant is held or discharged, the papers in the proceeding and any bail taken shall be transmitted to the clerk of the district court in which the prosecution is pending.

(d) Arrest of probationer or supervised releasee. If a person is arrested for a violation of probation or supervised release in a district other than the district having jurisdiction, such person must be taken without unnecessary delay before the nearest available federal magistrate judge. The person may be released under Rule 46(c). The federal magistrate judge shall:

(1) Proceed under Rule 32.1 if jurisdiction over the person is transferred to that district;

(2) Hold a prompt preliminary hearing if the alleged violation occurred in that district, and either (i) hold the person to answer in the district court of the district having jurisdiction or (ii) dismiss the proceedings and so notify that court; or

(3) Otherwise order the person held to answer in the district court of the district having jurisdiction upon production of certified copies of the judgment, the warrant, and the application for the warrant, and upon a finding that the person before the magistrate judge is the person named in the warrant.

(e) Arrest for failure to appear. If a person is arrested on a warrant in a district other than that in which the warrant was issued, and the warrant was issued because of the failure of the person named therein to appear as required pursuant to a subpoena or the terms of that person's release, the person arrested must be taken without unnecessary delay before the nearest available federal magistrate judge. Upon production of the warrant or a certified copy thereof and upon a finding that the person before the magistrate judge is the person named in the warrant, the federal magistrate judge shall hold the person to answer in the district in which the warrant was issued.

(f) Release or detention. If a person was previously detained or conditionally released, pursuant to chapter 207 of title 18, United States Code [18 USCS §§ 3141 et seq.], in another district where a warrant, information, or indictment issued, the federal magistrate judge shall take into account the decision previously made and the reasons set forth therefor, if any, but will not be bound by that decision. If the federal magistrate judge amends the release or detention decision or alters the conditions of release, the magistrate judge shall set forth the reasons therefor in writing.

Commentary

By Prof. Inga L. Parsons
New York University School of Law

When a person is arrested in a district other than the one where the charges are pending, that person must be brought before a magistrate judge without "unnecessary delay" for an initial appearance under FRCrP 5 and proceedings under FRCrP 40. (For a discussion of unnecessary delay and the defendant's rights at an initial appearance, *see* the Commentaries for FRCrP 5 and FRCrP 9.) There are four key issues that arise when someone is processed under FRCrP 40: (1) whether the person arrested is the actual individual wanted in the other district; (2) whether there is probable cause to hold that person; (3) whether that person will be removed to the charging jurisdiction in custody or allowed out on bail; and (4) whether the person will be permitted to plead guilty in the arresting district.

Identity Hearings under Rule 40

As to whether the person is the one wanted in the other jurisdiction, FRCrP 40 provides for an identity hearing where the government must show by a preponderance of the evidence that the arrested person is the individual wanted. Often the defense will waive an identity hearing where there is no issue as to the arrested individual being the wanted defendant. Demanding a hearing where identity is clear might antagonize the judge who will consider it a waste of court time. The better strategy might be to waive an identity hearing and save the battle (and the judge's good will) for getting the client out on bail. On the other hand, the defense may gain valuable discovery and the opportunity to examine government witnesses under oath if the identity hearing is held.

The warrant for an arrest under FRCrP 40 is accompanied by an affidavit sworn to by the arresting officer (usually a U.S. Marshal) detailing why this person is believed to be the defendant wanted in the charging jurisdiction. Counsel should review that document and interview the client to determine whether to request an identity hearing.

Preliminary Hearings under Rule 40

Once it is determined that the arrestee is the defendant wanted in the other jurisdiction and there is probable cause to hold that person pursuant to an indictment, information, or preliminary hearing under FRCrP 5.1, the defendant may be held to answer and removed to the charging jurisdiction. If the defendant is entitled to a preliminary hearing because no indictment or information was filed, the defendant can elect to have the preliminary hearing either in the arresting jurisdiction or the charging jurisdiction. Most preliminary hearings do not take place at either jurisdiction because the prosecution will usually seek and obtain an indictment before the preliminary hearing is held. In jurisdictions where the grand jury sits infrequently, a preliminary hearing is more likely to occur, and the sooner the preliminary hearing is scheduled, *i.e.*, at the initial appearance in the arresting jurisdiction, the less time the prosecution will have to seek an indictment.

Bail Hearings under Rule 40

Of great importance to the defendants is whether they will be removed to the charging jurisdiction in custody or released on the condition that they appear in the charging jurisdiction. If the defendants are released, they are responsible for getting to the other jurisdiction. An indigent defendant may be entitled to have the U.S. Marshals arrange for noncustodial transportation or the payment of transportation expenses. *See* 18 USCS § 4285. When a defendant is detained, the Bureau of Prisons will provide transportation (usually a long uncomfortable bus ride that stops at every federal correctional institution along the way). In some cases, a defendant may wish to return to the charging jurisdiction immediately. If that defendant is not entitled to bail or is unlikely to have bail set, the defendant can waive the identity hearing and consent to removal and detention without prejudice. Any preliminary hearing and bail hearing can be held in the charging jurisdiction.

In most cases the defendant will seek to be released on bail rather than be removed by the Bureau of Prisons to the jurisdiction where the charges are pending. In determining whether to set bail, the court considers the factors set out in the Bail Reform Act, including the nature and seriousness of the offense, any previous criminal record, risk of flight, etc., *see* 18 USCS § 3142. The magistrate judge will also consider whether the defendant was previously detained or conditionally released in the charging jurisdiction. FRCrP 40(f). The magistrate judge is guided by any previously set bail but is not bound by the charging jurisdiction's bail decision, and the judge can amend or alter those conditions provided it is in writing. *Id.* Most circuits require that an appeal of the magistrate judge's decision on bail be taken in the charging jurisdiction. *See, e.g., United States v. Evans*, 62 F.3d 1233 (9th Cir. 1995). In such circuits, if the magistrate judge in the arresting jurisdiction has denied bail, the appeal must be taken in the charging jurisdiction, and defense counsel should request an immediate hearing by phone with that district court judge. Otherwise, the bail issue will be essentially moot since the defendant will be transferred in custody to the charging jurisdiction to appeal the bail decision. If bail is granted, the prosecution should ask that the order of release be stayed pending appeal.

For defendants who reside in the charging jurisdiction, defense counsel should focus bail arguments on ties to that jurisdiction. Where the defendant lives in the arresting jurisdiction, defense counsel will need to craft a more complicated bail package. For example, if the defendant lives in New York and her only contact with the district where the prosecution is pending were phone calls to Florida in an insurance fraud scheme, her ties will be to the New York community and not to Florida. Defense counsel should ask for bail with a condition that the defendant appear on her own for the initial appearance in Florida, with a recommendation that the defendant be allowed to reside in New York during the pendency of the case provided she makes her Florida court appearances. The New York court cannot order that the defendant be allowed to return to New York; it is the Florida court that will consider the final bail at the defendant's initial appearance in that district. Obviously if the defendant is released in the arresting jurisdiction and shows up in the charging jurisdiction on her own, she is much more likely to get bail in that jurisdiction as well.

Psychologically, judges are reluctant to release defendants who are wanted elsewhere for fear they will not show up, although the standards for release are statutorily the same as in any bail hearing. It is less risky for judges simply to detain the defendant for removal to the charging jurisdiction. Defense counsel must understand that the bail bar is raised in a Rule 40 proceeding and must be prepared to offer significant resources or cosigners.

If the warrant issued in the charging jurisdiction was for failure to appear, the defendant is required to be held to answer upon proof of the warrant. FRCrP 40(e). The chances of getting bail in such cases are remote. Nevertheless, if there is no indication that the defendant knew of the court appearance or was trying to avoid prosecution, defense counsel should attempt to get the prosecutor in the charging jurisdiction to vacate any bench warrant and agree to a bail package that would allow the defendant to be released, notwithstanding the failure to appear. There are special considerations with respect to when a probationer or supervised releasee is arrested and brought in for a Rule 40 proceeding, and counsel should review those specific procedures set out in the rules. *See* FRCrP 40(d) and FRCrP 32.1.

Rule 20 Guilty Pleas

Also at the Rule 40 proceeding, the judge will advise the defendant of FRCrP 20, allowing for the defendant to plead guilty or nolo contendre to the charges in the district of arrest, rather than being removed to the district where the charges are pending. To plead in the arresting jurisdiction requires a written request from the defendant and approval from both United States Attorneys' offices. *See* the Commentary for FRCrP 20. Before appearing in front of the magistrate judge at the removal hearing, defense counsel should discuss with the client the possibility of pleading guilty in the arresting jurisdiction. If the defendant wants to take the case to trial, the defendant must do so in the charging jurisdiction. If the defendant is unsure about taking the case to trial, but wishes to stay in the arresting jurisdiction as long as possible, counsel should request a transfer of the case under FRCrP 20 in order to keep the defendant in that jurisdiction and to give the defendant time to consider pleading guilty pursuant to FRCrP 20. The defendant can always withdraw the request and have the case removed to the charging jurisdiction. *See* FRCrP 20. There may be strategic advantages to having the case sentenced by a judge in the arresting jurisdiction. For example, a small quantity of cocaine may seem like a trifle to a judge in the eastern district of New York where 50 percent of the criminal cases involve large quantities of narcotics, whereas the offense may seem more serious to a judge sitting in the district of Wyoming.

When the arrested person is represented by counsel in the charging jurisdiction, it is crucial that defense counsel contact that lawyer at the outset to discuss the various strategic decisions, particularly if the case will ultimately be litigated. If no counsel has been appointed or retained, defense counsel should facilitate an immediate assignment or retainer since there may be crucial decisions and investigations that could be compromised by delay.

Rule 41. Search and Seizure

(a) Authority to issue warrant. Upon the request of a federal law enforcement officer or an attorney for the government, a search warrant authorized by this rule may be issued (1) by a federal magistrate judge, or a state court of record within the federal district, for a search of property or for a person within the district and (2) by a federal magistrate judge for a search of property or for a person either within or outside the district if the property or person is within the district when the warrant is sought but might move outside the district before the warrant is executed.

(b) Property or persons which may be seized with a warrant. A warrant may be issued under this rule to search for and seize any (1) property that constitutes evidence of the commission of a criminal offense; or (2) contraband, the fruits of crime, or things otherwise criminally possessed; or (3) property designed or intended for use or which is or has been used as the means of committing a criminal offense; or (4) person for whose arrest there is probable cause, or who is unlawfully restrained.

(c) Issuance and contents.

(1) Warrant upon affidavit. A warrant other than a warrant upon oral testimony under paragraph (2) of this subdivision shall issue only on an affidavit or affidavits sworn to before the federal magistrate judge or state judge and establishing the grounds for issuing the warrant. If the federal magistrate judge or state judge is satisfied that grounds for the application exist or that there is probable cause to believe that they exist, that magistrate judge or state judge shall issue a warrant identifying the property or person to be seized and naming or describing the person or place to be searched. The finding of probable cause may be based upon hearsay evidence in whole or in part. Before ruling on a request for a warrant the federal magistrate judge or state judge may require the affiant to appear personally and may examine under oath the affiant and any witnesses the affiant may produce, provided that such proceeding shall be taken down by a court reporter or recording equipment and made part of the affidavit. The warrant shall be directed to a civil officer of the United States authorized to enforce or assist in enforcing any law thereof or to a person so authorized by the President of the United States. It shall command the officer to search, within a specified period of time not to exceed 10 days, the person or place named for the property or person specified. The warrant shall be served in the daytime, unless the issuing authority, by appropriate provision in the warrant, and for reasonable cause shown, authorizes its execution at times other than daytime. It shall designate a federal magistrate judge to whom it shall be returned.

(2) Warrant upon oral testimony.

(A) General rule. If the circumstances make it reasonable to dispense, in whole or in part, with a written affidavit, a Federal magistrate judge may issue a warrant based upon sworn testimony communicated by telephone or other appropriate means including facsimile transmission.

(B) Application. The person who is requesting the warrant shall prepare a document to be known as a duplicate original warrant and shall read such duplicate original warrant, verbatim, to the Federal magistrate judge. The Federal magistrate judge shall enter, verbatim, what is so read to such magistrate judge on a document to be known as the original warrant. The Federal magistrate judge may direct that the warrant be modified.

(C) Issuance. If the Federal magistrate judge is satisfied that the circumstances are such as to make it reasonable to dispense with a written affidavit and that grounds for the application exist or that there is probable cause to believe that they exist, the Federal magistrate judge shall order the issuance of a warrant by directing the person requesting the warrant to sign the Federal magistrate judge's name on the duplicate original warrant. The Federal magistrate judge shall immediately sign the original warrant and enter on the face of the original warrant the exact time when the warrant was ordered to be issued. The finding of probable cause for a warrant upon oral testimony may be based on the same kind of evidence as is sufficient for a warrant upon affidavit.

(D) Recording and certification of testimony. When a caller informs the Federal magistrate judge that the purpose of the call is to request a warrant, the Federal magistrate judge shall immediately place under oath each person whose testimony forms a basis of the application and each person applying for that warrant. If a voice recording device is available, the Federal magistrate judge shall record by means of such device all of the call after the caller informs the Federal magistrate judge that the purpose of the call is to request a warrant. Otherwise a stenographic or longhand verbatim record shall be made. If a voice recording device is used or a stenographic record made, the Federal magistrate judge shall have the record transcribed, shall certify the accuracy of the transcription, and shall file a copy of the original record and the transcription with the court. If a longhand verbatim record is made, the Federal magistrate judge shall file a signed copy with the court.

(E) Contents. The contents of a warrant upon oral testimony shall be the same as the contents of a warrant upon affidavit.

(F) Additional rule for execution. The person who executes the warrant shall enter the exact time of execution on the face of the duplicate original warrant.

(G) Motion to suppress precluded. Absent a finding of bad faith, evidence obtained pursuant to a warrant issued under this paragraph is not subject to a motion to suppress on the ground that the circumstances were not such as to make it reasonable to dispense with a written affidavit.

(d) Execution and return with inventory. The officer taking property under the warrant shall give to the person from whom or from whose premises the property was taken a copy of the warrant and a receipt for the property taken or shall leave the copy and receipt at the place from which the property was taken. The return shall be made promptly and shall be accompanied by a written inventory of any property taken. The inventory shall be made in the presence of the applicant for the warrant and the person from whose possession or premises the property was taken, if they are present, or in the presence of at least one credible person other than the applicant for the warrant or the person from whose possession or premises the property was taken, and shall be verified by the officer. The federal magistrate judge shall upon request deliver a copy of the inventory to the person from whom or from whose premises the property was taken and to the applicant for the warrant.

(e) Motion for return of property. A person aggrieved by an unlawful search and seizure or by the deprivation of property may move the district court for the district in which the property was seized for the return of the property on the ground that such person is entitled to lawful possession of the property. The court shall receive evidence on any issue of fact necessary to the decision of the motion. If the motion is granted, the property shall be returned to the movant, although reasonable conditions may be imposed to protect access and use of the property in subsequent proceedings. If a motion for return of property is made or comes on for hearing in the district of trial after an indictment or information is filed, it shall be treated also as a motion to suppress under Rule 12.

(f) Motion to suppress. A motion to suppress evidence may be made in the court of the district of trial as provided in Rule 12.

(g) Return of papers to clerk. The federal magistrate judge before whom the warrant is returned shall attach to the warrant a copy of the return, inventory and all other papers in connection therewith and shall file them with the clerk of the district court for the district in which the property was seized.

(h) Scope and definition. This rule does not modify any act, inconsistent with it, regulating search, seizure and the issuance and execution of search warrants in circumstances for which special provision is made. The term "property" is used in this rule to include documents, books, papers and any other tangible objects. The term "daytime" is used in this rule to mean the hours from 6:00 a.m. to 10:00 p.m. according to local time. The phrase "federal law enforcement officer" is used in this rule to mean any government agent, other than an attorney for the government as defined in Rule 54(c), who is engaged in the enforcement of the criminal laws and is within any category of officers authorized by the Attorney General to request the issuance of a search warrant.

Commentary

By Prof. Inga L. Parsons
New York University School of Law

FRCrP 41 governs search and seizure of property and people. It is important for both prosecutors and defense attorneys to know the detailed requirements of the rule and the substantial body of case law governing search and seizure issues. In litigating these issues, defense counsel must understand the prevailing perception that defendants go free by "getting off on a technicality." In reality, the "technicality" in most of these cases is a violation of the defendants' constitutional rights, typically their Fourth Amendment right to be free from unreasonable searches and seizures. Because the remedy for the "constable blundering" is suppression of the evidence from use in the government's case at trial under the exclusionary rule, the courts have continually eroded the protections of the Fourth Amendment to ensure that the "criminal" cannot go free. As a result, it is very difficult for the defense to prevail on a motion to suppress evidence. It is especially difficult to prevail in cases where the officers obtained the evidence pursuant to a warrant under FRCrP 41.

Warrants Generally

FRCrP 41 spells out the authority for obtaining a warrant, the necessary support for the warrant, and the form and terms of the warrant. Under the Fourth Amendment a warrant must be supported by probable cause. Probable cause is a determination that there is a substantial basis for finding fair probability that contraband, or other evidence of a crime, will be found in the place to be searched. It is based on the totality of the circumstances presented to the judge at the time. *See Illinois v. Gates*, 462 U.S. 213, 76 L.Ed.2d 527, 103 S.Ct. 2317 (1983).

Probable cause can be presented in person, by affidavit, over the phone, and even by facsimile provided it is given under oath. *See* FRCrP 41(c)(2) for the specific procedures for the use of various types of testimony. Allowing for the use of computer-generated transmission was considered in 1993, but it was ultimately rejected because it was believed to lack the authenticity of the handwriting that can be observed on a facsimile transmission. *See* Committee Notes 1993 Amendments. Probable cause can be based on hearsay although the court may require the affiant to appear in person. FRCrP 41(c)(1).

The warrant must identify the property or person to be seized, and it must name or describe the person or place to be searched. Any search must take place within a specified time period not to exceed ten days and ordinarily must be executed during the daytime—meaning 6:00 A.M. to 10:00 P.M. unless the court finds reasonable cause to allow it to be executed at night. *Id.* Search warrants related to narcotics offenses, however, can be served at any time if a judge is satisfied that there is probable cause to believe drugs will be found. *See* 21 USCS § 879. FRCrP 41 allows for anticipatory warrants for executions outside the district of the original request when the property or person is expected to move from the original district, such as luggage on an airplane. FRCrP 41(a).

Challenging the Warrant

Failure to follow the requirements of FRCrP 41 could lead to suppression of the evidence under the exclusionary rule, although FRCrP 41 no longer contains a specific exclusionary provision (having been deleted in the 1989 amendments). Given the numerous exceptions to the warrant requirement, it would be impossible to set out a black-and-white rule on exclusion today. When a search or seizure would be justified without a warrant, insufficiency of a search warrant becomes immaterial. Moreover, the Supreme Court provides an important safety net for the prosecution: if the executing officer relies on a defective warrant in good faith, the evidence will not be suppressed. *See United States v. Leon*, 468 U.S. 897, 82 L.Ed.2d 677, 104 S.Ct. 3405 (1984).

In some cases the defense may argue that the warrant was not supported by probable cause or the information was stale. Probable cause is a relatively low standard, and only requires that it persuade a person of reasonable caution to believe a crime is being committed or the evidence of a crime will be found at a particular place. Nevertheless, defense counsel should obtain a copy of the affidavit or other documents supporting the issuance of the warrant and review the copy for lack of probable cause or omissions. It will often contain valuable discovery as well.

Defense counsel should determine whether the affidavit contains more than a mere assertion that a statute has been violated, though not every element of the offense needs to be supported. Similarly, the affidavit cannot simply be a conclusory statement that the affiant believes there is probable cause to obtain a warrant; determination of probable cause is the role of a neutral and detached magistrate who assesses the facts underlying that belief. The court is not supposed to be a "rubber stamp" for the law enforcement officer. If the information relied on comes from an informant, the basis for the reliability of that information should be set out. Challenging the sufficiency of the affidavit at a minimum may provide the defense valuable discovery as to the source and content of government information. Prosecutors should avoid such challenges by including the basis for information such as why the informant is reliable without compromising the case investigation.

If the warrant is facially invalid or contains deliberate omissions, the defense may be able to get the fruits of the search excluded. Where the affidavit contains false statements, the defense might be entitled to a *Franks* hearing pursuant to *Franks v. Delaware*, 438 U.S. 154, 57 L.Ed.2d 667, 98 S.Ct. 2674 (1978), and ultimately invalidation of the warrant. To obtain a *Franks* hearing, the defense needs to make a "substantial preliminary showing" that the affidavit contained false information and the false information was submitted deliberately or from a reckless disregard of the truth. *Id.* If only part of the information is tainted but the remainder is sufficient to establish probable cause, the search usually will be considered valid.

A viable challenge to a search executed pursuant to a warrant is the warrant was not particularized as required or the search exceeded the scope of the warrant, *i.e.*, the places to be searched and the things to be seized. Defense counsel should obtain a copy of the return of the warrant, which details the evidence obtained, and compare it against the scope of the warrant. It may be that lawfully owned ammunition was seized during the search of an office for suspected wire fraud, although the warrant did not specify a search for firearms or ammunition. If the executing officers "flagrantly disregard" the terms of the warrant, a court could suppress all of the evidence recovered, even evidence that was properly described. *See, e.g., United States v. Medlin*, 842 F.2d 1194 (10th Cir. 1988) (court suppressed all evidence including firearms where ATF agents recovered 667 items in flagrant disregard of the scope of the warrant issued solely for firearms).

Avoiding Warrant Defects and Problems

Prosecutors and law enforcement officers can avoid many of these challenges by making sure that the warrant covers possible contraband including any fruits, instruments, or evidence of a crime such as money, firearms, etc. In setting out the terms of the warrant, the prosecutor must balance the need for particularization to avoid a "general search" against the possibility that the warrant will be too particularized to allow officers to take potential evidence.

In cases that involve mostly documents like mail fraud cases, the judge will usually allow a class of items to be seized such as business records if it is established they are expected to be "permeated with fraud." Prosecutors often use the catchall phrase "evidence of crime at this time unknown" on the warrant as long as it adequately limits the discretion of the executing officers. Attaching the affidavit to the warrant can often assist in particularizing the search. The good news for prosecutors is the courts understand that the warrants and affidavits must be viewed realistically and with common sense to avoid a "technicality." In addition, obvious contraband in plain view may be seized provided the officers are on the premises lawfully.

When documents are the target of the warrant, First Amendment rights are often implicated and the description of those documents must be met with "scrupulous exactitude." *See Stanford v. Texas*, 397 U.S. 476, 13 L.Ed.2d 431, 85 S.Ct. 506 (1965). Obscene materials present their own difficulties in this regard and counsel for both sides in these cases should be aware of the more exacting requirements.

Knock and Announce

In executing the warrant, officers must follow the federal statutory "knock and announce" provisions in 18 USCS § 3109 unless there are exigent circumstances involving the officers' safety, which justifies a "no knock" entry. Failure to give notice of purpose and authority before forced entry where there are no exigent circumstances is considered unreasonable and violative of the Fourth Amendment.

The remedy for violation of the knock and announce provision is exclusion of the evidence. *See, e.g., United States v. Becker*, 23 F.3d 1537 (9th Cir. 1994). Law enforcement officers can usually get around the "knock and announce" requirement by claiming exigent circumstances. Defense counsel should insist on individualized factual support for exigent circumstances, and should urge the court to reject a blanket, "It was a drug case, it is always dangerous" rationale. As the court stated in *Becker*, "While it is true that 'exigent circumstances' can justify immediate entry, incantation of that phrase does not dissolve the shield that our law provides." *Id.* at 1540.

Warrantless Searches and Seizures

Given the fact that a warrant is constitutionally prescribed and can be obtained relatively easily over the telephone (and now even by facsimile machine), it is surprising that more warrants are not obtained. It is no doubt because of the many exceptions to the warrant requirement, the expectation that judges will routinely credit the testimony of law enforcement officers, and a certain police culture where the rumored phrase in the ranks is that only rookies get warrants. It may also be due to a reluctance on the part of prosecutors to subject their law enforcement officers to yet another document under oath detailing case information when there are so many exceptions to the requirement to validate the search.

The exceptions to the warrant requirement that will usually validate a warrantless search include exigent circumstances, inevitable discovery, search incident to arrest, protective sweep, investigatory detentions, consent, etc. A detailed review of these exceptions and the underlying law is beyond the scope of this commentary, but federal practitioners should keep abreast of the state of Fourth Amendment jurisprudence to be effective litigators. The Supreme Court often takes certiorari on search and seizure issues and there are hundreds of circuit court decisions on these issues each year. FRCrP 41 itself has had several major amendments since enactment, which are indicative of the dynamic nature of search and seizure law. See generally J. W. Hall, *Search and Seizure*, 3d ed. (2000).

Motions to Suppress Generally

Despite the daunting task a defendant faces in trying to win a motion to suppress in federal court, there is generally much to be gained by filing the motion and obtaining a hearing, particularly if the case is going to go to trial. If nothing else, a hearing on the motion usually provides important discovery to the defense and the chance to examine the testifying officer. Prosecutors strive to avoid hearings and putting an officer on the stand in advance of trial. In some cases the prosecutor may decide not to introduce the evidence at trial in order to avoid the motion to suppress.

Filing the motion can sometimes give the defense leverage in negotiations, especially where there is some chance that the search will be invalidated. On the other hand, there are prosecutors who are willing to bargain before they have to respond to motions, and they may penalize a defendant by terminating an offer once motions are filed. Defense counsel needs to be aware of the practice within the district, as well as the individual prosecutor's custom with respect to filing motions and the motions' effect on negotiations.

Strategies in Interviewing the Defendant for Motions to Suppress

One of the best sources in determining whether there have been search and seizure violations is the defendant. Defense counsel should be prepared to conduct an extensive interview to determine the viability of a motion to suppress. In a case where there is a search of a car, for example, it may be that the police claim it was consent, but it looks to have been merely a response to governmental authority. Defense counsel must be aware of the important factors that are considered by the court in assessing the voluntariness of the consent and discuss the various factors with the defendant.

When interviewing the defendant on the search and seizure issues, it is better to ask open questions rather than closed. It is also important not to ask for legal conclusions from the client such as, "Did you give the officers consent to search the car." Instead counsel will get more neutral factual information by asking such questions as, "Where was the police car parked? Was it a marked police car? Were the police lights on? Was the siren used? Where was your car? Could you have backed up with the police car behind you? Where did the officer go after he got out of his car? Where was his partner standing? What was the first thing the officer said or did when he approached your car? What did you say or do? What was the very next thing that happened? How was the officer dressed? Did he carry a weapon? Did he show you his badge?" etc.

Strategies in Filing Supporting Affidavits

In moving to suppress evidence, the defendants have the initial burden to show that they have standing to make the claim, *i.e.*, that they had a reasonable expectation of privacy in the thing seized or the area searched. Establishing standing to make a Fourth Amendment claim often requires the defendants to admit ownership of the contraband or the container in which the contraband was found in derogation of their Fifth Amendment right against self-incrimination. The Supreme Court has effected a compromise that allows the defendants to make the incriminating assertions necessary to establish their right to bring a motion, but does not allow the prosecution to use that information in its case-in-chief to establish guilt. *See Simmons v. United States*, 390 U.S. 377, 19 L.Ed.2d 1247, 88 S.Ct. 967 (1968). Defense counsel must ensure that the information in the affidavit is not used inappropriately at trial.

There are important strategic considerations when the defendant or the case agent must swear to facts that support or counter a motion to suppress. Both sides should be cautious in unnecessarily committing an agent or client to a detailed account that can later be used to impeach the affiants should they take the stand and misstate a detail. For the defendant, the stakes are even higher since sworn statements by the defendant that are contradicted by law enforcement officers are often used to support obstruction of justice and perjury enhancements. Counsel should craft any declaration carefully to insure that only the minimal information needed to support or oppose the motion is included. *See* the Commentary for FRCrP 47.

Rule 12 Considerations

Motions to suppress evidence are governed by FRCrP 12 and must be raised prior to trial, or otherwise the issue is waived unless the court finds good cause. *See* FRCrP 12(b), (f). A motion to suppress is moot if the government does not intend to use the evidence at trial. FRCrP 12(d) provides that the defense may request notice of the government's intent to use specified evidence as early as the arraignment, and the government, in its discretion, may give notice of that intent. There is little to be lost by the defense submitting a detailed request for evidence under FRCrP 12(d). There is little to be gained by the prosecution not informing the defense of the evidence it intends to use as soon as possible. A delay in providing that information will ultimately delay any hearing, trial, or sentencing. Most of the evidence requested under FRCrP 12 is ultimately discoverable by the defense under FRCrP 16 anyway. *See* FRCrP 16.

Burdens of Proof

Once the defendants have met their burden to show they have standing to make a claim, the burden then shifts to the government to show that the evidence was obtained lawfully. Where there is a factual dispute as to the search and seizure of evidence, the judge ordinarily grants a hearing. Some judges may require the defendants to get on the stand first and assert their standing rights under oath subject to cross-examination in order to shift the burden to the government. In most districts, the defendant's affidavit suffices to meet the burden of going forward and the hearing begins with the government's burden to show that the evidence was obtained lawfully. Prosecutors should insist that the defendant take the stand first. The defense should avoid putting the client on the stand to meet the burden of going forward by countering that the defendant's affidavit is sufficient to shift the burden. Who has the initial burden at the hearing will depend on local practice and the individual judge's custom.

Suppression Hearing

The suppression hearing is not a trial on the issue of guilt. It is a hearing on the issue of the lawfulness of the search or seizure. The hearing is held before a judge and hearsay is admissible. Although it is wise to pin down certain testimony of the agents, most of the cross-examination of the officers should be open-ended questions to find out what happened. Bringing out the devastating impeachment of the officer by prior inconsistent statements during this hearing will be a waste. The judge is very unlikely to discredit the officer's testimony unless there is objective evidence of fabrication, and confronting the officer with the inconsistency at this pretrial stage will give the officer an opportunity to prepare for it for trial. Unless the hearing is in essence the trial where if the evidence comes in the defendant will be convicted, defense counsel should think of the suppression hearing as an opportunity to learn more about the case and to see how the officer testifies. It is also useful to pin down the officer on crucial facts so the officer does not have a "better recollection" at trial. *See also* the Commentary for FRCrP 12.

Prosecutors should be vigilant and object to the defense's questions that do not call for information related to the issue of the validity of the evidence. Judges dislike the use of these hearings for discovery purposes or "fishing expeditions," and are likely to side with the government unless the prosecutor has opened the door by having the officer testify about the investigations. Defense counsel should keep an ear out for broad questions from the prosecution on direct examination such as, "Why did you decide to arrest Mr. Jones that day?" which can open the scope of the cross to nearly everything that happened in the case.

When evidence is suppressed, it cannot be used in the government's case-in-chief. There are, however, a number of collateral uses for such evidence. If the defendant takes the stand at trial and makes statements inconsistent with the suppressed evidence, the evidence can be used to impeach the defendant's testimony. It cannot be used to impeach witnesses other than the defendant. The suppressed evidence can also be used at the defendant's sentencing and in certain civil proceedings. A person who is "aggrieved" by an unlawful search and seizure can move for return of the property if they may lawfully possess the property. *See* FRCrP 41(e) for the procedures on return of property. Much of the evidence seized, though, will be subject to the forfeiture laws and will not be returned. *See, e.g.,* FRCrP 32.2 and the Commentary for FRCrP 32.2.

Rule 42. Criminal Contempt

(a) Summary disposition. A criminal contempt may be punished summarily if the judge certifies that the judge saw or heard the conduct constituting the contempt and that it was committed in the actual presence of the court. The order of contempt shall recite the facts and shall be signed by the judge and entered of record.

(b) Disposition upon notice and hearing. A criminal contempt except as provided in subdivision (a) of this rule shall be prosecuted on notice. The notice shall state the time and place of hearing, allowing a reasonable time for the preparation of the defense, and shall state the essential facts constituting the criminal contempt charged and describe it as such. The notice shall be given orally by the judge in open court in the presence of the defendant or, on application of the United States attorney or of an attorney appointed by the court for that purpose, by an order to show cause or an order of arrest. The defendant is entitled to a trial by jury in any case in which an act of Congress so provides. The defendant is entitled to admission to bail as provided in these rules. If the contempt charged involves disrespect to or criticism of a judge, that judge is disqualified from presiding at the trial or hearing except with the defendant's consent. Upon a verdict or finding of guilt the court shall enter an order fixing the punishment.

Commentary

By Steven M. Statsinger
The Legal Aid Society, Federal Defender Division
Southern District of New York

A contempt citation can arise from just about any willful disregard of the court's authority. A federal court may punish as criminal contempt (1) "misbehavior of any person in its presence or so near thereto as to obstruct the administration of justice"; (2) "misbehavior of any of its officers in their official transactions"; and (3) "disobedience or resistance to its lawful writ, process, order, rule, decree, or command." 18 USCS § 401.

While this statute is quite broadly written, there are nevertheless some limits to its reach. Misbehavior in court only constitutes contempt if it actually obstructs justice, or at least presents an imminent threat to the administration of justice. The provision relating to disobedience of the court's order requires not only that the order be "lawful," but that it be unambiguous—that is, reasonably clear and specific. To be punished as criminal contempt an act must also be "willful." This means that the violation was deliberate, as opposed to accidental, inadvertent, or negligent.

(a) Summary procedures for direct contempts.

FRCrP 42(a) sets out the procedures for the summary disposition of what are known as "direct" criminal contempts: those acts committed in the actual presence of the court and seen and heard by the judge. The summary contempt power has been traditionally disfavored. It should be used only in those "exceptional circumstances" where "instant action is necessary to protect the judicial institution itself." *Harris v. United States*, 382 U.S. 162, 164, 167, 15 L.E.2d 240, 242, 243, 86 S.Ct. 352, 354, 356 (1965).

The summary contempt procedures of FRCrP 42(a) require the judge to prepare a certificate setting out with specificity the conduct that constituted the contempt and noting that the judge actually witnessed the conduct. FRCrP 42(a) permits summary adjudication of a contempt even if it is personal to the judge. However, it is preferable that the judge refer a personal contempt to a different judge for a trial under the procedures set out in FRCrP 42(b), unless there is a pressing need to adjudicate the contempt right away. *Offut v. United States*, 348 U.S. 11, 99 L.Ed. 11, 75 S.Ct. 11 (1954).

Since the summary procedure is intended only to address those urgent matters that must be resolved immediately, it is generally expected that summary proceedings under FRCrP 42(a) will result in an immediate finding of contempt and an immediate punishment. Accordingly, summarily citing attorneys after a trial is concluded for misconduct that occurred much earlier is disfavored. If the court does so, however, the attorneys are entitled to reasonable notice of the specific charges and an opportunity to be heard in their own behalf. *Taylor v. Hayes*, 418 U.S. 488, 42 L.Ed.2d 897, 94 S.Ct. 2697 (1974).

(b) Non-summary procedures.

FRCrP 42(b) details the procedures for all criminal contempts other than summary proceedings covered by FRCrP 42(a). The first, and most basic, requirement is notice. The court must provide notice to the defendant specifying the essential facts of the contempt charged, as well as the time and place of the hearing. The court must give the defendant a reasonable time for the preparation of a defense.

At the hearing the defendant has a right to be heard in defense or explanation, and to call defense witnesses. The defendant is also entitled to the assistance of counsel and to confront and cross-examine the adverse witnesses. The burden is on the prosecution to prove every element of the contempt beyond a reasonable doubt. FRCrP 42(b) specifies that the defendant is entitled to bail. It also requires that a different judge preside over the hearing if the contempt charged is personal to the judge who issued the citation.

(c) Jury trials in non-summary cases.

FRCrP 42(b) guarantees a jury trial in any case in which a federal statute provides for one, and several statutes do that. 18 USCS §§ 402 and 3691 require a jury trial on demand if the conduct constituting the contempt also violated a federal criminal statute or a criminal statute of the state in which the conduct occurred. However, these statutes contain two important exceptions. They apply only to the willful disobedience of a lawful court order under 18 USCS § 401(3), but not to the other types of contempt identified in § 401. And they do not apply at all if the order at issue was entered in any action or prosecuted in the name of, or in behalf of, the United States. 18 USCS § 3692 guarantees a jury trial in all contempt cases arising from injunctions or restraining orders in labor disputes. There is also a statutory right to a jury trial in certain criminal contempt cases arising from litigation under some of the federal civil rights statutes. *See* 42 USCS §§ 1995, 2000h.

Independent of any statute or rule, under the Sixth Amendment a court cannot sentence a contemnor to more than six months' imprisonment if the matter was tried without a jury, no matter how many contempt charges the defendant was convicted of in that proceeding. *Codispoti v. Pennsylvania*, 418 U.S. 506, 41 L.Ed.2d 912, 94 S.Ct. 2687 (1974).

(d) Authorized penalties.

The authorized penalties for criminal contempt are also governed by statute. 18 USCS § 401 sets no maximum penalty. It merely states that the penalty may be imprisonment or a fine, but not both. If the contempt falls within the narrow class of cases covered by 18 USCS § 402, then the authorized penalty is up to six months' imprisonment or a fine, or both. If the fine is to be paid to the United States, it cannot exceed $1,000.

The civil rights statutes noted above set out maximum sentences that are in most respects consistent with the other criminal contempt statutes. The United States Sentencing Commission has not promulgated a guideline specifically covering criminal contempt. The contempt guideline, USSG § 2J1.1, simply refer to USSG § 2X5.1, which provides that the court is to apply the "most analogous offense guideline" based on the underlying conduct. If there is no such guideline, the court is directed to 18 USCS § 3553(b), which requires a consideration of the sentencing factors set out in 18 USCS § 3553(a)(2).

(e) Appeals.

An order convicting a defendant of criminal contempt and imposing sentence is a final order and is appealable, even if the proceeding in which the contempt arose has not been concluded. Every aspect of the contempt can be reviewed by the appellate court—the findings of the court below, any procedural defects at the hearing, and the sentence imposed. Because there is no statutory maximum sentence for many contempts, criminal contempt presents an exception to the usual rule that an appellate court cannot modify the imposed sentence on the ground that it is excessive. *Yates v. United States*, 356 U.S. 363, 2 L.Ed.2d 837, 78 S.Ct. 766 (1958).

(f) Civil contempt.

It should be noted that FRCrP 42 sets out the applicable procedures for criminal contempt only. Civil contempt is governed by the Federal Rules of Civil Procedure as well as by various federal statutes, such as 28 USCS § 1826 (recalcitrant witnesses). A contempt citation should state with clarity whether the contemnor is being held in civil or in criminal contempt. If it does not, the surest way to determine whether the contempt is civil or criminal is to identify the purpose of the punishment. If the purpose of the contempt is remedial, that is, it is intended to coerce the contemnor to act, then it is civil. If its purpose is to punish the offender, then the contempt is criminal. A single citation can have both criminal and civil features. For example, a recalcitrant witness might be held in criminal contempt as punishment for disobedience, and also be imprisoned to coerce compliance, a civil sanction. An appellate court will treat as criminal a citation that has both civil and criminal components.

X. General Provisions

Rule 43. Presence of the Defendant

(a) Presence required. The defendant shall be present at the arraignment, at the time of the plea, at every stage of the trial including the impaneling of the jury and the return of the verdict, and at the imposition of sentence, except as otherwise provided by this rule.

(b) Continued presence not required. The further progress of the trial to and including the return of the verdict, and the imposition of sentence, will not be prevented and the defendant will be considered to have waived the right to be present whenever a defendant, initially present at trial, or having pleaded guilty or nolo contendere,

(1) is voluntarily absent after the trial has commenced (whether or not the defendant has been informed by the court of the obligation to remain during the trial),

(2) in a noncapital case, is voluntarily absent at the imposition of sentence, or

(3) after being warned by the court that disruptive conduct will cause the removal of the defendant from the courtroom, persists in conduct which is such as to justify exclusion from the courtroom.

(c) Presence not required. A defendant need not be present:

(1) when represented by counsel and the defendant is an organization, as defined in 18 U.S.C. § 18;

(2) when the offense is punishable by fine or by imprisonment for not more than one year or both, and the court, with the written consent of the defendant, permits arraignment, plea, trial, and imposition of sentence in the defendant's absence;

(3) when the proceeding involves only a conference or hearing upon a question of law; or

(4) when the proceeding involves a reduction or correction of sentence under Rule 35(b) or (c) or 18 U.S.C. § 3582(c).

Commentary

By Prof. Inga L. Parsons
New York University School of Law

FRCrP 43 lists when the presence of the defendant is required, including at arraignment, any plea, trial, verdict, and sentencing. The rule has two competing purposes: to protect the defendant's constitutional right to be present at all stages of trial while preventing the defendant from precluding trial or sentence by fleeing. Once the trial has begun with the defendant present, if the defendant voluntarily absents himself, the verdict and sentence (except in a capital case) can go forward without him. If the trial has not commenced, the defendant cannot be tried in absentia. *United States v. Crosby*, 506 U.S. 255, 122 L.Ed. 2d 25, 113 S.Ct. 748 (1993). If the offense is a misdemeanor, the defendant can consent to have the arraignment, plea, trial, and even sentence imposed in absentia. *See* the Commentary for FRCrP 58.

Defendant's Presence at Trial

FRCrP 43 does not specify what exactly is meant by the presence of the defendant at trial other than to include impaneling the jury and the verdict. Much of the litigation of FRCrP 43 has involved the exclusion of the defendant at side bars and discussions on jury instructions. If the defendant wishes to be present during these colloquies, the defendant ordinarily must make a request or it can be deemed a waiver of her presence at these conferences. At its core, this issue is one of counseling. The attorney should explain to the defendant in advance of hearing or trial what role the attorney will play, what role the jury will play, what role the judge will play, and what role the defendant will play. For example, the defense attorney can explain why it may be beneficial to allow the lawyers to question the jurors outside the hearing of the defendant to ensure more candid responses to provide better information to exercise peremptory challenges.

When the Defendant's Presence Is Not Required

If the proceeding involves solely a legal issue such as a constitutional challenge, the defendant's presence is not required. FRCrP

43(c)(3). However, there is often much to be gained by having the defendant present even when only purely legal matters are going to be discussed. First, it signals to the judge the defendant's interest in the outcome. Second, it demonstrates to the defendant the attorney's commitment and efforts in the case. Third, if the case does not go to trial, it may be one of the few opportunities for the defendant to feel like she had her day in court. If the defendant's presence is going to be waived, counsel should discuss this with the defendant in advance and get the defendant's consent. At a hearing when the defendant is not going to be present, defense counsel should state for the record that the defendant waives her presence given the purely legal nature of the proceeding.

Strategies Regarding the Defendant's Absence

Counsel must not in any way advise the defendant to flee or to absent herself. Jokes are often bandied about how attorneys put posters of beautiful beaches in the Dominican Republic in their offices since there is no extradition treaty with that country. Obstruction of justice is no joke and counsel needs to be careful not to give the wrong impression for fear defendants will take seriously what was meant to be in jest. The defendant should be advised that if she flees, she would give up her right to appeal any conviction.

When the defendant does not appear at trial after having been present, defense counsel should ask for at least one day's adjournment to call family members, check local hospitals, run an arrest sheet, etc., to determine if the defendant did, in fact, voluntarily absent herself. Following that, defense counsel should request a hearing to determine whether the absence is voluntary, because if it is inconclusive, that may prevent prejudicial instructions from being given to the jury on the issue. At some point the defense may want to have the judge instruct the jury that the defendant is unable to attend the trial. If the judge insists on a more forceful instruction, the defense should request that the judge advise the jury that the defendant has a right not to be present and that the jury should not give any weight to the defendant not being physically in court.

The prosecution should request a consciousness of guilt instruction advising the jurors that the fact of the defendant's flight allows the jurors to draw an inference of guilt. Defense counsel should object to a consciousness of guilt charge. At a minimum, the defense should require the government to meet the Fifth Circuit's four-prong test: (1) that the defendant's absence shows flight; (2) such flight shows consciousness of guilt; (3) the consciousness of guilt is about the crime charged; and (4) the consciousness of guilt about the crime charged shows actual guilt as to that offense. *United States v. Myers*, 550 F.2d 1036, 1049–50 (5th Cir. 1977).

Strategies Regarding the Defendant's Presence

When the defendant is present, particularly during a jury trial, the defense attorney should counsel the defendant that the jury will be watching him/her closely. We live in a visual society, and what is seen with the eye is often much more compelling than what is heard by the ear. The defendant should be advised about the importance of her demeanor: no funny faces, no rolled eyes, no shaking of the head, no finger across the throat when the informant testifies (true story). The defendant should sit straight, not be afraid to look jurors in the eyes (but not stare at them, either) and appear interested in the outcome.

Defense counsel should make clear to the defendant the importance of being at the trial, on time. The defendant should also be within nudging distance from counsel in case the defendant nods off or makes an inappropriate gesture. It is also helpful to have the defendant within reach to be able to place a hand on the defendant's shoulder or whisper in her ear on occasion to signal to the jury a connection of trust and confidence between counsel and client. It should be subtle; group hugs or anything too contrived will backfire. Defense counsel should be mindful where the defendant is placed vis-a-vis the jury and others at the defense table. Even slightly different placements can send drastically different messages: protection by counsel from the overreaching government; or as far from counsel as possible because who wants to sit by someone who did that?

What the defendant wears at trial is also important—dress for acquittal. Defendants who are tried in prison jumpsuits will look like criminals to the jury. At a minimum, prison garb gives an appearance of dangerousness because the jury can deduce that the defendant was not let out on bail. If the defendant is in custody, it is essential that arrangements be made for appropriate court attire to be brought to the detention center and cleared through the Bureau of Prisons. Defense counsel should do this in advance, because it may take a few days to have the clothing approved. If for some reason court clothes are misplaced, etc., the defense should ask for a short recess before the jury is brought into court to ensure the defendant is properly dressed.

Many defense lawyers keep a closet of various-sized suits and dresses in the event the defendant shows up in a fluorescent red satin pajama set (true story) or leaves her suit on the prison bus. Defense counsel should avoid telling a defendant such things as "wear what you wear to church on Sunday," because the lawyer's view and the defendant's view may be very different. Instead, counsel should be specific: suit and tie, sweater and slacks, long-sleeved dress with collar and pearls. No gum. No nose ring. No jacket with the gang emblem on the back. It is also important to have the detained defendant out of the handcuffs before the jury is brought into court.

Removing the Defendant from Court

Although the defendant has a constitutional right to be present at trial, under FRCrP 43, the court can remove a disruptive defendant from the courtroom after fair warning. If the defendant is given a warning, defense counsel should immediately ask for a brief recess to "talk turkey" to the client. The defendant's political agenda may clearly be to challenge the entire criminal justice system by disrupting the process; the defendant should be counseled against using this behavior toward that end in this forum. Defense counsel should acknowledge the legitimacy of the defendant's aims—challenging the system, but suggest that the means will be simply playing into the "oppressor's" hands by giving the judge power to exclude the defendant from her own trial. Oftentimes it may be helpful to explain to the defendant that a more effective strategy might be to test the government's evidence by cross-examining and impeaching the witnesses. Otherwise, the defendant's behavior will distract the jury from the government's burden and lack of proof. Moreover, if the defendant gives the jury a reason to dislike her, it will be easier to convict the defendant on her behavior in the courtroom, rather than proof that may have otherwise given the jury a reasonable doubt as to the defendant's guilt.

In short, client disruption at trial or at any other court appearance is a counseling issue with the defendant. Ideally, courtroom behavior and the client's agenda will be handled in advance of the proceeding. Defense counsel should be open with the defendant about strategic considerations in terms of courtroom demeanor and visual appearance and how they relate to a better chance of acquittal. Defense counsel should avoid making the issue one of obedience from the defendant; rather, it should be demonstrated how it is in the defendant's best interest to make a good impression in front of the jury. Why give the prosecution an undeserved weapon of bad behavior in the courtroom to use to convict the defendant, especially if that is needed to bolster a weak case?

Rule 44. Right to and Assignment of Counsel

(a) Right to assigned counsel. Every defendant who is unable to obtain counsel shall be entitled to have counsel assigned to represent that defendant at every stage of the proceedings from initial appearance before the federal magistrate judge or the court through appeal, unless the defendant waives such appointment.

(b) Assignment procedure. The procedures for implementing the right set out in subdivision (a) shall be those provided by law and by local rules of court established pursuant thereto.

(c) Joint representation. Whenever two or more defendants have been jointly charged pursuant to Rule 8(b) or have been joined for trial pursuant to Rule 8(b) or have been joined for trial pursuant to Rule 13, and are represented by the same retained or assigned counsel or by retained or assigned counsel who are associated in the practice of law, the court shall promptly inquire with respect to such joint representation and shall personally advise each defendant of the right to the effective assistance of counsel, including separate representation. Unless it appears that there is good cause to believe no conflict of interest is likely to arise, the court shall take such measures as may be appropriate to protect each defendant's right to counsel.

Commentary

By Prof. Inga L. Parsons
New York University School of Law

Right to Counsel

If accused of a felony or a misdemeanor that imposes actual jail time, a criminal defendant has a right to counsel. *See Johnson v.*

Zerbst, 304 U.S. 458, 82 L.Ed. 1461, 58 S.Ct. 1019 (1938) and *Scott v. Illinois*, 440 U.S. 367, 59 L.Ed.2d 383, 99 S.Ct. 1158 (1979). In misdemeanors and other minor offenses the judge may determine in advance that no jail will be imposed, and in those cases the defendant does not have a right to counsel. *See* the Commentary for FRCrP 58.

The right to counsel arises under the Sixth Amendment and is triggered by the initiation of adversarial judicial proceedings, which ordinarily means the filing of formal charges in a complaint, information, or indictment. A defendant clearly has a right to counsel at an arraignment and a bail hearing, but a defendant ordinarily does not have a right to counsel at a lineup or other pretrial identification hearing. *See, e.g., United States v. Tolliver*, 569 F.2d 724 (2d Cir. 1978). Defense counsel should still make the request to be present at any lineup, since prosecutors may permit the presence of defense counsel even if it is not mandated.

Even before the Sixth Amendment right to counsel attaches, the defendant may request counsel under the Fifth Amendment providing it is a clear and unequivocal demand. *See Davis v. United States*, 512 U.S. 452, 129 L.Ed.2d 362, 114 S.Ct. 2350 (1994). Defense counsel should review any post-arrest statements made before initiation of the charges where the defendant has mentioned an attorney for a possible Fifth Amendment violation. Even where the defendant fails to essentially state in no uncertain terms "I want my lawyer now"—necessary for a clear violation—the fact that a lawyer was not present and there was some discussion as to having an attorney may bear on the voluntariness of the defendant's statements under a totality of the circumstances analysis.

Assignment of Counsel

For defendants who are unable to obtain counsel, FRCrP 44 provides for the assignment of counsel "at every stage in the proceedings from initial appearance through appeal." FRCrP 44(a). The defendants can waive appointment of counsel and represent themselves, known as proceeding pro se or pro per. *See Faretta v. California*, 422 U.S. 806, 45 L.Ed.2d 562, 95 S.Ct. 2525 (1975). In cases where the defendant elects to proceed without an attorney, judges ordinarily assign a lawyer, known as standby counsel, to sit at counsel table to assist the pro se defendant. Standby counsel is not appointed as an attorney but as an expert to the court under 5 USCS § 3109.

The Criminal Justice Act (CJA) passed in 1964 in the wake of *Gideon v. Wainwright*, 372 U.S. 335, 9 L.Ed.2d 799, 83 S.Ct. 792 (1963) sets out the procedures and policies for establishing effective representation for indigent defendants in federal court. Judicial districts have adopted their own plans for providing indigent representation through the use of federal public defenders, community defender organizations, and CJA panel attorneys—or a combination of the three. In many districts the federal public defender or community defender is given the first assignment in an indigent defense case. Where there are codefendants or cases where the public defender has a conflict of interest, the case is usually assigned to a private attorney who is a member of the CJA panel and who will be reimbursed by the court.

The CJA provides for appointment of counsel for a number of defendants other than those who are facing initial charges, *e.g.*, defendants facing violation of probation or supervised release, a material witness in custody, a defendant subject to a mental condition hearing. *See* 18 USCS § 3006A(a)(1). In some cases judges will appoint counsel even prior to an initial proceeding such as when a person is called before a grand jury and has received a target letter. Where a defendant is not indigent and is unable to obtain counsel for reasons other than financial, the court may still appoint counsel. *See, e.g., United States v. White*, 529 F.2d 1390, 1394 (8th Cir. 1976).

An effective defense requires not only an attorney but also the use of investigative, expert, and other services. If the court determines the defendant is indigent for assignment of counsel purposes, that ordinarily entitles that defendant to have expert services paid for by the court as well as the costs of complying with subpoenas; this often convinces a judge that the defendant is unable to pay a fine or make restitution. *See* 18 USCS § 3006A(e), FRCrP 17(b), and 18 USCS § 3572(a)(1), (2). Some of these expenses may need prior authorization if they exceed a certain amount such as the $300 limit on expert services. *See* 18 USCS § 3006A(e). Even if a defendant has private counsel, if the defendant can demonstrate an inability to pay for expert services, the court can approve payment for such services. *Id.*

Financial Affidavit Considerations

In order to request appointed counsel, the defendant must complete a financial affidavit called a CJA Form 23. It is usually available in both Spanish and English. The purpose of the form is to provide the necessary financial information for the judge to determine whether the defendant has enough income and assets to afford an attorney. Courts typically use the adjusted figures for the lower living standard income level, which are published each year in the Federal Register. Given the expectation that defending a case in federal court will usually be very expensive, most magistrate judges take a generous view in assessing a defendant's ability to afford counsel.

CJA Form 23 is not well drafted and it is important that defense counsel go through the affidavit with the defendant. The form should be completed accurately and thoroughly. There have been times when defendants have been denied counsel because they have misunderstood what was being asked on the form or did not include all of their debts or dependents. The following are a number of problematic areas that require special review by counsel.

Earnings. The CJA 23 form asks for earnings per month. If earnings are known only per hour or per week, that should be clearly marked on the form, *e.g.*, "$7.00 per hour." or "$156 per week". The defendant should describe any ambiguity of the employment for the court's review, *e.g.*, "$260/week but only work two weeks per month." One of the trickiest questions under earnings is the request for spousal income. The question is "If married is your spouse employed?" Many defendants read this as asking whether they are married. A clear indication that the defendant was confused is an answer of "no" to this question, meaning "I am married but my spouse is unemployed," and then a check in the box marked "single" indicating marital status. Similarly, if the answer to spousal income is marked "yes" but the amount entered for the spouse's income is "$0," it is likely the defendant misunderstood the question.

Juveniles. Defendants under twenty-one years old are asked to include parental income even though defendants are generally defined as juveniles if they have not attained the age of eighteen. 18 USCS § 5031. If the defendant under twenty-one does not live with or receive income from a parent, that should be noted on the form. If the defendant is a juvenile, the CJA 23 form should be completed under a John or Jane Doe, and the financial affidavit and other court papers should be subsequently sealed pursuant to 18 USCS § 5038.

Assets. The financial affidavit requires a listing of assets. Clients who are unable to afford an attorney and are requesting the appointment of counsel ordinarily do not have real property, but they often have a car. The estimated value of the car should be its current market value, not the original purchase price. A useful question is to ask the defendant, "If you had to sell the car tomorrow to get money for a lawyer, how much do you think you could get for it?" Sometimes the defendant owns a home but the equity in the home, the assessed value minus the mortgage, is de minimus. The amount of the mortgage and the monthly payment should be listed in the debts section so the judge can assess the available equity. There is a very small line asking for cash on hand or money in a savings account. That question is often missed because it is sandwiched between two larger questions. If the savings account or other asset is jointly owned, that should be indicated on the form.

Dependents. Make sure that the client has listed all dependents whom they actually support. Dependents can include children, parents, aunts, uncles, nieces, nephews, etc. If the defendant sends money back home to Trinidad to support a family member, that information should be included. The questions asking about dependants on the CJA 23 form are very confusing. The form asks for the defendants' relationship to the dependents. In practice, the defendants naturally list the dependents' relationship to themselves, *e.g.*, "son," "daughter," "wife," etc.; that is what the judges expect despite the language on the form.

Expenses/Debts. Defendants often understate their debts and expenses. It is important particularly where the defendant makes a decent salary and has some real property, that the defendant list all debts and expenses including car loans, house mortgages, personal and student loans, outstanding credit card charges, department store charges, mortgages, utilities, children's tuition, transportation, etc.

Miscellaneous. The form is signed under the penalties of perjury. The defendant should be advised to be thorough and accurate. If there are concerns about listing unlawfully obtained income, the defendant may be better off obtaining private counsel rather than requesting appointment of counsel and making incriminating statements on the form. Should the defendants knowingly put down something false, they could be prosecuted for perjury or for making false statements under 18 USCS § 1001. The signature line is clearly marked at the end of the document. There is an unmarked second line adjacent to the signature line that is blank, which is used for the date.

Compensation of Attorneys

An attorney assigned to represent a defendant under the CJA should obtain a copy of the Guidelines for the Administration of the Criminal Justice Act from the clerk of the court. These guidelines will advise an attorney on compensation amounts, reasonable and necessary expenses, how to submit claims, etc. In brief, appointed counsel compensation is claimed on a CJA Form 20 (CJA Form 30 in capital cases), which is referred to as a CJA voucher. These vouchers must be submitted to the court clerk no later than forty-five days after the final disposition of the case unless there is good cause for the delay. Counsel should check the form for accuracy since errors can result in a return of the form and a delay in payment.

There are limits on case compensation although the presiding judge may certify compensation in excess of the district limits when the case involves extended or complex representation. If an appointed attorney is going to claim an amount in excess of the district court's hourly rate or maximum case amount, a memorandum in support of the claim needs to be submitted. Case compensation limits do not apply to capital cases. Compensation may include necessary and reasonable travel and out-of-pocket expenses including transcripts, legal research, telephone calls, copying costs, etc. Travel time does not ordinarily include time spent at a hotel, and reimbursement may be apportioned if the travel was for more than one client. Appointed counsel should be aware that many expenses will not be reimbursed such as general office overhead or personal items like suits or food. Counsel should check the guidelines as to whether a particular expense will be reimbursed by the court before incurring the expense particularly because some expenses require prior court authorization.

Conflicts of Interests

When two defendants in the same case have the same lawyer, the court must inquire as to the actual or possible conflict of interests that would prevent either defendant from receiving competent Sixth Amendment representation, known as a Rule 44(c) inquiry. *See* FRCrP 44(c). A Rule 44(c) conflict precludes not only joint representation by the same attorney but representation by attorneys in the same firm or associated in the practice of law. Institutional defenders are considered one law firm for the purposes of FRCrP 44(c).

In some cases the defendants might insist on having the same counsel despite an actual conflict of interest. This typically occurs when the defendants are married or have had the same attorney for a long period of time. In addition to assigning or suggesting separate counsel to both defendants, the judges will also talk to the defendants of the advisability of joint representation.

The defendants may seek to waive their rights to conflict-free counsel. A waiver is done only after the judge has separately questioned each defendant as to the rights he or she is giving up and the possible disadvantages with respect to joint representation, namely the inability of counsel to assert certain defenses, to conduct certain cross-examinations, and to make certain arguments as a result of the joint representation. The waiver must be clear, unequivocal, and unambiguous. Even after the defendants are clearly aware of the conflict and the possible consequences of joint representation but still wish to waive the right to conflict-free counsel, the judge may still reject the request if the court believes that joint representation would be ineffective representation under the Sixth Amendment. *See, e.g., Wheat v. United States*, 486 U.S. 153, 109 L.Ed.2d 140, 108 S.Ct. 1692 (1988).

Before a Rule 44(c) inquiry, defense counsel should prepare each defendant for questioning by the judge, similar to any waiver or plea. The judge will ask the defendant standard background questions including the age and education of each defendant. The judge will ask about the voluntariness of the defendant's waiver, whether the defendant is under the influence of a controlled substance or alcohol, suffers from a mental impairment or illness, or has been threatened or coerced in any way to waive a right. The judge will ask defense counsel if they know of any reason why the defendant is not competent to enter a waiver. The judge will then personally address each defendant, often in separate hearings, to ensure that the defendant is aware of the possible and/or actual conflicts and the foreseeable prejudices from joint representation. The judge will advise the defendants that not all possible consequences can be divined and that later on more conflicts might arise that may preclude certain defenses and strategies. Because defense strategies and theories of the case may be discussed during the colloquy, defense counsel should ask for an in camera hearing outside the presence of the prosecution.

Rule 45. Time

(a) **Computation.** In computing any period of time the day of the act or event from which the designated period of time begins to run shall not be included. The last day of the period so computed shall be included, unless it is a Saturday, a Sunday, or a legal holiday, or, when the act to be done is the filing of some paper in court, a day on which weather or other conditions have made the office of the clerk of the district court inaccessible, in which event the period runs until the end of the next day which is not one of the aforementioned days. When a period of time prescribed or allowed is less than 11 days, intermediate Saturdays, Sundays and legal holidays shall be excluded in the computation. As used in these rules, "legal holiday" includes New Year's Day, Birthday of Martin Luther King, Jr., Washington's Birthday, Memorial Day, Independence Day, Labor Day, Columbus Day, Veterans Day, Thanksgiving Day, Christmas Day, and any other day appointed as a holiday by the President or the Congress of the United States, or by the state in which the district court is held.

(b) **Enlargement.** When an act is required or allowed to be done at or within a specified time, the court for cause shown may at any time in its discretion (1) with or without motion or notice, order the period enlarged if request therefor is made before the expiration of the period originally prescribed or as extended by a previous order or (2) upon motion made after the expiration of the specified period permit the act to be done if the failure to act was the result of excusable neglect; but the court may not extend the time for taking any action under Rules 29, 33, 34, and 35, except to the extent and under the conditions stated in them.

(c) **[Rescinded]**

(d) For motions; affidavits. A written motion, other than one which may be heard ex parte, and notice of the hearing thereof shall be served not later than 5 days before the time specified for the hearing unless a different period is fixed by rule or order of the court. For cause shown such an order may be made on ex parte application. When a motion is supported by affidavit, the affidavit shall be served with the motion; and opposing affidavits may be served not less than 1 day before the hearing unless the court permits them to be served at a later time.

(e) Additional time after service by mail. Whenever a party has the right or is required to do an act within a prescribed period after the service of a notice or other paper upon that party and the notice or other paper is served by mail, 3 days shall be added to the prescribed period.

Commentary

By Prof. Inga L. Parsons
New York University School of Law

The title of FRCrP 45 is elegant in its simplicity: Time. Unfortunately, computing time in federal district court is far from simple, which is obvious after reading the convoluted text of FRCrP 45. In plain English, when a time period is eleven days or more, all days count except when the final date is on a holiday or weekend; then the time period is extended to the next business day. If the time allotted is ten days or less, for example the ten days in which the prosecution must hold a preliminary examination if the defendant is in custody, interim weekends and holidays are not counted. Bottom line, the moving party gets the maximum number of business days available for short time periods; with a ten-day time period that is a full two weeks of working business days. There is also an allowance for days when weather conditions or other conditions (like acts of God) make the clerk of the district court inaccessible. *See* FRCrP 45(a). Holidays include the obvious ones listed in the Rule, other declared federal holidays and holidays observed in the state in which the district court is seated. *Id.* Groundhog Day and Flag Day are not excluded.

The clock starts to run the day after the triggering event. For example, if the initial appearance was on Tuesday, February 6, 2001, the last day for holding the preliminary hearing would be

Wednesday, February 21, 2001: Wednesday, February 7, Thursday, February 8 and Friday, February 9 all count; Saturday, February 10, Sunday, February 11, do not count; Monday through Friday (February 12–16) of the following week count; the next weekend does not count; Monday, February 19, does not count because it is President's Day—a legal holiday; Tuesday, February 20 counts (day 9); and Wednesday, February 21 (day 10) counts and is the last day for holding the hearing (or obtaining an indictment in lieu of a preliminary hearing). Thursday, February 22 is beyond the deadline for holding the preliminary hearing and the case would ordinarily be dismissed. Ticking off days like this is essential to avoid missing deadlines. In short, do the math. It is helpful to keep a page from a calendar in the case file showing the time calculations.

Excusable Neglect

The district court can enlarge a time period before the time expires with or without motion or after the expiration of the time period upon a showing of excusable neglect. Extensions under FRCrP 29, 33, 34, and 35 are excepted. FRCrP 45(b). All but FRCrP 35(a) allow for extensions within the seven-day time period, but because the court is without jurisdiction to hear motions under those particular rules when the time has expired, the court cannot extend the time period no matter how excusable the neglect or worthy the case. *See* the Commentary for FRCrP 29 (Motion for judgment of acquittal), the Commentary for FRCrP 33 (New trial), Commentary for FRCrP 34 (Arrest of judgment), and the Commentary for FRCrP 35 (Correction or reduction of sentence), for further discussion.

"Excusable neglect" is assessed by taking into account all relevant circumstances surrounding the party's failure to meet the deadline, including danger of prejudice to the opposing side, length of the delay and its potential impact on the judicial proceedings, reason for the delay, including whether it was within the reasonable control of the moving party, and whether the moving party acted in good faith. *See Pratt v. Philbrook*, 109 F.3d 18 (1st Cir. 1997) construing *Pioneer Investment Services Company v. Brunswick Associates*, 507 U.S. 380, 123 L.Ed.2d 74, 113 S.Ct. 1489 (1993).

Notice of Appeal Time Calculations

There is a wrinkle in time calculations when it comes to filing a notice of appeal. A notice of appeal must be filed within ten days from the date of the judgment or from the date of the entry of an appealable order such as an order to dismiss the indictment, an order denying bail, an order denying a motion to withdraw a guilty plea, or an order denying a motion for new trial. The problem is that exclusion of holidays under the Federal Appellate Rules is different than exclusions under the Federal Rules of Criminal Procedure. As discussed, FRCrP 45(a) excludes interim holidays and weekends for time periods of less than eleven days. FRAP 26(a) excludes interim holidays and weekends when the time period is less than seven days. Because appellate rules govern the filing of a notice of appeal, defense counsel has fewer days to file a notice of appeal than would be available under FRCrP 45. For example, if the judgment were rendered on Tuesday, February 6, 2001, an appeal would need to be filed by Friday, February 16, 2001—five days earlier than would be calculated under FRCrP 45 because holidays and weekends count in time periods of more than six days under the appellate rules.

In cases of excusable neglect or good cause the court can extend the time to file an appeal (even after the time has expired) up to thirty days. FRAP 4(b)(4). But where experienced lawyers have failed to file appellate papers because of miscalculation from using time calculation under the Federal Rules of Criminal Procedure instead of the appellate rules, that has been found to not be excusable neglect. *See, e.g., United States v. Guy,* 140 F.3d 735 (7th Cir. 1998) (experienced federal practitioner's failure to file a timely appeal due to reliance on federal criminal procedure time calculations rather than federal appellate rules was not excusable neglect, although inexperienced state practitioner's failure to file as a result of this same reliance was excusable neglect).

The best practice is not to cut it close. File the papers well within the time period. When an extension is available, such as within the seven-day period for filing post-trial motions under FRCrP 29, 33, and 34, counsel should automatically request a thirty-day or longer extension at the time of the verdict to avoid delay problems. Even if the lawyer does not think he or she will need the extra time, ask for it anyway—one can always file early. (Remember those thirty days include weekends and holidays).

Speedy Trial Act

Time calculations are obviously important under the Speedy Trial Act. Trial is supposed to commence within seventy days from the defendant's initial appearance or the filing of the charging document whichever is later. *See* 18 USCS § 3161(c)(1). At each court appearance, counsel for both sides should count the days off the speedy trial calendar. Be sure to know what days are excluded under the Act. *See* 18 USCS § 3161(h). If there is any doubt, defense counsel should ask the court at the pretrial conferences to have the government state on the record how much time has elapsed under the Speedy Trial Act. Speedy trial motions should be filed strategically and only when it is certain that the time has expired. One defendant filed a motion to dismiss under the Speedy Trial Act on the Monday following the expiration of the seventy-day period which had fallen on the preceding Saturday. Since the seventieth day was on a Saturday, the next business day the trial could have started was that Monday. However, the filing of a pretrial motion excludes time under the Act (*see* 18 USCS § 3161(h)(1)(F)) so that Monday was excluded from the speedy trial clock calculations as a result of the filed motion. Had the defendant waited to file the motion until that Tuesday, the case could have been dismissed. *See United States v. Bruckman*, 874 F.2d 57, 62 (1st. Cir. 1989).

Time for Filing Motions

FRCrP 45 also speaks to the timing for the filing of motions. Most judges have their own rules regarding motion schedules and there are local district court rules as well; consequently FRCrP 45 is little used. However, if not otherwise specified, FRCrP 45 provides that motions with affidavits need to be filed five days before any hearing and opposition papers filed one day beforehand. FRCrP 45(d). As a practical matter, most courts would want motions much earlier to allow adequate time for the opposition to respond as well as for the moving party to reply. A typical motion schedule would be moving papers filed one month in advance of hearing, opposition papers filed two weeks afterward, reply papers filed one week later and the hearing held one week after the reply is received. A month-long motion schedule gives the parties adequate time to file and to respond and also gives the court time to review the papers in advance of the hearing.

When service is effected by mail, the receiving party has an additional three days added to any prescribed period in which to respond; therefore to avoid delay, the moving party should mail the papers at least three days in advance. FRCrP 45(e). Many parties effect service by facsimile if the other party is willing to accept service in that manner.

Rule 46. Release From Custody

(a) **Release prior to trial.** Eligibility for release prior to trial shall be in accordance with 18 USC § 3142 and 3144.

(b) **Release during trial.** A person released before trial shall continue on release during trial under the same terms and conditions as were previously imposed unless the court determines that other terms and conditions or termination of release are necessary to assure such person's presence during the trial or to assure that such person's conduct will not obstruct the orderly and expeditious progress of the trial.

(c) **Pending sentence and notice of appeal.** Eligibility for release pending sentence or pending notice of appeal or expiration of the time allowed for filing notice of appeal, shall be in accordance with 18 USC § 3143. The burden of establishing that the defendant will not flee or pose a danger to any other person or to the community rests with the defendant.

(d) **Justification of sureties.** Every surety, except a corporate surety which is approved as provided by law, shall justify by affidavit and may be required to describe in the affidavit the property by which the surety proposes to justify and the encumbrances thereon, the number and amount of other bonds and undertakings for bail entered into by the surety and remaining undischarged and all the other liabilities of the surety. No bond shall be approved unless the surety thereon appears to be qualified.

(e) **Forfeiture.**

(1) **Declaration.** If there is a breach of condition of a bond, the district court shall declare a forfeiture of the bail.

(2) **Setting aside.** The court may direct that a forfeiture be set aside in whole or in part, upon such conditions as the court may impose, if a person released upon execution of an appearance bond with a surety is subsequently surrendered by the

Rule 46. Release From Custody

surety into custody or if it otherwise appears that justice does not require the forfeiture.

(3) Enforcement. When a forfeiture has not been set aside, the court shall on motion enter a judgment of default and execution may issue thereon. By entering into a bond the obligors submit to the jurisdiction of the district court and irrevocably appoint the clerk of the court as their agent upon whom any papers affecting their liability may be served. Their liability may be enforced on motion without the necessity of an independent action. The motion and such notice of the motion as the court prescribes may be served on the clerk of the court, who shall forthwith mail copies to the obligors to their last known addresses.

(4) Remission. After entry of such judgment, the court may remit it in whole or in part under the conditions applying to the setting aside of forfeiture in paragraph (2) of this subdivision.

(f) Exoneration. When the condition of the bond has been satisfied or the forfeiture thereof has been set aside or remitted, the court shall exonerate the obligors and release any bail. A surety may be exonerated by a deposit of cash in the amount of the bond or by a timely surrender of the defendant into custody.

(g) Supervision of detention pending trial. The court shall exercise supervision over the detention of defendants and witnesses within the district pending trial for the purpose of eliminating all unnecessary detention. The attorney for the government shall make a biweekly report to the court listing each defendant and witness who has been held in custody pending indictment, arraignment or trial for a period in excess of ten days. As to each witness so listed the attorney for the government shall make a statement of the reasons why such witness should not be released with or without the taking of a deposition pursuant to Rule 15(a). As to each defendant so listed the attorney for the government shall make a statement of the reasons why the defendant is still held in custody.

(h) Forfeiture of property. Nothing in this rule or in chapter 207 of title 18, United States Code, shall prevent the court from disposing of any charge by entering an order directing forfeiture of property pursuant to 18 U.S.C. 3142 (c)(1)(B)(xi) if the value of the property is an amount that would be an appropriate sentence after conviction of the offense charged and if such forfeiture is authorized by statute or regulation.

(i) Production of statements.

(1) In general. Rule 26.2(a)–(d) and (f) applies at a detention hearing held under 18 U.S.C. § 3142, unless the court, for good cause shown, rules otherwise in a particular case.

(2) Sanctions for failure to produce statement. If a party elects not to comply with an order under Rule 26.2(a) to deliver a statement to the moving party, at the detention hearing the court may not consider the testimony of a witness whose statement is withheld.

Commentary

By Prof. Inga L. Parsons
New York University School of Law

The Bail Reform Act Generally

FRCrP 46 pertains to release of the defendant from custody but in most cases directs the reader to the Bail Reform Act codified in 18 USCS §§ 3142–3161. *See, e.g.*, FRCrP 46(a). FRCrP 46 itself provides little guidance. A federal practitioner must become well acquainted with the Bail Reform Act to represent a defendant effectively in federal court. Certainly the issue of whether the defendant will be released or in custody during the pendency of the proceedings is most important to the defendant. The good news for defendants is that in federal court pretrial release is "encouraged" in many cases and often the prosecution will consent to bail. *See* FRCrP 46 1966 Advisory Committee Notes. The bad news for defendants is that for federal drug offenses and crimes of violence a defendant can be detained not only for risk of flight but also for potential dangerousness, and there is a rebuttable presumption that the defendant is a risk of flight and a danger to the community for most of these offenses. *See* 18 USCS § 3142(e)–(f); *see also United States v. Salerno*, 481 U.S. 739, 95 L.Ed.2d 697, 107 S.Ct 2095 (1986).

The Bail Reform Act requires judges to first consider releasing the defendants on their own recognizance (referred to as ROR) or releasing the defendants on an unsecured personal recognizance bond (referred to as a PRB). *See* 18 USCS § 3142(b). Only if this release is inadequate to assure the defendant's presence in court and the safety of the community, can the judge consider adding restrictive conditions such as requiring the defendant to remain in a family member's custody, report to pretrial services on a regular basis, or attend a substance abuse program. *See* 18 USCS § 3142(c) for a list of conditions. Detention is the last resort except in rebuttable presumption cases.

In short, the court releases a defendant unless it determines there are no conditions or combinations of conditions that would assure the defendant's presence in court and the safety of the community. The factors the court looks to in making its determination are detailed at 18 USCS § 3142(g) and include the nature and circumstances of the offense, the weight of the evidence against the defendant, the history and characteristics of the defendant including family ties, employment, financial resources, substance abuse, criminal record, and whether the defendant's release would pose a danger to a person or the community.

Preparing for Bail

The issue of bail arises in most cases at the initial appearance before the magistrate judge, which is held pursuant to FRCrP 5. If defense counsel has been retained or appointed in advance of the initial appearance, there are important preparations to be done. Defense counsel should interview the client in-depth, focusing on the release factors set out in 18 USCS § 3142(g). Defense counsel should also determine all bail resources including cash, property (even jewelry and stocks), and financially responsible persons (referred to as FRPs or sureties) who would be willing to co-sign a bond or take custody of the defendant. If there is real property and the case is one where the posting of substantial security is anticipated, a recent assessment of the property may be required. Documentation on the property that shows proof of ownership and value should be brought to court. Ideally, the FRPs should be asked to come to court with proof of their income and assets. If the judge orders the bond be secured by FRPs, this can be met more immediately if they are in court, and it also visually demonstrates to the judge support for the defendant as well as ties to the community. In federal court, the defendant no longer has to post the full amount of the bond through a bail bondsmen. Instead, the federal court holds the bond and the defendant posts any requisite security. Some judges will even take wedding rings and other items of sentimental value to assure the presence of the defendant. The defendant will be required to surrender all travel documents and should bring any passport or visas to the initial appearance.

If defense counsel's first exposure to the case is the day of the initial appearance, a similar interview and investigation should be done to the extent possible given the time constraints of the court appearance. In cases where the prosecution is seeking detention, it may be better to hold off the judge's determination of bail until resources and FRPs can be marshaled, even though the defendant will have to stay in custody during the meantime. This also provides additional time to try to work out a negotiated bail with the prosecution.

In some cases it may be possible to have bail set and have the defendant released even before all conditions are met. Judges will sometimes approve a premature release (usually if the prosecution consents and it is not a serious rebuttable presumption case) as long as a date is given when all bail conditions must be met or the defendant will be returned to custody or a bench warrant will issue for failure to appear. If the condition is a relatively minor one, such as surrendering a passport when the defendant has signed a substantial bond, judges are likely to give the defendant twenty-four hours to go home and get the passport. In other cases, usually rebuttable presumption cases, the defense may want to consent to detention without prejudice in order to bring a motion for bail at a later date if defense counsel does not believe they will have enough time to marshal the resources necessary to overcome the presumption by the date of the detention hearing, which must be held within five days.

Defense counsel may be tempted to consent to detention without prejudice because the attorney is convinced that there is no way the defendant will be released—often where the defendant has a serious criminal record or is in the country illegally. Even in those cases it is usually better to have the detention hearing and at least hear the government's proffers, which could lead to discovery of important information about the case. The prosecution may have to call witnesses to support its assertions, and those witnesses would be under oath and subject to cross-examination. Although judges may allow the prosecution to proceed by proffer, for certain assertions some judges will require live testimony. Defense counsel should request that witnesses be called. The prosecution would also have to turn over any statements of the witnesses pursuant to FRCrP 26.2. FRCrP 46(i). Prosecutors may want to consider consenting to a high bail to avoid disclosing witnesses where that is likely. For defense counsel, contesting bail provides an opportunity to fight hard for the client, demonstrate a commitment to the defense, and establish good client rapport even where release is highly unlikely.

Pretrial Services Interview

Before the initial appearance, the defendant ordinarily will be interviewed by the Pretrial Services Office to determine whether the defendant is at risk of flight and/or a danger to the community. The Pretrial Services Office issues a brief report setting forth the charges, the defendant's prior record (in some jurisdictions the "rap sheet" is attached to the report), bail resources, and, importantly, a recommendation as to whether the defendant should be released, and, if so, on what conditions. If counsel has been retained, it may be helpful to be present at the interview, particularly since counsel may have useful information on potential cosigners and may be able to provide confirmation of the client's assets and resources. In many cases the interview is held without counsel but the substance of the report is confidential and is to be used solely for bail purposes. Although the statute provides that regulations may be promulgated allowing for release of the bail information to specified individuals/entities such as probation officers and law enforcement agencies (in limited circumstances and for criminal justice research), no such regulations have been promulgated to date. *See* 18 USCS § 3153(c). In any event, information contained in the report is not admissible on the issue of guilt unless it is a crime committed to obtain pretrial release or for failure to appear. *Id.*

Although the parties are entitled to a copy of the pretrial services report, most jurisdictions require that the report be returned at the end of the bail hearing. Any information contained in the report, which is helpful to the defense, should be written down in the file. It is especially important to note whether the defendant tested positive for controlled substances and made any incriminating statements. Should the government attempt to use that information to establish the defendant's knowledge of narcotics, for instance, the defense should object that the prosecution is precluded under the Bail Reform Act. See 18 USCS § 3153(c)(3).

Detention Hearings Generally

The best of all worlds is to get the government to consent to a reasonable bail and avoid a detention hearing. Even if the prosecution wants more security than the defense is prepared to offer, it is important that the defense get the prosecution to say on the record that there are conditions that could assure the defendant's presence in court and the safety of the community. The parties can then argue to the judge what those conditions should be.

One of the "reforms" of the Bail Reform Act was to insure that people were not kept in custody simply because they did not have money. The Act specifically states that the "judicial officer may not impose a financial condition that results in the pretrial detention of the person." 18 USCS § 3142(c)(2). Although the judge can justify financial conditions as necessary to assure the defendant's presence in court and the safety of the community, once bail is set, if the defense can demonstrate an inability to meet a financial condition, often the judge will agree to a lower amount to avoid conflicting with § 3142(c)(2).

A detention hearing is not required in every case. Unless it is a crime of violence, an offense carrying life imprisonment or death, a drug offense with a maximum of ten years or more (essentially any federal drug felony), a felon with two violent or drug priors, or the case involves a serious risk of flight or obstruction of justice, the government is not entitled to a detention hearing and bail must be set. See 18 USCS § 3142(f)(1). Although subsection (f)(1) covers a wide range of cases, both parties need to assess whether a detention hearing is required. If the defendant is accused solely of having brought a firearm from another state, for example, and there is no risk of flight or obstruction of justice, the prosecution could not seek detention.

Once it is established that the prosecution is entitled to seek detention, the issue is whether the hearing will go forward immediately. The defense may request a continuance for up to five days and the prosecution can request a continuance for up to three days (these time periods do not include holidays and weekends). 18 USCS § 3142(f)(2). It is usually better to be prepared fully for the hearing rather than risk having the judge impose an order of detention or release based on half a presentation and then have to overcome that order later on.

In most cases the judge will ask at the outset what the government's position is on bail. If the government is seeking detention, the judge will inquire whether it is a rebuttable presumption case and if not, whether the government is proceeding on risk of flight or dangerousness to the community (or both). When the judge neglects to ask, defense counsel should insure that the prosecutor states specifically on what grounds the prosecution is relying in seeking detention. Prosecutors prefer to proceed on risk of flight rather than danger to the community because the burden of proof for risk of flight is preponderance of the evidence, but for danger to the community the burden of proof is by clear and convincing evidence. *See* 18 USCS § 3142(f)(2).

Rebuttable Presumption Cases

Similarly, judges usually will rule on risk of flight and may not reach the issue of danger to the community. A judge who is asked to find a danger to the community is also likely to find a risk of flight to insulate the bail order from review at the higher standard.

In rebuttable presumption cases, some judges will require the defense to go first once it is determined that the presumption applies, since in those cases the defense technically has the burden to rebut the presumption. Defense counsel should try to insist that the prosecution set out all of the facts it relies on first so the defense can make a consolidated response. In addition to arguing that the presumption is rebuttable, defense counsel is usually benefitted by offering a concrete proposal. Defense counsel should be aware of the "going rate" for the district as to bail in such cases. Asking for bail without offering a specific package can be dangerous because even if the judge is persuaded that bail can be set, the conditions may be impossible for the defendant to make. The following is a typical defense response:

"Your Honor, although there is presumption of risk of flight and danger to the community, the presumption is rebuttable. Mr. Jones is a lifelong resident of the community. He is a thirty-eight-year-old U.S. citizen, married with two children. His wife is present in court today. Mr. Jones's immediate and extended family all live in the metropolitan area. Seven of them are in court today. Mr. Jones has worked for the postal service for fifteen years. His only other brush with the law involved simple possession of marijuana six years ago for which he received a suspended sentence. Although this offense involves narcotics, thus triggering the presumption, there are no allegations of actual violence or the presence of any weapons. Moreover, the evidence linking Mr. Jones to the offense relies solely on the uncorroborated testimony of a confidential informant. If Your Honor were to detain Mr. Jones, the defense would request that the confidential informant come before this court and testify under oath subject to cross-examination. In addition, as Your Honor is well aware, pursuant to 18 USCS § 3142 (j), nothing in the Bail Reform Act shall be construed as modifying or limiting the presumption of innocence. The defense believes that a $200,000 personal recognizance bond cosigned by three financially responsible people, Mr. Jones's father who is a retired school superintendent with a pension, Mr. Jones's mother who currently works as a nurse at the VA hospital, and Mr. Jones's brother who is a sanitation worker with the city, is sufficient. All three are present in court with proof of income and are prepared to sign today. If necessary, Mr. Jones's father would put up his home, which has an equity value of over $65,000. Mr. Jones would submit to strict pretrial supervision."

Order of Release

If the defendant is released, the court will issue a release order that includes any special conditions and advises the defendant both of the penalties for failure to appear and committing an offense while out on bail. *See* 18 USCS § 3142(h). The court must also advise the defendant of the crimes of witness tampering, obstruction of justice, etc. *See* 18 USCS § 3142(h)(2)(C). Defense counsel should tell the defendant that if the defendant is found guilty of bail jumping, any jail sentence for that offense is required to be run consecutively and any crime committed while out on bail must also run consecutively to the original offense sentence. *See* 18 USCS §§ 3146(b)(2), 3147.

Detention Order

If the defendant is detained, the court must issue an order of detention including findings of fact and statement of reasons for detention. 18 USCS § 3142(i). These reasons will be helpful if counsel decides to reopen the hearing or appeal the order. The judge can also permit the temporary release of a person in custody for the preparation of the defense or for "another compelling reason." *Id.* In practice, the compelling reason for allowing such a release is almost always when the defendant becomes a cooperating witness for the government and must meet with the prosecution and case agents away from prison.

Special Release Conditions and Considerations

Pretrial services administer a drug test by testing the defendant's urine at the pretrial interview. If the defendants test positive for narcotics, they will be subject to drug testing as a condition of bail. If the defendants do not test positive and there is no evidence of drug use, the defense should object to the imposition of a drug testing release condition. Where the defendant has a substance abuse problem the defense may want to propose having the defendant submit to in-house drug treatment as an alternative to detention.

If possible, the defense should try to get "regular" pretrial service supervision rather than "strict" pretrial supervision. Strict pretrial supervision usually means the defendant has to report daily to the pretrial office, sometimes in person. Regular pretrial supervision may only require a weekly telephone call. The defense should also try to get generous travel restrictions such as the ability to travel within the continental United States or even foreign countries if that is necessary for the defendant's employment. The standard condition when a bail is set is usually that the defendant must remain in the jurisdiction unless receiving prior permission to travel beyond that jurisdiction.

Defense counsel should avoid offering real property to secure a bond unless it is absolutely necessary. Judges require proof of the value of the property, and some may insist on a current assessment, which can be costly, and the paperwork can delay release. Some prosecutors will demand deeds and signing over liens to the government in advance. Defense counsel should object to actions by the prosecution; such actions are more appropriate for a real estate agent in the sale of a house rather than an officer of the court seeking security of a bond. The government is not there to obtain the property. It is the risk of losing the property that compels the defendant's presence in court and the reason for requiring the property as security.

As a last resort the defense can offer that the defendant wear an electronic monitoring device while in home detention. This can be expensive to operate and prosecutors usually object because the defendant can often make it out of the state before the person is discovered to be missing. If electronic monitoring and home confinement are ordered, defense counsel should make certain that the defendant is still able to attend employment, medical, religious, and legal appointments.

If the defendant is detained but requires medical or psychological treatment, defense counsel should ensure that the detention order or separate medical order includes specific treatment. This will help the defendant to get services from the Bureau of Prisons, and counsel can return to the judge to enforce the court's order if services are not provided.

Sureties and Securities

FRCrP 46(d) requires that every surety be justified by affidavit, which may include detailing the property and encumbrances and liabilities of the surety. The requirement of an affidavit may be relaxed in some jurisdictions, and a verbal representation in court or a proffer by counsel may be sufficient justification. Counsel should determine what the local practice is with respect to the justification of sureties.

Before offering sureties or FRPs, defense counsel should interview the people to discover their financial situation and also their relationship to the defendant, plus their knowledge of the facts of the case. Under FRCrP 46 the surety must be qualified, and prosecutors will try to interview the surety to confirm assets and to further the investigation of the case. In some instances it may be wiser for the defense not to proffer a particular FRP whose testimony may compromise the defendant and the merits of his case even if the FRP's bank account might assure release. The better practice is to try to get the judge to approve the surety on the record at the bail hearing so the prosecution does not have the opportunity to interview the surety privately. Prosecutors should demand the opportunity to interview the FRPs before the court approves them.

Prosecutors have used the FRP interviews not only to further the investigation, but in some cases to discourage potential cosigners from signing in order to keep a defendant in custody when bail has been set over the prosecutor's objection. If there is a dispute as to the adequacy of the surety, the issue will be resolved by the judge. In most cases judicial intervention is unnecessary because the prosecutors will be successful in dissuading the FRPs from signing, often by emphasizing that if the defendants fail to come to court, the sureties could lose their life savings, be unable to send their children to college, and will owe the government hundreds of thousands of dollars, possibly for the rest of their lives. Prosecutors have been known to focus on potential cosigners' immigration status if they are non-U.S. citizens and to suggest that this status could be compromised by signing a bond. Once the FRP declines to sign, defense counsel has few options except to "debrief" the FRP on what the prosecutor said and to explain realistically what the consequences would be if the defendant were to fail to appear when the prosecutor has exaggerated those consequences. In some cases defense counsel may wish to have the judge explain to the potential FRP what the consequences would be if the defendant did not appear in court. Again, the better practice is to try to get the judge to approve the surety on the record at the bail hearing so that the prosecution does not have the opportunity to interview the surety privately.

If the court in convinced that the money or property used to secure bail was obtained from illegitimate sources, the court may decline to accept it. Prosecutors should review the source of the monies carefully because a hearing to determine its legitimacy, known as a Nebbia hearing from *United States v. Nebbia*, 357 F.2d 303 (2d Cir. 1966), could provide discovery to the prosecution and an opportunity to put sureties on the stand and prevent them from signing a bond. *See also* 18 USCS § 3142(g)(4). Conversely, defense counsel should know what monies will be used and the source of those monies before they are offered as bail. It is within the court's discretion to hold a hearing; the prosecution is not entitled to a hearing on the source of the funding. *See, e.g.*, *United States v. O'Brien*, 895 F.2d 810 (1st Cir. 1990).

Sureties or FRPs should be advised that they will be jointly and severally liable for the full amount of the bond should the defendant fail to come to court as required. FRCrP 46(e) provides further details on the forfeiture of bond for failure to appear.

Appealing, Revoking, or Amending a Bail Decision

There is a right to a district court review of a magistrate's bail determination. 18 USCS § 3145(b). Usually the district court judges are less sympathetic to the defense than the magistrate judges because most bail decisions are made by magistrate judges who have a sense of what a case is worth and which defendants are good and bad risks. District court judges tend to think any defendant where the prosecution moves for detention is a bad risk, and they review the magistrate judge's decision de novo. If a bail decision is adverse to counsel's position and the attorney intends to seek district court review, counsel should ask for a stay of the bail order pending that review.

A bail decision of the district court is appealable to the court of appeals. 18 USCS § 3145(c). The appeal is interlocutory; otherwise the issue of release would be moot once the defendant was convicted and sentenced under the original release or detention order. *See* 18 USCS § 3731. The standard of review for an appeal of the district court decision is not set out in the Bail Reform Act and circuits differ on the level of deference; thus, counsel should familiarize themselves with the standard in their jurisdiction.

Often more useful and successful for the defense than a review or appeal is the reconsideration of bail. A bail hearing may be reopened any time before trial if there is new information. 18 USCS § 3142(f)(2). New information could mean one more cosigner was found or an extra ten dollars discovered. In practice, it does not take much to get the hearing reopened. It may be that the magistrate judge has changed or the case is now with the district court judge who may be more likely to rule in a particular party's favor. The judge's decision on bail may depend on the posture of the case. If the defense has a strong motion to suppress, defense counsel can argue that the defendant has little incentive to flee while the issue is pending. If the defendant qualifies for substantial reductions under the drug guidelines, the defendant may have less incentive to flee. Once bail is granted and the defendant shows up, it is harder to justify detention even if the defendant loses the suppression hearing. Getting bail may take six bites of the apple and ten FRPs before a judge will finally relent, but defendants will appreciate the effort. The bail orders can be amended on motion of the defense or the prosecution. 18 USCS § 3142(c)(3). If the defendant commits other offenses or violates the conditions of bail, the prosecution can move to have the bail revoked. The procedures and sanctions for violating the terms of release are set out at 18 USCS § 3148.

Post-Trial Detention

It is obviously harder to obtain bail after conviction. Some violent crimes and drug offenses require a mandatory revocation unless there are exceptional reasons why detention would not be appropriate. *See* 18 USCS § 3143(a)(2), (b)(2); 18 USCS § 3145(c). In mandatory detention cases the defense may be able to persuade a judge to delay formal imposition of a judgment of conviction to give the defendant some time to at least go home one last time, particularly where the defendant has made all court appearances. The defense may be able to obtain bail pending sentencing if there is a substantial likelihood a motion for acquittal or a new trial will be granted, or if the government is not seeking jail time and the court finds by clear and convincing evidence that the defendant will not flee or endanger the community. *See* 18 USCS § 3143(a)(2).

Once the defendant is sentenced to a term of incarceration, it becomes even more difficult to remain out on bail pending appeal. Violent and drug offenses where jail time is imposed require mandatory detention unless there are exceptional reasons that compel release. 18 USCS § 3143(b)(2); 18 USCS § 3145(c). Otherwise, the defense must show by clear and convincing evidence that the defendant will not flee or endanger the community and that the appeal raises a substantial question of law or fact likely to result in a favorable disposition for the defendant. *See* 18 USCS § 3143(b)(1).

Rule 47. Motions

An application to the court for an order shall be by motion. A motion other than one made during a trial or hearing shall be in writing unless the court permits it to be made orally. It shall state the grounds upon which it is made and shall set forth the relief or order sought. It may be supported by affidavit.

Commentary

By Prof. Inga L. Parsons
New York University School of Law

Motions Generally

When making an application to a district court for an order, the request is generally made by written motion. *See* FRCrP 47. Oral motions are more appropriately brought at trial or hearing or as the court permits. In some cases judges will accept a motion in letterform and "so order" the letter. Each district has local rules that often specify the form of motion papers and the formality of those filings. *See* FRCrP 57. Judges also have individual standing orders that describe their requirements for motions. Before filing a motion with the court, an attorney must review the local rules, administrative orders, and standing orders of the particular court. *See* FRCrP 49 for the service and filing of motions. FRCrP 12 governs pretrial motions.

Form of the Motion

Although the formality of motions varies from district to district, a typical formal motion consists of a notice of motion, a motion supported by affidavit or declaration, and a memorandum of law. The notice of motion informs the court and opposing counsel of the nature of the issue and the anticipated date for submissions and any hearing. The motion states the specific relief requested and a summary of the grounds for relief. The motion is usually supported by an averment, either by affidavit or declaration. An affidavit is sworn to and notarized, and a declaration is signed under the penalties of perjury. Some districts will allow the use of declarations while other districts require formal notarized affidavits. Attorneys should know the local rules of the district and the custom of the court.

The memorandum of law typically contains a preliminary statement setting forth the procedural posture of the case, a factual background, and the legal arguments raised by the motion. In some districts the notice of motion and motion are combined, or the memorandum of law is combined with the attorney's affidavit for expediency.

FRCrP 47 does not require that a motion be supported by an affidavit, only that it "may" be supported by affidavit. Some circuits insist that in order to put a fact in issue, the party with the burden of going forward must do so through personal knowledge sworn under the penalties of perjury. *See, e.g., United States v. Gillette*, 383 F.2d 843 (2d Cir. 1967). An attorney's affidavit is insufficient where the personal knowledge rests with the client or agent. Where the opposing party fails to place a fact in issue through sworn testimony, litigants should insist on the filing of sworn affidavits or declarations, or request that the judge deny the request for a hearing and/or dismiss the motion outright.

Supporting Affidavit Considerations

There are important strategic considerations when the defendant or the case agent must swear to facts to support or counter a motion. The inexperienced attorney is often tempted to include all of the facts in the case in the affidavit. That is a usually a mistake, particularly at the outset of the matter when certain facts will not be known and many of the known facts will be in dispute. Both sides should be cautious in committing an agent or client to a detailed account unnecessarily because that can later be used to impeach the affiant should the affiant take the stand and misstate a detail. For the defendant the stakes are even higher since sworn statements by the defendant contradicted by law enforcement officers are often used to support obstruction of justice and perjury enhancements.

There is an additional concern in cases where the defendant moves for suppression of evidence. In order to meet the burden of going forward on that motion, the defendant must aver that the defendant had a reasonable expectation of privacy in the thing seized or the area searched. *See* the Commentary for FRCrP 41. Establishing standing to make a Fourth Amendment claim often requires that the defendant admit to ownership of the contraband or the container in which the contraband was found in derogation of the defendant's Fifth Amendment right against self-incrimination. The Supreme Court has effected a compromise that allows the defendant to make the incriminating assertions necessary to establish the right to bring a motion, but does not allow the prosecution to use that information in its case-in-chief to establish guilt. *See Simmons v. United States*, 390 U.S. 377, 19 L.Ed.2d 1247, 88 S.Ct. 967 (1968). Defense counsel must ensure that the information is not used inappropriately at trial.

Counsel should craft any declaration carefully to insure that only the minimal information needed to support or oppose the motion is detailed, while indicating that an attorney prepared the declaration with just the relevant facts included. Moreover, detailed affidavits are not ordinarily necessary because the facts the judge will rely on in assessing the motion will be those brought out under oath and subject to cross-examination at the hearing. Indeed, counsel must be vigilant that all the necessary facts included in the affidavits and declarations are elicited at the hearing through testimony since the affidavits are not considered testimony.

In some cases there will be no factual dispute because the facts are not contested or are stipulated to for the purposes of the motion. In such cases a hearing may be unnecessary. The judge is in a position to rule on the basis of the legal briefing in the memoranda of law as if the motion were one for civil summary judgment. Prosecutors in particular wish to keep law enforcement agents off the stand and will look first to whether the party has standing to make the motion, and second to whether a hearing is avoidable. Defendants, on the other hand, can gain much from a hearing. Even if at the end of the day the judge credits the testimony of the law enforcement officer and denies the motion, the defense will usually obtain valuable discovery and an opportunity to pin down the officer's testimony.

Memoranda of Law Considerations

The initial memorandum of law contains argument based on the facts set out in the affidavits. Affidavits should not contain argument, only the facts in support of the argument. Some lawyers will not include a statement of facts in the memorandum of law and will rely solely on the attached affidavits. The better practice is to include a brief statement of facts taken from the various affidavits and cite to those affidavits. This saves the judge (or law clerk) from having to go back and forth from the memorandum of law to the attached affidavits. A factual statement also allows the attorney to choose the important facts and put them in desirable order in a persuasive narrative. The factual statement is like an opening statement at trial—it should not be waived. In some cases where the facts are not well known it may be better to submit both a cursory memorandum of law and a detailed post-hearing memorandum applying the law to the facts established at the hearing.

In preparing the memorandum of law many judges will admonish lawyers that a "brief" should be just that—short and to the point. It is good advice. Much of the verbiage in motions is "lawyerese" and attorneys should strive for plain English and short sentences. Make sure the law is good and the arguments sound. Too often parties rely on exaggerated language such as "clearly," "undeniably," and "without a doubt" in an attempt to make their point. If the issues were so clear, the case would be disposed of and there would be no need for motions. The argument should be persuasive and forceful but not histrionic. Similarly, inexperienced attorneys will be tempted to attack opposing counsel personally for whatever claims are contained in their papers and to respond with indignation and righteousness. This is unprofessional and distracts from the quality of the argument. Counsel should be careful not to misstate the facts or the law. If it appears as an intentional misstatement or "stretch," a judge is likely to discredit the entire motion.

Judges are human and are affected by visual professionalism. Just as one would not wear a crumpled suit and loose tie to an interview for a judicial clerkship, a motion should be neat and clean. The motion should be easy to read and well organized. A list of citations as may be included in appellate briefs is not ordinarily required in district court motions although many practitioners include a table of contents particularly for lengthy motions. Pages should be numbered and citations checked. In a word . . . proofread. Spelling and grammatical errors are distracting and suggest sloppiness, which could color a judge's view of the quality of the attorney and the attorney's argument. A judge who used to sit in the Central District of California would consider a split infinitive a personal affront and view the lawyer's arguments with much greater skepticism. In the computer age of automatic spell check programs and grammar check programs, it is entirely avoidable. If nothing else, make sure the judge's name is spelled correctly.

Judges will often use one side's papers as a starting point to write their opinions. Counsel should strive to have it be their motion. Even though the government's submissions are often the starting point, particularly where the judge is denying a motion to suppress, judges will still use defense papers that are "judicial," *i.e.,* well written, well researched, and carefully analyzed. Ideally a memorandum of law should read as if it were the judge's written opinion.

Motions In Limine

In cases that are scheduled to go to trial, a motion in limine is often brought requesting the judge exclude or allow the introduction of certain evidence. In limine means at the threshold, and often the motions are made before or near the beginning of trial to determine what evidence will be allowed. The sooner the issue is resolved the more time each side will have to prepare their case although some issues will not ripen until trial.

A motion in limine does not involve the suppression of evidence under the Exclusionary Rule. By the time a motion in limine is raised the evidence usually will have been determined to have been obtained lawfully, otherwise there would be no need for a motion in limine. Despite a finding that the evidence was lawfully obtained, there are many other reasons to keep the evidence out of the trial, *e.g.,* reliability or the impact on the jury's ability to be fair and impartial.

Most of the issues surrounding a motion in limine involve the Federal Rules of Evidence, such as whether the prosecution can offer statements made by the alleged child victim to a psychiatrist, whether the shocking autopsy photos can be shown to the jury, or whether a letter from the defendant to his wife can be admitted. It is helpful to think of a motion in limine as a motion in limbo.

Before the issue is resolved, counsel must speculate on what the defense should be if the child witnesses is not called, how to examine the coroner without the photographs, and how to advise the defendant whether to take the stand if the letter comes in. A request to the judge to rule on the issue will make trial preparations easier and more efficient. Waiting until the first day of trial for the judge to decide is not advised. There will be little time to adapt opening arguments and trial strategies based on the ruling, and judges will be reluctant to take a lot of time with preliminary issues when jurors are waiting.

Motions in limine are frequently made in letter form and even orally. Whether to make a formal motion in limine will depend on the judge, the local rules of the district, and also the complexity of the argument. If the analysis is whether the probative value of the autopsy photos to show defensive wounds outweighs the prejudice from the gory emotional impact, a lengthy memorandum of law is probably unnecessary. But if the issue is whether the testimony of a child complainant in a sexual assault case can be introduced through her psychiatrist rather than having the child take the stand, it will need to be thoroughly briefed well in advance of trial. Counsel may also want to request an opportunity to make oral arguments on the issue.

Rule 48. Dismissal

(a) By attorney for government. The Attorney General or the United States attorney may by leave of court file a dismissal of an indictment, information or complaint and the prosecution shall thereupon terminate. Such a dismissal may not be filed during the trial without the consent of the defendant.

(b) By court. If there is unnecessary delay in presenting the charge to a grand jury or in filing an information against a defendant who has been held to answer to the district court, or if there is unnecessary delay in bringing a defendant to trial, the court may dismiss the indictment, information or complaint.

Commentary

By Prof. Inga L. Parsons
New York University School of Law

Dismissal by the Prosecution—FRCrP 48(a)

The government may dismiss a charge or a case, referred to by the common law phrase of nolle prosequi, or "nolle" for short. The dismissal is made pursuant to FRCrP 48(a) and requires leave of the court. FRCrP 48(a). It would be rare for a judge to deny the government's motion to dismiss before trial unless the judge determined that the prosecutor was trying to harass or deliberately prejudice the defendant through charging, dismissing, and then recharging. Most federal judges give great deference to prosecutorial discretion in deciding whether to bring or to continue to bring charges.

FRCrP 48(a) does not provide whether the prosecutor's dismissal is with or without prejudice. A dismissal that is not specified is treated as without prejudice, and the government can indict again for the same offense providing it does so within the statute of limitations. Defense counsel should endeavor to have the case dismissed with prejudice to preclude the government from recharging.

FRCrP48(a) Strategic Consideration

After the trial starts, the prosecution cannot dismiss a case or a count without the consent of the defendant. FRCrP 48(a). When double jeopardy has attached (at the time the jurors are sworn at a jury trial or the swearing of the first witness at a bench trial), if the defense does not consent and the defendant is acquitted on the count or counts, a retrial would be barred. If the defense consents to the prosecution's request to dismiss during trial after double jeopardy has attached, the government could retry the defendant. *See* the Commentary for FRCrP 26.3.

Defense counsel must understand that the prosecutor's seemingly noble offer to dismiss a count because a witness cannot be found or a key witness has lied is often in the government's strategic best interest if it can get the defense to consent, since the government could retry the defendant. The defense should ask that the prosecutor state on the record that the dismissal will be with prejudice. If the prosecutor's objective is to avoid an acquittal (possibly a personal record issue) but has no intention of retrying the case, the prosecutor may be willing to dismiss with prejudice. If the prosecutor intends to retry with better evidence or other witnesses, defense counsel must assess the risk that the jury will convict even where the government's case has soured.

Dismissal by the prosecution pursuant to FRCrP 48(a) often arises when there is a federal prosecution and it is discovered that the defendant's conduct has already been adjudicated in another jurisdiction. If a case is adjudicated at the state level, there is no legal bar to the federal government prosecuting the defendant in federal court on the same conduct providing there is federal jurisdiction. Double jeopardy does not bar a subsequent prosecution under the dual sovereignty doctrine even when the defendant is acquitted of the charges at the state level. However, the Department of Justice has an internal policy that precludes initiation of a federal prosecution following a state prosecution unless there is an independent compelling federal interest. This DOJ position is called the Petite Policy because it was recognized by the Supreme Court in *Petite v. United States*, 361 U.S. 529, 4 L.Ed.2d, 80 S.Ct. 45 (1960). Because the Petite Policy is an internal agency policy, it is not enforceable by the courts against the government. However, if the government seeks to vacate a judgment on the grounds that the prosecution violated its own Petite Policy, courts will grant such requests. *See Thompson v. United States*, 444 US 248, 62 L.Ed.2d 457, 100 S.Ct. 512 (1980). When there has been a previous prosecution on the same conduct, defense counsel should notify the government detailing why a subsequent prosecution lacks a compelling independent federal interest, plus any other mitigating circumstances, to convince the government to dismiss the federal case.

Dismissal by the Court for Unnecessary Delay—FRCrP 48(b)

FRCrP 48(b) provides for dismissal by the court if there is "unnecessary delay" in indicting the defendant who has been "held to answer" or in bringing the defendant to trial. "Held to answer" generally means once the defendant has been arrested; pre-arrest delay is not covered by FRCrP 48(b). *See, e.g., United States v. Marion*, 404 United States 307, 30 L.Ed.2d 468, 92 S.Ct. 455 (1971). Dismissal for delay under FRCrP 48 does not require a Sixth Amendment speedy trial violation or a statutory violation of the Speed Trial Act. The rule is broader, though similar considerations are at play. In cases where the court finds unnecessary delay under FRCrP 48, the court may dismiss the charges, though in some circuits the court must warn the government of a possible dismissal beforehand. *See, e.g., United States v. Towill*, 548 F.2d 1363, 1369 (9th Cir. 1977).

What Constitutes Unnecessary Delay

As with other rules using the term "unnecessary delay," FRCrP 48(b) fails to define the term. *See also* FRCrP 4, 5, and 9. The Advisory Committee Notes to FRCrP 5 provide that unnecessary delay must be "determined in light of all the facts and circumstances of the case." Four factors emerge in considering unnecessary delay: length of delay, reason for delay, whether the defendant timely asserted his rights, and whether the defendant was prejudiced by the delay. *See, e.g., United States v. Jones*, 91 F.3d 5, 7 (2d Cir. 1966) *citing Barker v. Wingo*, 407 U.S. 514, 530, 33 L.Ed.2d 10, 92 S.Ct. 2182 (1972)).

The kinds of delay that have been found "patently too long" involve delays of a number of years rather than a number of months. *See, e.g., United States v. Baron*, 336 F.Supp. 303, 305 (S.D.N.Y. 1971) (six-year post-indictment delay of trial was "by any standard shockingly long"). Even when a delay is too long, a dismissal is rarely granted, absent a showing of prosecutorial misconduct. *See, e.g., United States v. Simmons*, 338 F.2d 804 (2d Cir. 1964). Many courts require that the delay be "purposeful," "culpable," "oppressive," "vexatious," or done to secure an "unfair advantage."

See, e.g., Mull v. United States, 402 F.2d 571, 573 (9th Cir. 1968).

Showing Prejudice From Delay

To prevail on a motion to dismiss the charges, the defense also must be able to articulate and substantiate actual identifiable prejudice to the defense case. Prejudice to the defense can include whether witnesses have died or memories have faded; whether there is an increased chance of misidentification; whether any physical evidence is no longer available or compromised; whether the defendant's ability to investigate the case has been impaired; and whether the defendant or key witnesses have deteriorating health or advancing age, and are now unfit or unable to stand trial or testify at trial. These prejudice factors should be couched in terms of impairing the defendant's ability to present an adequate defense. Even a showing of prejudice or misconduct will often not be enough, however, if the defendant is not in custody and has not requested a speedy trial.

Dismissing with or without Prejudice

If counsel can persuade the court to dismiss the case or charges, the next hurdle for the defense is to persuade the court to dismiss with prejudice. A dismissal with prejudice will preclude refiling of any of the dismissed charges. In deciding whether dismissal will be with or without prejudice, the following factors are usually considered: (1) the seriousness of the offense; (2) the facts and circumstances that led to the dismissal; (3) the impact of a reprosecution on the administration of justice; and (4) any prejudice to the defendant. *See United States v. Taylor*, 487 U.S. 326, 333, 101 L.Ed.2d 297, 108 S.Ct. 2413 (1988).

Once a court has found unnecessary delay, the defense has gone a long way toward establishing the factors meriting a dismissal with prejudice. Although not necessarily entitled to a hearing depending on the circuit, the defense should request a hearing on the issue of prejudice. The hearing is an opportunity for defense counsel to learn more about the prosecution's case should defense counsel be unsuccessful in getting the case dismissed.

In their arguments on the issue of unnecessary delay and the appropriate remedy, both parties should obtain a copy of the district court's plan regarding speedy trial concerns and mandates for the prompt disposition of criminal cases pursuant to 18 USCS §

3165 and FRCrP 50. These plans, which are available to the public, will often provide information to assist both counsels in making and responding to challenges for undue delay. For example, some plans may require the U.S. Attorney's Office to exert extra vigilance and oversight on speedy trial issues, which may be useful in the defense's arguments. *See* the Commentary for FRCrP 50.

Rule 49. Service and Filing of Papers

(a) Service: when required. Written motions other than those which are heard ex parte, written notices, designations of record on appeal and similar papers shall be served upon each of the parties.

(b) Service: how made. Whenever under these rules or by an order of the court service is required or permitted to be made upon a party represented by an attorney, the service shall be made upon the attorney unless service upon the party personally is ordered by the court. Service upon the attorney or upon a party shall be made in the manner provided in civil actions.

(c) Notice of orders. Immediately upon the entry of an order made on a written motion subsequent to arraignment the clerk shall mail to each party a notice thereof and shall make a note in the docket of the mailing. Lack of notice of the entry by the clerk does not affect the time to appeal or relieve or authorize the court to relieve a party for failure to appeal within the time allowed, except as permitted by Rule 4(b) of the Federal Rules of Appellate Procedure.

(d) Filing. Papers required to be served shall be filed with the court. Papers shall be filed in the manner provided in civil actions.

(e) Filing of Dangerous Offender Notice. (Abrogated)

Commentary

By Prof. Inga L. Parsons
New York University School of Law

FRCrP 49 governs the service and filing of motion papers and other documents. Written motions and similar papers must be served on each of the parties; this includes service on opposing counsel and codefendants. Service is ordinarily made on the attorney for the party unless the court orders otherwise. FRCrP 49(b). The manner of service in a criminal case is accomplished in the same manner as in a civil case whose rules provide for delivering or mailing a copy to the last known address. *See* FRCP 5(b). Note that in time calculations, a party receiving mailed papers has three days added to any prescribed period for a response. *See* FRCrP 45.

It is a good idea to prepare the original motion (stamped "original" on the upper right-hand corner) and have it blue-backed. A blue-backing is a preprinted litigation form that is attached to the motion or any proposed order showing the case name, case number, parties in the litigation, and date of service. Some districts may require formal blue-backing, so lawyers should check local rules and court custom. A blue-backed copy also should be prepared for opposing counsel with an additional copy for each codefendant. In some districts there is less formal motion practice, and oral motions or letter motions are accepted. Counsel should be familiar with the local rules and judges' rules with respect to any special instructions on the filing of motion papers.

Ordinarily, service of motion papers is first made on the opposing party. If this copy is delivered in person, the original motion should be stamped by that office to show proof of service. Have the office stamp all other copies as well, including the original copy that will be filed with the court. If the copy to opposing counsel is mailed, defense counsel should prepare an affidavit of mailing. Once a copy is served on opposing counsel, the original motion with the stamp of proof of service, a certificate of service, or an affidavit of mailing can be filed with the court clerk. The date the court clerk receives these papers is what constitutes when a motion is filed.

The court clerk is determined to be "always open" for the filing of any motion or other documents. *See* FRCrP 56. The clerk's office is open during business hours on all days except weekends, listed holidays, and other days designated by local rule. *Id.* When the clerk's office is closed, federal courthouses have twenty-four-hour late-night depositories that automatically stamp the date and time. Papers filed in night depositories are considered to have been filed in the district court as of the time and date stamp. In order to be timely filed on a particular date, a filing must be time stamped no later than 11:59 P.M. on that day.

When filed in person, counsel should ask to have the clerk stamp not only the filed original, but to stamp the other copies to show that they are true copies of the original filed with the clerk; these copies are known as conformed copies. Overall, counsel should make sure to have the original copy for the clerk, copies for opposing counsel and codefendants, a courtesy copy for the judge, a file copy, and a working copy for counsel.

Rule 50. Calendars; Plan for Prompt Disposition

(a) **Calendars.** The district courts may provide for placing criminal proceedings upon appropriate calendars. Preference shall be given to criminal proceedings as far as practicable.

(b) **Plans for achieving prompt disposition of criminal cases.** To minimize undue delay and to further the prompt disposition of criminal cases, each district court shall conduct a continuing study of the administration of criminal justice in the district court and before United States magistrate judges of the district and shall prepare plans for the prompt disposition of criminal cases in accordance with the provisions of Chapter 208 of Title 18, United States Code.

Commentary

By Prof. Inga L. Parsons
New York University School of Law

Calendars and Continuances

The district court controls its calendar and has wide discretion in setting case dates. *See* FRCrP 50(a). FRCrP 50 gives priority to criminal cases in the court's calendar. The conventional wisdom is that delay helps the defense: memories fade, witnesses move, prosecutors leave, etc. Continuances are often sought and granted when there is a substitution of counsel, critical witnesses are unavailable, discovery or investigation is prolonged, or the defendant must undergo treatment or an examination, etc. Denying a party's request for a continuance is reviewed under the very difficult abuse of discretion standard.

Speedy Trial Act Considerations

The calendaring of a criminal case must accommodate the provisions of the Speedy Trial Act requiring that a defendant be brought to trial within seventy days from the date the indictment or information is filed, or the initial presentment before the magistrate judge, whichever is later. *See* 18 USCS § 3161(c)(1).

Time needed to consider and dispose of various matters including pretrial motions, competency hearings, etc., can be excluded from speedy trial calculations and toll the seventy-day period. *See* 18 USCS § 3161(h) for a list of specific exclusions. Adjournments not specifically delineated in the Speedy Trial Act can be excluded if the ends of justice outweigh the public and the defendant's interest in a speedy trial. *See* 18 USCS § 3161(h)(8)(A). This "interests of justice" catchall exclusion cannot be granted retroactively; thus, most federal judges will exclude the time until the next court date for a specified reason and under the general catchall.

Judges will seek the consent of the defendant for exclusions and continuances under the Speedy Trial Act. If the defense anticipates making a speedy trial argument under the Speedy Trial Act, FRCrP 48, or the Sixth Amendment, defense counsel should object to any continuances and exclusions and request an immediate trial. Of course, when the request for the continuance is on the defendant's motion, defense counsel should be prepared to consent to an exclusion of time under the Speedy Trial Act.

Strategies for Seeking a Continuance

If the defendant is not in custody, it is usually not very difficult to get a continuance at the outset of a case providing the defense is willing to consent to exclusion of time. It is always a good idea to get opposing counsel to consent to the continuances in advance since judges are more likely to grant a request when there is no objection. Even with both parties in agreement, however, a continuance is not assured because the court retains the duty to see that not only the defendant's but also the public's right to a speedy trial is protected. When the defendant is in jail, the judge may require more of a basis for a continuance and to have the defendant state personally on the record that the defendant does not object to the continuance. In any event, unless the defense consents, trial cannot begin less than thirty days from the date the defendant first appears, even when the defendant is in custody. *See* 18 USCS § 3161(c)(2).

In seeking a continuance of a hearing or trial date, counsel must be prepared to provide a good reason for needing the continuance, and ideally it should be linked to a trial right such as the right to counsel or the right to confrontation. For example, if the government turned over three boxes of witness statements the night before trial, the defense can argue that additional time is needed to prepare due to the unexpected amount of materials. Without this additional time, counsel can proffer that they will be unable to cross-examine witnesses competently, and therefore, the defendant will not have effective assistance of counsel or an effective right of confrontation. Prior written requests from the defense to the prosecution asking to receive the material earlier can add to the reasonableness of the defense's request for a continuance. Defense counsel should craft discovery demands and requests for statements under 18 USCS § 3500 (Jencks material) keeping in mind the potential use of this documentation is to bolster a motion for a continuance.

Before seeking a continuance, counsel should ensure that they have done "due diligence" that would justify a continuance. Specifically, counsel should demonstrate the efforts made to prevent the need for the continuance and the exhaustion of alternatives. If a witness is unavailable except for a certain period, if the defense has obtained an affidavit from the witness showing that the witness will be undergoing heart surgery at the time, if defense has detailed the importance of the testimony to the case, if defense sought the request the day after being notified of the day of the surgery and offered to proceed by deposition testimony, the judge is more likely to grant the continuance. If the continuance is needed because counsel only tried to reach the witness the morning of the trial and discovered the witness was unavailable, judges are less likely to grant the request.

Continuances should be requested as soon as possible; last minute requests are more likely to be denied absent extraordinary unforeseeable circumstances. Certainly, seeking a continuance on the day of trial is extremely risky and counsel should be prepared to proceed if the request is denied. Moreover, once a jury is impaneled, judges are particularly reluctant to grant continuances that will keep the jurors waiting and prolong the trial. Ideally, counsel should try to avoid having to request continuance by working with opposing counsel and persuading the judge to set reasonable motion and trial schedules in order to leave plenty of time for adequate preparation.

Prompt Disposition Plans

FRCrP 50(b) requires each district to prepare a plan for the prompt disposition of cases. Much of the original FRCrP 50(b) regarding plans for prompt disposition was deleted with the enactment of the Speedy Trial Act of 1974 that included provisions for implementing district plans. *See* 18 USCS §§ 3165–3171. Districts are still required to conduct studies and prepare plans regarding the disposition of cases under FRCrP 50, but most of the specifics with respect to when cases must be prosecuted and remedies for failure to bring a defendant to trial in a timely manner are now covered by the Speedy Trial Act. *See generally* 18 USCS §§ 3161–3174. Litigants should be familiar with the provisions of the Speedy Trial Act and the specifics of the plan of the district in which they are litigating, particularly in cases where there has been a delay in the proceedings. Prosecutors should be aware of any special obligations required of the government under the district plan.

The plans are considered regulatory and do not give rise to a separate speedy trial right compelling dismissal, although the courts have discretion to dismiss an indictment with prejudice for noncompliance with the plan. *See, e.g., United States v. Novelli*, 544 F.2d 800 (5th Cir 1977). In arguing for dismissal of the charges and misconduct, or deliberate delay by the prosecution either due to unnecessary delay or violations of the Speedy Trial Act, a district's disposition plan may provide helpful language in making those arguments or in defending those arguments. For further discussion of dismissal of cases on speedy trial grounds and unnecessary delay, *see* the specific provisions of the Speedy Trial Act at 18 USC 3162(a)(1), FRCrP 48 and the Commentary for FRCrP 48.

Rule 51. Exceptions Unnecessary

Exceptions to rulings or orders of the court are unnecessary and for all purposes for which an exception has heretofore been necessary it is sufficient that a party, at the time the ruling or order of the court is made or sought, makes known to the court the action which that party desires the court to take or that party's objection to the action of the court and the grounds therefor; but if a party has no opportunity to object to a ruling or order, the absence of an objection does not thereafter prejudice that party.

Commentary

By Steven M. Statsinger
The Legal Aid Society, Federal Defender Division
Southern District of New York

FRCrP 51 explains in general terms what is required to preserve for appellate review the errors that occur in trial court. The consequences of failing to preserve an error can be severe. Errors not properly noticed in the trial court will be reviewed on appeal only under the highly restricted plain error standard set out in FRCrP 52(b); some errors might even be deemed waived entirely.

The first sentence of FRCrP 51 abolishes the need for the now somewhat archaic practice of registering an exception to an action of the trial court, to which counsel has already objected.

To preserve an error, counsel "at the time the ruling or order of the court is made or sought," must make known to the court "the action which he desires the court to take or his objection to the action of the court and the grounds therefor." Thus, all that is required is a contemporaneous objection accompanied by a stated reason.

This general provision applies to all trial court rulings, although there are many additional specific preservation rules in other areas. FRCrP 12(b) lists a number of claims that must be raised in a pretrial motion. If they are not, they cannot be raised on appeal. FRCrP 30 has a special preservation rule for errors in jury instructions: "No party may assign as error any portion of the charge or omission therefrom unless that party objects thereto before the jury retires to consider its verdict, stating distinctly the matter to which that party objects and the grounds of the objection." FRCrP 32(b)(6) prescribes time periods within which objections to a presentence report must be registered. The court can only entertain objections made outside this time period for good cause shown. FRCrP 32(b)(6)(D).

The Federal Rules of Evidence contain their own preservation rules. Where the objectionable ruling pertains to admitting evidence, FRE 103(a)(1) requires a "timely objection or motion to strike" that states "the specific ground of objection, if the specific ground was not apparent from context." Where the objectionable ruling is one excluding evidence, FRE 103(a)(2) requires an offer of proof that makes known "the substance of the evidence," unless it is "apparent from the context within which questions were asked." It can be particularly difficult to negotiate the preservation rules when the objection centers on the conduct of, as opposed to the rulings of, the judge. Under FRE 614(c), a party can wait to object to the court's interrogation of a witness, or the calling of its own witness, until "the next available opportunity when the jury is not present." If a district judge has designated a magistrate judge to make findings on a pretrial matter pursuant to 28 USCS § 636(b)(1), a party must file written objections to those findings within ten days, otherwise they are unreviewable. 28 USCS § 636(b)(1)(C).

FRCrP 51 presupposes that a party has been given an opportunity to register an objection. If there is "no opportunity to object to a ruling or order, the absence of an objection does not prejudice" the party. This occurs most commonly in two situations: (1) the court deprives counsel of the opportunity to register an objection, and (2) the information necessary to register an objection is not available until it is too late.

An objection that has been overruled should be renewed every time evidence similar to the objectionable evidence is offered. To avoid the repeated disruptions that can result from such multiple objections, counsel should ask the court for a continuing objection.

If there are multiple defendants, an objection registered on behalf of one defendant does not automatically apply to the others; thus all counsel must join in any objections with which they agree. Some courts will permit the parties to place on the record early in the proceedings an "all for one" agreement under which all defendants join in any defendant's objections throughout the trial.

Rule 52. Harmless Error and Plain Error.

(a) Harmless error. Any error, defect, irregularity or variance which does not affect substantial rights shall be disregarded.

(b) Plain error. Plain errors or defects affecting substantial rights may be noticed although they were not brought to the attention of the court.

Commentary

By Steven M. Statsinger
The Legal Aid Society, Federal Defender Division
Southern District of New York

FRCrP 52 sets the parameters for two of the most important issues in appellate practice—harmless error and plain error.

(1) Harmless error analysis. FRCrP52(a): Surely the backbone of any appellate brief is the "harmless error" analysis. This is the portion of the argument that shows the appellate court how the error committed by the trial court prejudiced the outcome of the case, and why, therefore, the judgment should be reversed.

FRCrP 52(a) contains the harmless error standard for all errors that were properly objected to in the trial court. The rule uses a general formulation to cover a wide range of issues, providing that any error that "does not affect substantial rights shall be disregarded" by the reviewing court. Federal courts have recognized three types of error, and each error requires a different showing to satisfy this standard.

(a) Nonconstitutional trial errors.

Nonconstitutional trial errors are those that occur during a trial that do not implicate important constitutional rights. Included in this category are erroneous evidentiary rulings, defects in the jury instructions, and other procedural issues. For these errors, a reversal is warranted if the error had "substantial and injurious effect or influence in determining the jury's verdict." *Kotteakos v. United States*, 328 U.S. 750, 776, 90 L.Ed. 1557, 1572, 66 S.Ct. 1239, 1253 (1946). Although the government bears the burden of demonstrating an absence of prejudice, the defendant's brief should nevertheless affirmatively show how the defense case was prejudiced. Such an argument should analyze the error in the context of the record as a whole, focusing on the magnitude of the error, the strength of the government's case, and the impact of the error on the outcome of the trial.

(b) Constitutional trial errors.

Constitutional trial errors are those that implicate the guarantees contained in the Fourth, Fifth, Sixth, and Fourteenth Amendments. Where a constitutional error has occurred, the burden on the government is higher. It must establish to the reviewing court's satisfaction that the error was "harmless beyond a reasonable doubt." *Chapman v. California*, 386 U.S. 18, 24, 17 L.Ed.2d 705, 711, 87 S.Ct. 824, 828 (1967). Once again, although the burden of persuasion is on the prosecution, the defense counsel must still make a harmless error argument of their own. In arguing that the error was not harmless beyond a reasonable doubt, the defense should again stress the magnitude of the error and analyze it in light of the impact it had on the verdict and the strength of the government's case.

(c) "Structural" error.

There is also a small number of what are known as "structural" errors, for which reversal is automatic, and no showing of prejudice is required. Structural errors are those "affecting the framework within which the trial proceeds, rather than simply an error in the trial process itself." *Arizona v. Fulminante*, 499 U.S. 279, 310, 113 L.Ed.2d 302, 331, 111 S.Ct. 1246, 1265 (1991). A partial list of errors that the Supreme Court has found to be structural would include the following : (1) a lack of federal subject matter jurisdiction, (2) racial discrimination in the selection of the grand or petit jury, (3) the complete denial of counsel in a felony case, (4) the denial of a jury trial where the defendant is charged with a crime that is not a petty offense, (5) double jeopardy violations, (6) a biased judge, (7) the denial of a public trial, (8) the denial of the right to self-representation, and (9) constitutionally defective reasonable-doubt jury instructions.

(d) Tactical considerations.

Often a single error can be characterized in more than one way. When this occurs, counsel should make every effort to take advantage of the more favorable harmless error standard. For example, the improper admission of hearsay can be thought of as a nonconstitutional trial error because it is usually a straightforward violation of one of the Federal Rules of Evidence. But hearsay violations can also implicate a defendant's rights under the Confrontation Clause of the Sixth Amendment, and hence can be thought of as constitutional errors, which are subject to a more favorable harmless error standard.

(e) Sentencing errors.

The harmless error concept also applies to sentencing errors, but the standards tend to be applied less rigorously. Generally, if the defense can show that but for the sentencing error, the sentence, or at least the applicable guideline range, would have been lower, the requirements of FRCrP 52(a) will be met.

(f) Collateral review.

In *Brecht v. Abrahmson*, 507 U.S. 619, 123 L.Ed.2d 353, 113 S.Ct. 1710 (1993), the Supreme Court applied the Kotteakos standard to constitutional errors considered on collateral review in habeas corpus proceedings. The Court recognized that on direct review such errors are subject to a harmless error standard that is more favorable to the defendant, but held that the distinctions between collateral and direct review warranted the differing standards.

(g) Plain error.

FRCrP 52(b): This provision provides for limited appellate review of those errors not properly objected to in the trial court. The reviewing court cannot notice such errors unless they "[affect] substantial rights."

(i) Waiver versus forfeiture.

Preliminarily, a distinction must be drawn between forfeiture and waiver. An appellate court will not review errors that have been waived. For the most part, silence alone will not constitute a waiver because waiver is usually defined as the voluntary relinquishment of a known right. Waivers generally occur in writing, as in a plea agreement, but may also occur orally. There a few issues, however, that can be waived by mere silence. The matters listed in FRCrP 12(b), which covers pretrial motions, will be deemed waived if the appropriate motion is not made. Similarly, a valid guilty plea waives any nonjurisdictional defect in the proceedings, even if there was no express waiver of the issue in the allocution. The only way to preserve a nonjurisdictional issue if the client pleads guilty is by entering into a conditional plea agreement pursuant to FRCrP 11(a)(2).

(ii) The plain error standard.

Errors that have not been waived, but were not objected to, are considered forfeited, and are subject to plain error review under FRCrP 52(b). The Supreme Court has set out a three-part definition of plain error. First, there must be an error. Second, the error must be plain. And third, the error must have affected substantial rights. *United States v. Olano*, 507 U.S. 725, 123 L.Ed.2d 508, 113 S.Ct. 1720 (1993).

The first *Olano* requirement is the most straightforward. Presumably, by the time plain error analysis occurs, the appellate brief will have already identified the issue complained of and explained why it was an error. If the particular claim was waived in the trial court, however, it is not an error within the meaning of *Olano*.

The second requirement is that the error be plain, which means "clear" or "obvious." This is most easily satisfied when a higher court has already identified the particular issue as an error, or when the trial court's ruling flatly contradicts an applicable statue or rule. Even if the law was not clear at the time of the trial, an error can be deemed plain as long as the law is settled at the time of the appeal.

The third requirement is the defendant must show that the error affected a substantial right. This would most commonly be accomplished by demonstrating that the error affected the outcome of the proceedings, although *Olano* has left open the possibility that there might be a small category of forfeited errors so serious that they can be corrected without need for a showing of prejudice. It should be noted that if an error is preserved and FRCrP 52(a) applies, the government bears the burden of showing an absence of prejudice. For plain error, however, the burden is on the defendant to make an affirmative showing of prejudice.

Even when the three requirements are met, a reversal for plain error is discretionary, not mandatory. In *Johnson v. United States*, 520 U.S. 461, 469–70, 137 L.Ed.2d 718, 728–29, 117 S.Ct. 1544, 1550 (1997), the Court held that a reviewing court may only exercise this discretion when the error "seriously affect[s] the fairness, integrity, or public reputation of judicial proceedings." While the courts of appeal occasionally reverse for plain error, the

Supreme Court has yet to find that any particular error meets this standard.

Rule 53. Regulation of Conduct in the Court Room

The taking of photographs in the court room during the progress of judicial proceedings or radio broadcasting of judicial proceedings from the court room shall not be permitted by the court.

Commentary

By Prof. Inga L. Parsons
New York University School of Law

Despite its broad title, FRCrP 53 is a very specific rule relating to the photographing and broadcasting of courtroom proceedings. Rules regarding the judge's ability to control the courtroom are elsewhere. *See, e.g.,* FRCrP 43(b)(3) (allowing the court to remove a disruptive defendant after proper warning); FRCrP 57(b) ("A judge may regulate practice in any manner consistent with federal law, these rules, and local rules of the district").

FRCrP 53 states in mandatory terms that the taking of photographs and radio broadcasting of judicial proceedings in the courtroom is prohibited. FRCrP 53. Although the rule does not specifically say "no cameras," it has been construed to include the latest camera and videotaping technologies. Nevertheless, the issue of broadcasting federal court proceedings continues to resurface in the wake of such highly publicized cases as *United States v. McVeigh*, 931 F.Supp. 753 (D. Colo. 1996) (involving the bombing of the federal building in Oklahoma).

Most states allow for some broadcasting of criminal cases. The seminal Supreme Court cases that address the issue have been state court cases, one where the Supreme Court seemed close to declaring a constitutional ban on cameras as per se violative of the defendant's right to a fair trial in *Estes v. Texas*, 381 U.S. 532, 14 L.Ed.2d 543, 85 S.Ct 1628 (1965) and one softening that position in *Chandler v. Florida*, 449 U.S. 560, 66 L.Ed.2d 740, 101 S.Ct 802 (1981) to a case-by-case analysis reviewing the actual impact and the level of technological intrusiveness on the proceedings. There has been experimentation with cameras in the courtroom in civil cases in federal court, but the federal judiciary has rejected changes to its canons and procedures, which would allow cameras in the courtroom. There are proposals pending to amend the rules to allow for some videoconferencing where parties are unable to physically attend a court session.

Proponents of cameras in the courtroom tend to be the media and certain crime victims and their families, though child victims and rape victims are more likely to request a closed proceeding. Recently proposed victim's rights legislation could overrule FRCrP 53, in part by providing camera access in high profile cases where the trial is moved and the victim's families are unable to attend the trial in person. There is a debate on the impact of cameras in the courtroom with respect to the defendant's case. Some attorneys have maintained that cameras in the courtroom would promote justice since the government and judge would be subject to public scrutiny. Most defense attorneys are opposed to cameras in the courtroom as compromising a defendant's right to a fair trial.

Given the present state of the law, defendants are unlikely to succeed in the rare cases where they wish to have their own trials videotaped. FRCrP 53 prohibits broadcasting and is not limited to cases where the defense objects. Defendants who have argued that FRCrP 53 is discretionary have failed to persuade the court. *See, e.g., United States v. Kerley*, 753 F.2d 617 (7th Cir. 1985). Defendants have also argued unsuccessfully that the Federal Rules of Criminal Procedure are "intended to provide for the just determination of every criminal proceeding," and FRCrP 2 gives the court discretion to consider cameras in the courtroom on an individual case basis despite the language of FRCrP 53. Circuit courts have rejected "interpreting" FRCrP 53 and FRCrP 2 as giving them discretion. *Id.* Arguments based on the First and Sixth Amendment have met with a similar fate. The federal courts have consistently maintained that a limitation of access is not a violation of the First or Sixth amendments since trials are still open to the public and the press may attend and report. *See, e.g., United States v. Kerley*, 753 F.2d 617 (7th Cir. 1985); *United States v. Hastings*, 695 F.2d 1278 (11th Cir. 1983).

Rule 54. Application and Exception

(a) Courts. These rules apply to all criminal proceedings in the United States District Courts; in the District Court of Guam; in the

District Court for the Northern Mariana Islands, except as otherwise provided in articles IV and V of the covenant provided by the Act of March 24, 1976 (90 Stat. 263); and in the District Court of the Virgin Islands; in the United States Courts of Appeals; and in the Supreme Court of the United States; except that the prosecution of offenses in the District Court of the Virgin Islands shall be by indictment or information as otherwise provided by law.

(b) Proceedings.

(1) Removed proceedings. These rules apply to criminal prosecutions removed to the United States district courts from state courts and govern all procedure after removal, except that dismissal by the attorney for the prosecution shall be governed by state law.

(2) Offenses outside a district or state. These rules apply to proceedings for offenses committed upon the high seas or elsewhere out of the jurisdiction of any particular state or district, except that such proceedings may be had in any district authorized by 18 USC § 3238.

(3) Peace bonds. These rules do not alter the power of judges of the United States or of United States magistrate judges to hold to security of the peace and for good behavior under Revised Statutes, § 4069, 50 U.S.C. § 23, but in such cases the procedure shall conform to these rules so far as they are applicable.

(4) Proceedings before United States magistrate judges. Proceedings involving misdemeanors and other petty offenses are governed by Rule 58.

(5) Other proceedings. These rules are not applicable to extradition and rendition of fugitives; civil forfeiture of property for violation of a statute of the United States; or the collection of fines and penalties. Except as provided in Rule 20(d) they do not apply to proceedings under 18 USC, Chapter 403—Juvenile Delinquency—so far as they are inconsistent with that chapter. They do not apply to summary trials for offenses against the navigation laws under Revised Statutes §§ 4300–4305, 33 USC §§ 391–396, or to proceedings involving disputes between seamen under Revised Statutes, §§ 4079–4081, as amended, 22 USC §§ 256–258, or to proceedings for fishery offenses under the Act of June 28, 1937, c. 392,

50 Stat 325–327, 16 USC §§ 772–772i, or to proceedings against a witness in a foreign country under 28 USC § 1784.

(c) Application of terms. As used in these rules the following terms have the designated meanings.

"Act of Congress" includes any act of Congress locally applicable to and in force in the District of Columbia, in Puerto Rico, in a territory or in an insular possession.

"Attorney for the government" means the Attorney General, an authorized assistant of the Attorney General, a United States attorney, an authorized assistant of a United States Attorney, when applicable to cases arising under the laws of Guam the Attorney General of Guam or such other person or persons as may be authorized by the laws of Guam to act therein, and when applicable to cases arising under the laws of the Northern Mariana Islands the Attorney General of the Northern Mariana Islands or any other person or persons as may be authorized by the laws of the Northern Marianas to act therein.

"Civil action", refers to a civil action in a district court.

The words "demurrer," "motion to quash," "plea in abatement," "plea in bar" and "special plea in bar," or words to the same effect, in any act of Congress shall be construed to mean the motion raising a defense or objection provided in Rule 12.

"District court" includes all district courts named in subdivision (a) of this rule.

"Federal magistrate judge" means a United States magistrate judge as defined in 28 U.S.C. §§ 631–639, a judge of the United States or another judge or judicial officer specifically empowered by statute in force in any territory or possession, the Commonwealth of Puerto Rico, or the District of Columbia, to perform a function to which a particular rule relates.

"Judge of the United States" includes a judge of a district court, court of appeals, or the Supreme Court.

"Law" includes statutes and judicial decisions.

"Magistrate judge" includes a United States magistrate judge as defined in 28 U.S.C. §§ 631–639, a judge of the United States, another judge or judicial officer specifically empowered by statute in force in any territory or possession, the Commonwealth of Puerto

Rico, or the District of Columbia, to perform a function to which a particular rule relates, and a state or local judicial officer, authorized by 18 U.S.C. § 3041 to perform the functions prescribed in Rules 3, 4, and 5.

"Oath" includes affirmations.

"Petty offense" is defined in 18 U.S.C. § 19.

"State" includes District of Columbia, Puerto Rico, territory and insular possession.

"United States magistrate judge" means the officer authorized by 28 U.S.C. §§ 631–639.

Commentary

By Prof. Inga L. Parsons
New York University School of Law

The Federal Rules of Criminal Procedure (the Rules) govern procedure in criminal proceedings in the courts of the United States enumerated in FRCrP 54, which includes the District of Guam, the Virgin Islands, and the District for the Northern Mariana Islands. *See* FRCrP 1; FRCrP 54(a).

There are certain exceptions to the application of the rules. In the Virgin Islands, for example, trial may proceed by information; an indictment is not required. FRCrP 54(a). If an attorney will be practicing in a court outside the United States, but under federal jurisdiction, a careful reading of FRCrP 54 is necessary. Helpful to this endeavor will be the stylistic amendments to FRCrP 54 that are set to be codified by the end of 2001, which will combine FRCrP 54 with FRCrP 1 and make the application provisions of FRCrP 54 more accessible and easier to understand. Significant terms for the Rules are defined in FRCrP 54(c) such as what is meant by "Attorney for the government," "Law," and "State"; attorneys should be familiar with those terms, for example, the term "State" encompasses the District of Columbia and Puerto Rico.

The Rules do not apply to extradition proceedings, civil forfeiture, or the collection of fines. *See* FRCrP 54(b)(5). Habeas corpus proceedings are regarded as civil proceedings and thus not governed by the Rules. Military proceedings are not ordinarily subject to the Rules either.

Juvenile delinquency proceedings are governed by the procedures set out in the juvenile delinquency provisions of the criminal code (18 USCS §§ 5031–5042) and may be governed by the Rules to the extent the Rules are not inconsistent with those provisions. The one specific federal criminal procedure rule applying to a juvenile is FRCrP 20(d) regarding the transfer of a juvenile's case from the charging jurisdiction to the jurisdiction of arrest. See FRCrP 20(d).

Misdemeanors are subject to the Rules to the extent provided by FRCrP 58, which has special provisions applying specifically to misdemeanors and other petty offenses in federal court. See FRCrP 58 and the Commentary for FRCrP 58.

State offenses removed to federal court are governed by the Rules, except state law governs dismissal by the prosecutor. FRCrP 54(b)(1). In general, state law controls the substantive law of transferred state cases, including states cases assimilated into the federal system pursuant to 18 USCS § 13. Procedure is governed by federal law. See, e.g., *United States v. Wilmer*, 799 F.2d 495, 499–500 (9th Cir. 1986). If a person is arrested in a federal park for unlicensed operation of a vehicle, that is strictly a state crime because there is no federal unlicensed operation offense. In order to prosecute the case in federal court, the state offense is assimilated into the federal system because the offense occurred on federal property. Federal procedural and constitutional law applies to the offense, including the law on Fourth and Fifth Amendment rights, e.g., whether a defendant's statement is admissible. In some states a defendant's statement would be suppressed or not admitted under that state's constitution, but would be admissible under the federal constitution. Such cases may be transferred to the federal system so the evidence will be allowed. State substantive law applies to the elements of the assimilated state offense, e.g., what is meant by the term operation of a vehicle. The Federal Rules of Evidence would apply to the hearings and trial of transferred and assimilated cases.

Rule 55. Records

The clerk of the district court and each United States magistrate judge shall keep records in criminal proceedings in such form as the Director of the Administrative Office of the United States

Courts may prescribe. The clerk shall enter in the records each order or judgment of the court and the date such entry is made.

Commentary

By Prof. Inga L. Parsons
New York University School of Law

Accessing Records

District court records are kept by the clerk of court; magistrate records may or may not be kept separately depending on the particular district's practice. Most federal court case documents are public records and are available through the clerk's office without court order except for sealed documents, documents relating to juveniles in criminal cases and grand jury materials, and other documents made confidential by order of law.

The clerk also keeps a docket sheet that includes the orders and judgment of the court. FRCrP 55. For example, if at the initial appearance the judge appointed counsel for the defendant, ordered the defendant detained, and set a date for a preliminary hearing, those orders will be listed along with the date they were entered. In reviewing a case file it is useful to look first at the docket sheet to see what has happened in the case.

A number of courts have an electronic system called PACER, which stands for Public Access to Court Electronic Records. Through PACER an attorney (or other registered user) can dial in to a district court computer or access the court's Web site and retrieve official electronic case information. The records are transferred in a matter of minutes for a fee with the going rate at sixty-cents-per-minute access fee for dial-in requests or seven cents per page for the Internet service for information downloaded from the Web site. To use PACER a person must first subscribe and obtain a user identification and password by calling the PACER Service Center at 1-800-676-6856, or registering through the U.S. courts Web site at http://pacer.psc.uscourts.gov/. There is no fee for subscribing.

A few federal courts have a system called Case Management/Electronic Case Files (CM/ECF). CM/ECF courts have case file documents in electronic format and can accept filings over the Internet if local rules permit such filings. Case file documents are kept in electronic format and can be transmitted to the requesting party over the Internet through the PACER system described above.

In addition, a party can file documents using conventional word processing software converted to PDF and logging onto the court's Web site. Upon filing the electronic document, the party receives an automatic verification confirming receipt, and the other parties in the case also receive e-mail notification. There are no additional fees for electronically filed documents over the existing document filing fees. CM/ECF systems provide each litigant one free electronic copy of the documents in the case.

When a practitioner needs a court document from a district without PACER or CM/ECF, usually the fastest way to get it is to go directly to the district court clerk's office. To obtain the case record a picture identification is required (and typically lots of quarters) unless the courthouse has up-to-date copier machines that can tally the number of individual copies made and charge for all copies. If copies are obtained through the court clerk, either in person or over the phone, a fee of fifty cents per page is charged and an additional fee of $15 may be assessed if the information is not readily available.

Sealing and Expunging Records

If the proceeding has been historically open to the press and public access plays a "significant positive role" in the proceeding, sealing a proceeding triggers First Amendment issues and requires the movant to meet the standards set forth in *Press-Enterprise Co. v. Superior Court*, 464 U.S. 501, 78 L.Ed.2d 629, 104 S.Ct. 819 (1984) (known as the Press-Enterprise I standard). See *Press-Enterprise Co. v. Superior Court (Press-Enterprise II)*, 478 U.S. 1, 92 L.Ed.2d 1, 106 S.Ct. 2735 (1986). The Press-Enterprise I standard requires the court to determine (1) if there is substantial probability of prejudice compelling closure; (2) even if there is a substantial probability the court must consider alternatives such as partial sealing; (3) if the alternatives are insufficient the court must find that the prejudice from an open proceeding outweighs the First Amendment right of access; and (4) any sealing order must be narrowly tailored. Courts need to make specific findings on the record to seal the proceedings and cannot make such findings after the fact. Counsel should ensure that the court's findings are timely and complete to effect a proper sealing of the proceedings.

Although in many states dismissed cases, deferred cases, and certain convictions are automatically sealed by statute, in federal court it is more difficult to get case records sealed, and extremely difficult to get arrest records expunged even when the case has been dismissed outright. As to arrest records, federal law requires the Attorney General to acquire and retain criminal records, *see* 28 USCS § 534(a), and there is no federal statute providing for the expungement of an arrest. Although most courts have recognized that expungement of an arrest record and an order to return fingerprints and photographs lies within the equitable discretion of a federal court, in practice expungement is an extreme remedy where the defendant must show extraordinary circumstances such as where there is government impropriety or the defendant will suffer particularized harm. *See, e.g., United States v. Schnitzer*, 567 F.2d 536 (2d Cir. 1977) (rabbinical student failed to show harsh or unique consequences to justify expungement of arrest record after dismissal of indictment). Even after an acquittal, expungement is difficult to obtain as long as there was a proper finding of probable cause. Where cases have been dismissed outright before indictment, arrest records may still be maintained if the rights and duties of law enforcement officials outweigh the balance of the equities of privacy for the individual.

In some cases defense counsel can try to seek to have records segregated so they are accessible only for legitimate law enforcement purposes and not available to other sources such as the board of education if the client is seeking a teaching position. *See, e.g., United States v. Doe*, 935 F.Supp. 978 (SDNY 1996) (court ordered partial expunction of records by physically removing the records from central criminal files and placing them in a separate storage facility). Despite the heavy burden, defense counsel loses little by requesting an expungement, and in an appropriate case may be able to convince the government to consent, particularly where the request is for partial expungement that would still allow law enforcement access to the records.

Juvenile cases are sealed as a matter of law and are not to be disclosed except as directed by 18 USCS § 5038. Defense counsel should ensure that all juvenile records are properly sealed. If the defendant is convicted of a one-time simple possession of a controlled substance offense under 21 USCS § 844, the defendant may be eligible for a special disposition that does not result in a conviction or a public record of disposition. *See* 18 USCS § 3607. If the defendant was under twenty-one at the time of the simple possession offense, the defendant is further eligible for a total expungement of the record and would not have to acknowledge the arrest. *See* 18 USCS § 3607(c).

Rule 56. Courts and Clerks

The district court shall be deemed always open for the purpose of filing any proper paper, of issuing and returning process and of making motions and orders. The clerk's office with the clerk or a deputy in attendance shall be open during business hours on all days except Saturdays, Sundays, and legal holidays, but a court may provide by local rule or order that its clerk's office shall be open for specified hours on Saturdays or particular legal holidays other than New Year's Day, Birthday of Martin Luther King, Jr., Washington's Birthday, Memorial Day, Independence Day, Labor Day, Columbus Day, Veterans Day, Thanksgiving Day, and Christmas Day.

Commentary

See the Commentary for FRCrP 49.

Rule 57. Rules by District Courts

(a) In general.

(1) Each district court acting by a majority of its district judges may, after giving appropriate public notice and an opportunity to comment, make and amend rules governing its practice. A local rule shall be consistent with—but not duplicative of—Acts of Congress and rules adopted under 28 U.S.C. § 2072 and shall conform to any uniform numbering system prescribed by the Judicial Conference of the United States.

(2) A local rule imposing a requirement of form shall not be enforced in a manner that causes a party to lose rights because of a nonwillful failure to comply with the requirement.

(b) Procedure when there is no controlling law. A judge may regulate practice in any manner consistent with federal law, these rules, and local rules of the district. No sanction or other disadvantage may be imposed for noncompliance with any requirement not in federal law, federal rules, or the local district rules unless the alleged violator has been furnished in the particular case with actual notice of the requirement.

(c) Effective date and notice. A local rule so adopted shall take effect upon the date specified by the district court and shall remain in effect unless amended by the district court or abrogated by the judicial council of the circuit in which the district is located. Copies of the rules and amendments so made by any district court shall upon their promulgation be furnished to the judicial council and the Administrative Office of the United States Courts and shall be made available to the public.

Commentary

By Prof. Inga L. Parsons
New York University School of Law

Local Rules

An attorney practicing in a federal district court should be aware of the local rules of that court. These rules, provided for in FRCrP 57, govern court procedure and practices, and may be enforceable against an attorney providing the attorney has actual notice of the rule and has willfully failed to comply with the requirements. *See* FRCrP 57(a)(2)–(b). Although it would be the rare case that an attorney would be sanctioned for an initial failure to comply with a local rule, to maintain credibility and professionalism before the presiding judge the attorney must know and follow the local rules.

Local rules often cover discovery matters, filing requirements, assignment of judges, transfer of cases, and, importantly, the form of pleadings and motions. The local rules may also make the Code of Professional Responsibility controlling in a particular district. *See United States v. Barnett*, 814 F.Supp. 1449, (D. Alaska 1992). Many districts make their local rules available online for easy access through the Internet.

In addition to the local rules, many judges have standing orders describing their individual practices. A number of judges, for example, require the parties to attempt to resolve their discovery disputes in advance and seek court intervention only as a last resort. Counsel are often admonished not to copy the judge on discovery exchanges. As soon as the judge is assigned to a case, a lawyer should review the judge's standing. A good lawyer knows the law; a great lawyer knows the judge, or at a minimum, the judge's standing orders.

Regulation of Proceedings

In situations where there is no controlling law, FRCrP 57 allows a judge to regulate practice in "any manner consistent with federal law, these rules, and local rules of the district." FRCrP 57(b). On one hand, this broad judicial authority provides important litigative opportunities for the criminal practitioner. Under this section, for example, a party can seek to have the judge require disclosure of witness lists, to sequester witnesses, to send exhibits and the indictment to the jury, to allow the jurors to view the "scene of the crime," or to stay a concurrent civil proceeding that might impact a criminal trial. *See, e.g., Bunn v. United States*, 260 F.2d 313 (8th Cir. 1958) (sequestration of witnesses during a trial is within the trial court's discretion). On the other hand, a judge may use this authority adversely to a party by requiring counsel to disclose peremptory challenges to the jury, by asking probing questions of a party's witness, by limiting attorney examinations and closing arguments, or by precluding certain witnesses.

Although there are times when it will be crucial to object even to the actions of a judge to preserve the issue, counsel should be aware that a judge's rulings under FRCrP 57(b) are reviewed under the abuse of discretion standard so most decisions under this authority will be upheld on appeal.

Rule 58. Procedure for Misdemeanors and Other Petty Offenses

(a) Scope.

(1) **In general.** This rule governs the procedure and practice for the conduct of proceedings involving misdemeanors

Rule 58. Procedure for Misdemeanors and Other Petty Offenses

and other petty offenses, and for appeals to district judges in such cases tried by United States magistrate judges.

(2) Applicability of other Federal Rules of Criminal Procedure. In proceedings concerning petty offenses for which no sentence of imprisonment will be imposed the court may follow such provisions of these rules as it deems appropriate, to the extent not inconsistent with this rule. In all other proceedings the other rules govern except as specifically provided in this rule.

(3) Definition. The term "petty offenses for which no sentence of imprisonment will be imposed" as used in this rule, means any petty offenses as defined in 18 U.S.C. § 19 as to which the court determines, that, in the event of conviction, no sentence of imprisonment will actually be imposed.

(b) Pretrial procedures.

(1) Trial document. The trial of a misdemeanor may proceed on an indictment, information, or complaint or, in the case of a petty offense, on a citation or violation notice.

(2) Initial appearance. At the defendant's initial appearance on a misdemeanor or other petty offense charge, the court shall inform the defendant of:

(A) the charge, and the maximum possible penalties provided by law, including payment of a special assessment under 18 U.S.C. § 3013, and restitution under 18 U.S.C. § 3663;

(B) the right to retain counsel;

(C) the right to request the appointment of counsel if the defendant is unable to obtain counsel, unless the charge is a petty offense for which an appointment of counsel is not required;

(D) the right to remain silent and that any statement made by the defendant may be used against the defendant;

(E) the right to trial, judgment, and sentencing before a district judge, unless:

(i) the charge is a Class B misdemeanor motor-vehicle offense, a Class C misdemeanor, or an infraction; or

(ii) the defendant consents to trial, judgment, and sentencing before a magistrate judge;

(F) the right to trial by jury before either a United States magistrate judge or a district judge, unless the charge is a petty offense; and

(G) the right to a preliminary examination in accordance with 18 U.S.C. § 3060, and the general circumstances under which the defendant may secure pretrial release, if the defendant is held in custody and charged with a misdemeanor other than a petty offense.

(3) Consent and arraignment.

(A) Plea before a United States magistrate judge. A magistrate judge shall take the defendant's plea in a Class B misdemeanor charging a motor-vehicle offense, a Class C misdemeanor, or an infraction. In every other misdemeanor case, a magistrate judge may take the plea only if the defendant consents either in writing or orally on the record to be tried before the magistrate judge and specifically waives trial before a district judge. The defendant may plead not guilty, guilty, or with the consent of the magistrate judge, nolo contendere.

(B) Failure to consent. In a misdemeanor case—other than a Class B misdemeanor charging a motor-vehicle offense, a Class C misdemeanor, or an infraction—magistrate judge shall order the defendant to appear before a district judge for further proceedings on notice, unless the defendant consents to trial before the magistrate judge.

(c) Additional procedures applicable only to petty offenses for which no sentence of imprisonment will be imposed. With respect to petty offenses for which no sentence of imprisonment will be imposed, the following additional procedures are applicable:

(1) Plea of guilty or nolo contendere. No plea of guilty or nolo contendere shall be accepted unless the court is satisfied that the defendant understands the nature of the charge and the maximum possible penalties provided by law.

(2) Waiver of venue for plea and sentence. A defendant who is arrested, held, or present in a district other than that in which the indictment, information, complaint, citation or violation notice is pending against that defendant may state in writing a wish to plead guilty or nolo contendere, to waive venue and trial in the district in which the proceeding is pending, and to consent to disposition of the case in the district in which that defendant was arrested, is held, or is present. Unless the defendant thereafter pleads not guilty, the prosecution shall be had as if venue were in such district, and notice of the same shall be given to the magistrate judge in the district where the proceeding was originally commenced. The defendant's statement of a desire to plead guilty or nolo contendere is not admissible against the defendant.

(3) Sentence. The court shall afford the defendant an opportunity to be heard in mitigation. The court shall then immediately proceed to sentence the defendant, except that in the discretion of the court, sentencing may be continued to allow an investigation by the probation service or submission of additional information by either party.

(4) Notification of right to appeal. After imposing sentence in a case which has gone to trial on a plea of not guilty, the court shall advise the defendant of the defendant's right to appeal including any right to appeal the sentence. There shall be no duty on the court to advise the defendant of any right of appeal after sentence is imposed following a plea of guilty or nolo contendere, except that the court shall advise the defendant of any right to appeal the sentence.

(d) Securing the defendant's appearance; payment in lieu of appearance.

(1) Forfeiture of Collateral. When authorized by local rules of the district court, payment of a fixed sum may be accepted in suitable cases in lieu of appearance and as authorizing the termination of the proceedings. Local rules may make provision for increases in fixed sums not to exceed the maximum fine which could be imposed.

(2) Notice to Appear. If a defendant fails to pay a fixed sum, request a hearing, or appear in response to a citation or violation notice, the clerk or a magistrate judge may issue a notice for the defendant to appear before the court on a date certain. The notice may also afford the defendant an additional opportunity to pay a fixed sum in lieu of appearance, and shall be served upon the defendant by mailing a copy to the defendant's last known address.

(3) Summons or Warrant. Upon an indictment or a showing by one of the other documents specified in subdivision (b)(1) of probable cause to believe that an offense has been committed and that the defendant has committed it, the court may issue an arrest warrant or, if no warrant is requested by the attorney for the prosecution, a summons. The showing of probable cause shall be made in writing upon oath or under penalty for perjury, but the affiant need not appear before the court. If the defendant fails to appear before the court in response to a summons, the court may summarily issue a warrant for the defendant's immediate arrest and appearance before the court.

(e) Record. Proceedings under this rule shall be taken down by a reporter or recorded by suitable sound equipment.

(f) New trial. The provisions of Rule 33 shall apply.

(g) Appeal.

(1) Decision, order, judgment or sentence by a district judge. An appeal from a decision, order, judgment or conviction or sentence by a district judge shall be taken in accordance with the Federal Rules of Appellate Procedure.

(2) Decision, order, judgment or sentence by a United States magistrate judge.

(A) Interlocutory appeal. A decision or order by a magistrate judge which, if made by a district judge, could be appealed by the government or defendant under any provision of law, shall be subject to an appeal to a district judge provided such appeal is taken within 10 days of the entry of the decision or order. An appeal shall be taken by filing with the clerk of court a statement specifying the decision or order from which an appeal is taken and by serving a copy of the statement upon the adverse party, personally or by mail, and by filing a copy with the magistrate judge.

(B) Appeal from conviction or sentence. An appeal from a judgment of conviction or sentence by a magistrate judge to a district judge shall be taken within 10 days after entry of the judgment. An appeal shall be taken by filing with the clerk of court a statement specifying the judgment from which an appeal is taken, and by serving a copy of the statement upon the United States Attorney, personally or by mail, and by filing a copy with the magistrate judge.

(C) Record. The record shall consist of the original papers and exhibits in the case together with any transcript, tape, or other recording of the proceedings and a certified copy of the docket entries which shall be transmitted promptly to the clerk of court. For purposes of the appeal, a copy of the record of such proceedings shall be made available at the expense of the United States to a person who establishes by affidavit the inability to pay or give security therefor, and the expense of such copy shall be paid by the Director of the Administrative Office of the United States Courts.

(D) Scope of appeal. The defendant shall not be entitled to a trial de novo by a district judge. The scope of appeal shall be the same as an appeal from a judgment of a district court to a court of appeals.

(3) Stay of execution; release pending appeal. The provisions of Rule 38 relating to stay of execution shall be applicable to a judgment of conviction or sentence. The defendant may be released pending appeal in accordance with the provisions of law relating to release pending appeal from a judgment of a district court to a court of appeals.

Commentary

By Prof. Inga L. Parsons
New York University School of Law

Federal Misdemeanors Generally

Federal misdemeanors are generally defined as offenses carrying no more than one year imprisonment and are further broken down into three classes: Class A (more than six months but no more than one year imprisonment), Class B (more than thirty days up to six months imprisonment), and Class C misdemeanors (more than five days up to thirty days imprisonment). *See* 18 USCS § 3581(b). There is also an offense category called an infraction that carries a penalty of no more than five days imprisonment.

18 USCS § 3581(b)(9). A "petty offense" is defined as a Class B or C misdemeanor or an infraction. 18 USCS § 19. A violation is not a crime and does not subject the defendant to imprisonment but only to a potential fine, forfeiture, or civil penalty.

Most offenses prosecuted in federal court are felonies. There are a number of federal misdemeanors defined in the United States Code, usually involving low-level versions of more serious federal offenses such as theft of government property. *See, e.g.,* 18 USCS § 641 (defining the taking of property valued at $1,000 or less as an A misdemeanor). When there is concurrent state jurisdiction over such offenses, often there is little federal interest to prosecute such "small potatoes" cases. As a result, many federal practitioners have little experience with misdemeanors and need to be aware of the different procedures and rules.

Misdemeanor Jurisdiction

The magistrate judge has original jurisdiction over Class B misdemeanors charging motor vehicle offenses, all Class C misdemeanors, and infractions. 18 USCS § 3401(g). A magistrate judge has concurrent jurisdiction with the federal district court over any other federal misdemeanor. *See* 18 USCS § 3401(b). In cases where there is concurrent jurisdiction, the defendant has a right of election between magistrate court and district court. 18 USCS § 3401(b). Where the defendant is charged with an offense over which the magistrate has original jurisdiction, there is no right of election and the case will almost always remain in magistrate court. However, in rare cases the district court may order that a misdemeanor be heard before the district court upon the court's own motion or a petition by the government where the case is complex, involves a novel issue, etc. 18 USCS § 3401(f).

Even in cases where the defendant can elect to proceed in district court, it is often to the defendant's advantage to keep the case in magistrate court where the magistrate judges are familiar with the practices and culture of misdemeanor litigation. On the other hand, where there is some confidence that the higher court will view the case as relatively trifling compared to a felony or the district judge pool is better for the defense, it may be advisable to proceed in district court.

When the defendants have the right of election, they need to be advised that they have a right to have the case prosecuted before a district court judge, including any plea, trial, judgment, or sentencing, and should be counseled as to the advisability of keeping the case in magistrate court. If the defendants wish to proceed in magistrate court, the defendants will have to execute a form expressly consenting to proceed in magistrate court and waiving their right to proceed in district court. FRCrP 58(b)(3); 18 USCS § 3401(b). Such consent and waiver must be made in writing or orally on the record. *Id.* Like any waiver, the judge will question the defendant on whether the waiver of the right to proceed in district court is knowing and voluntary, and defense counsel must prepare the client for the colloquy with the judge.

When misdemeanors are prosecuted in federal court they are specifically governed by FRCrP 58, as well as generally by the Federal Rules of Criminal Procedure. FRCrP 58 sets forth special procedures for misdemeanor cases and should be reviewed carefully by the federal misdemeanor practitioner.

Application of Other Federal Rules and Laws to Misdemeanors

In many ways Class A misdemeanors are more closely related to felonies in terms of rights and procedures than to petty offenses. Like felonies, Class A misdemeanors require a judicial finding of probable cause pursuant to FRCrP 4. Petty offenses do not require a court finding of probable cause unless the defendant is to be detained or there is a bench warrant issued for non-appearance. *See* FRCrP 58(d). Defendants charged with an A misdemeanor are entitled to a jury trial (although each side is allotted only three peremptory challenges rather than the ten for the defense and six for the government in a felony trial, *see* FRCrP 24(b)). Petty offenses are tried before a magistrate judge because there is no right to a jury trial for an offense carrying six months or less, even if the potential cumulative penalty is the same or even greater than an A misdemeanor. *Lewis v. United States*, 518 U.S. 322, 135 L.Ed.2d 590, 116 S.Ct. 2163 (1996).

The Bail Reform Act, the Speedy Trial Act, and the Federal Sentencing Guidelines apply to A misdemeanors but not to petty offenses. *See* FRCrP 58(b)(2)(G); 18 USCS § 3172(2); USSG § 1B1.9 (18 USCS Appx § 1B1.9). Unlike felonies, however, an A misdemeanor can proceed by a prosecutor's information or complaint; a petty offense can proceed by a violation notice. Both A misdemeanor and petty offense appeals are taken to the district court judge in the first instance rather than the Court of Appeals. FRCrP 58(g)(2).

The practice in many magistrate courts is to commence the prosecution of most misdemeanor offenses, even A misdemeanors, through the issuance of a violation notice because police officers usually issue the violation notices at the time of arrest and often are unaware of the level of the offense. Before a defendant may be tried on a Class A misdemeanor, however, the violation notice must be superseded with an information or complaint, or the defense should file a motion to dismiss for a defect in the prosecution.

Federal Petty Offenses Generally

Petty offenses (*i.e.*, Class B misdemeanors or lower) may be prosecuted on a summons or violation notice that looks something like a traffic ticket typically given to the defendant at the time of the alleged incident. The violation notice usually sets forth a statement of the reasons for the charge on the back of the original notice, which is kept by the law enforcement agents and ultimately filed with the court. This officer's statement may not be on the copy of the ticket issued to the defendant. FRCrP 58(d)(3) lays down a requirement of probable cause that the judge must find in issuing a warrant or summons, something that happens in the event the defendant does not show up for the initial appearance.

FRCrP 58 does not require the magistrate judge to find probable cause in the pleadings at an initial appearance for a petty offense, as is required for A misdemeanors and felony cases pursuant to FRCrP 4. Nevertheless, some magistrate judges may be persuaded to dismiss a case outright where there appears to be insufficient evidence set out in the officer's written statement to support a finding of probable cause. As a result, defense counsel should always review the statement—not just in A misdemeanor cases—to determine whether it sufficiently connects the particular defendant to the crime charged. Should defense counsel determine that the statement is inadequate, counsel can try to move for dismissal of the charges or, at a minimum, use it in negotiations.

Many petty offenses are handled like a traffic ticket where a fine can be paid in lieu of an appearance. For petty offenses deemed more serious, there is a mandatory court appearance usually marked "MC" where a fine would be listed. In petty offense cases for which the magistrate judge has determined in advance of hearing or trial that no sentence of imprisonment will be imposed, the court may follow such provisions of the Federal Rules of Criminal Procedure "as it deems appropriate" to the extent not inconsistent with FRCrP 58. FRCrP 58(a)(2). There are less formal procedures for these so-called "non-jail petty offenses" set out in FRCrP 58, including that a defendant may plead guilty in the district of arrest even if the case is being charged in another district and that sentencing will ordinarily proceed immediately after any plea to a non-jail petty offense without awaiting a pretrial investigation. See FRCrP 58(c).

It is not uncommon for the court to dispense with formal proceedings like an initial appearance or an arraignment for non-jail petty offense cases. Instead, such cases are frequently negotiated with a representative from the prosecuting agency such as an officer from the National Park Service or an officer from the Department of Veterans Affairs. Often these dispositions take place without an attorney, a prosecutor, or even a judge present. In some districts it is the newest assistant United States attorneys who negotiate directly with the defendants to dispose of the cases and no defense counsel is present. If it is a case where the judge has determined in advance that no jail will be imposed, the defendant is not entitled to an attorney. See Scott v. Illinois, 440 U.S. 367, 59 L.Ed.2d 383, 99 S.Ct. 1158 (1979). Correlatively, if the defendant lacked an attorney the court may not impose a jail sentence. See Argersinger v. Hamlin, 407 U.S. 25, 32 L.Ed.2d 530, 92 S.Ct 2006 (1972).

If the court fails to state specifically in advance that jail will not be imposed, and if the court has neglected to follow the dictates of FRCrP 58(b) such as holding a formal initial appearance or arraignment, the defense should argue that the court is estopped from imposing a sentence of imprisonment. In most cases, the issue is not one of the length of a jail sentence but the imposition of a fine and/or a period of probation. The battleground is typically over the amount of the fine and whether any probation should be supervised or unsupervised.

Code of Federal Regulation Violations

A number of governmental agencies bring misdemeanor cases into federal court such as the National Park Service, the

Department of Veterans Affairs, the United States Army, and the General Services Administration. Most of these agencies have promulgated regulations to govern behavior on federal property and these offenses are listed in the Code of Federal Regulations (CFR). Any offense under the CFR is presumed to be a B misdemeanor unless stated otherwise because the general penalties section of most CFR titles describes the maximum penalties for the majority of offenses as up to six months in jail—the federal definition of a B misdemeanor. *See, e.g.*, 38 CFR 1.218(b) (penalties provision for Veterans Affairs violations), 36 CFR 1.3 (penalties provision for National Park Service violations).

If the defendant is charged under the CFR even for a seemingly minor offense such as being in the park after dark or spitting on the sidewalk, the defendant is still facing a B misdemeanor with all the consequences of a criminal conviction. Unaware of the general penalties provision that makes the offenses B misdemeanors, the agency representative or new assistant will often offer a plea to a CFR offense assuming it is an infraction or violation. Defense counsel should always double check the penalties and ensure that the disposition is a true federal violation or infraction, or elicit an offer of a plea to an assimilated state violation so that the defendant does not unwittingly plead to a B misdemeanor.

Many of the CFRs and enabling legislation require that in order for a defendant to be prosecuted under the regulations, the government must conspicuously post notice of the rules and regulations. For example, the General Services Administration (GSA) may "make all needful rules and regulations for the government of the property under their charge and control . . . Provided, that such rules and regulations shall be posted and kept posted in a conspicuous place on such property." 40 USCS § 318a. Even in cases where the defendant has clearly committed the offense, courts have overturned the conviction because the regulations were not conspicuously posted. *See, e.g., United States v. Strakoff,* 719 F.2d 1307 (5th Cir. 1983) (overturning defendant's conviction due to GSA's failure to post regulations in a conspicuous place on federal property).

A number of the CFR provisions are poorly drafted and various legal defenses may arise due to the inartful wording, notably constitutional challenges for overbreadth and vagueness. For example, "unwarranted loitering, sleeping or assembly" is prohibited on

Veterans Affairs property as well as "loud, abusive or improper language." *See* 38 CFR 1.218(a)(5). Although a federal judge is unlikely to strike down a federal regulation in its entirety, defense counsel may be successful in having the judge add elements such as mens rea, an intent to disturb, and other elements increasing the prosecution's burden at trial.

If an attorney is retained or appointed for a petty offense, it is crucial for counsel to learn both the culture of the petty offense court and standard offers on various offenses. For attorneys who are accustomed to handling felonies, the fact that an offense is a misdemeanor may seem like a bargain and an attorney may automatically advise the client to plead to the offenses as charged. Upon investigation of the court culture, counsel may learn that most offenses are disposed of by lesser dispositions such as a deferral of prosecution, a violation, or unsupervised probation. Law school clinics operating in the misdemeanor system are often in the role of an institutional defender and are a good source of information for attorneys unfamiliar with local misdemeanor practice.

Assimilated Crimes

A number of the misdemeanors and petty offenses that are brought into federal court are state offenses that are assimilated into the federal system because the conduct took place on federal property such as on an army base or at a Veterans Affairs hospital. *See* 18 USCS § 13. The prosecutor may charge assimilated state crimes where there is no governing federal law and the offense occurred "within the special maritime and territorial jurisdiction of the United States." 18 USCS § 7.

If an otherwise state offense is specifically set forth as a federal crime, the state offense cannot be assimilated. Defense counsel could move to dismiss the assimilated offense and have it recharged as a federal offense. It may be to the defendant's advantage, however, to have a state offense assimilated rather than have the defendant charged with the federal offense. For example, in New York a state disorderly conduct is a violation; whereas, a federal disorderly conduct charged under the CFR is a B misdemeanor. Nevertheless, the parties can agree to proceed on a state assimilated offense. While such a plea is arguably to an offense over which the court lacks subject matter jurisdiction, the fact that it is made in the context of a negotiated settlement means that the defendant is waiving whatever jurisdictional issues might arise. Alternatively, if a case were to be tried with an improperly assimilated offense for which federal statutory authority applies, a motion to dismiss for lack of subject matter jurisdiction would properly lie, and defense counsel should inform the court of the defect if doing so would be in the defendant's best interest.

With assimilated offenses, counsel should verify that the property where the offense is alleged to have occurred is, indeed, federal property. Some property presumed to be federal is actually state land, and the extent of the federal government's right or authority over that property may need to be determined by a lease contract or easement rights. Property abutting federal land appearing to be federal property may, in fact, be state property; for example, the sidewalks in New York are owned by the city, even those directly in front of the federal courthouse.

For assimilated crimes, state law determines the elements of offenses. Federal law, including the United States Constitution, the Federal Rules of Criminal Procedure, and the Federal Rules of Evidence, govern the process and procedures including motions to suppress. Although some state constitutions and case law may be more favorable to defendants than federal law on search and seizure issues, interpretations of the state constitutions regarding police misconduct are not controlling in assimilated cases. *See, e.g., United States v. Wilmer*, 799 F.2d 495 (9th Cir. 1986). Furthermore, assimilated crimes carry an imprisonment penalty derived from state law, but the fines are governed by 18 USCS § 3572 up to the maximum imposed by state law. Some state offenses have mandatory minimum fines or penalties. Since there is no mandatory fine in the federal system, use of the mandatory minimum fine would expand the scope of the Federal Criminal Code and would therefore be unlawful.

Collateral Consequences from Misdemeanor Convictions

Even petty offense convictions can result in significant collateral consequences. Defense counsel must be aware of any immigration consequences a disposition may have when the defendant is not a U.S. citizen before a plea is effected or the defendant is advised with respect to taking a case to trial. For example, any drug offense (except for a single conviction for simple possession of thirty grams or less of marijuana) will result in automatic deportation. Defense counsel may be able to negotiate for disorderly conduct to avoid a criminal conviction on a drug offense or other offense that might result in deportation.

Petty offenses can result in criminal history points under the Federal Sentencing Guidelines and counsel should review the list of offenses that count and do not count under Chapter 4, particularly if the defendant has a pending federal case. *See* USSG § 4A1.2(c)(1) (18 USCS Appx § 4A1.2(c)(1)). Importantly, convictions for driving while intoxicated or under the influence are counted. *See* USSG § 4A1.2(c)(1) (18 USCS Appx § 4A1.2(c)(1)), Commentary at n. 5. Some diversionary dispositions such as Adjournments in Contemplation of Dismissal may count if there is an admission of guilt (in open court), or a finding of guilt in a judicial proceeding. *See* USSG 4A1.2(f) (18 USCS Appx § 4A1.2(f)).

When the defendant is charged with a driving offense, one of the concerns will often be whether a conviction or plea will result in points on the defendant's license. Depending on the particular jurisdiction, the agencies ordinarily do not send driving convictions, which might result in "points" on a client's license to the Department of Motor Vehicles. Defense counsel should seek an affirmative agreement that the agency will not send the conviction to the attention of the state authorities. If it is of real concern to the defendant, it may be advisable for the client to plead to a nondriving offense or violation such as a disorderly conduct, which would not have license consequences.

For military defendants a major concern is loss of military privileges. In cases where the defendant is charged with theft from the commissary or the Post Exchange (PX), the usual practice is the defendant's PX card is confiscated by the arresting officers. The defendant's privileges are suspended for six months and can be restored following the six-month period upon application. In the meantime, the defendant can apply to have a restricted card returned, which will have a sticker indicating that the card cannot be used at the PX or commissary. The sticker can be removed at the end of the six-month period. Defendants convicted of even a violation may lose their housing privileges on a military base and/or right of access to the base. Defense counsel should investigate other possible military consequences before an enlisted defendant enters a plea or is advised whether to take a case to trial.

Rule 59. Effective Date

These rules take effect on the day which is 3 months subsequent to the adjournment of the first regular session of the 79th Congress, but if that day is prior to September 1, 1945, then they take effect on September 1, 1945. They govern all criminal proceedings thereafter commenced and so far as just and practicable all proceedings then pending.

Commentary

There is no Commentary for FRCrP 59.

Rule 60. Title

These rules may be known and cited as the Federal Rules of Criminal Procedure.

Commentary

There is no Commentary for FRCrP 60.